Digital Audio Operations

Digital Audio Operations

Francis Rumsey

Focal Press
London & Boston

Focal Press
An imprint of Butterworth–Heinemann Ltd
Halley Court, Jordan Hill, Oxford OX2 8EJ

 PART OF REED INTERNATIONAL P.L.C.

OXFORD LONDON GUILDFORD BOSTON
MUNICH NEW DELHI SINGAPORE SYDNEY
TOKYO TORONTO WELLINGTON

First published 1991

British Library Cataloguing-in-Publication Data

Rumsey, Francis
    Digital Audio Operations
    I. Title
    621.389
ISBN 0 240 51311 8

Library of Congress Cataloging in Publication Data

Applied for

Typeset by Designer Publishing, Guildford
Printed and bound by Hartnolls Ltd, Bodmin, Cornwall

Preface

Digital audio is now well established in the field of professional recording and broadcasting, and is here to stay, without a doubt. Many operators and engineers were brought up with analogue systems and may find that they need to adapt their skills to the new technology, in order that they may use it to best advantage, obtain the best sound quality, and avoid costly mistakes. For most such operators it is not necessary to know the detailed theory of digital audio, but rather to know enough about 'how it works' to be able to use it properly, fault-find when it goes wrong, and then to know how to use digital equipment in larger systems where problems such as synchronisation and interfacing may arise. *Digital Audio Operations* is dedicated to just that person, and it aims to put over the principles of digital audio together with a wealth of operational advice and guidance concerning today's principal recording and broadcasting systems.

Intentionally, this book does not dwell too heavily on theory, as there are already two good books in this area: John Watkinson's *The Art of Digital Audio*, also from Focal Press, and Ken Pohlmann's *Principles of Digital Audio*. Where greater detail has been felt to be necessary it has been assigned to 'Fact File' boxes, which may be either read or passed-by as the needs of the reader dictate. There is also an appendix covering the principles of conversion to and from the digital domain, together with a discussion of oversampling and noise shaping.

Digital Audio Operations is concerned with practical situations. What is the likely effect of errors and how can they be minimised? How can two dissimilar systems be made to communicate? How can digital audio be locked to video of different standards? How can a marginal tape be made to replay? Without hesitation, this book is concerned more with recording and broadcasting systems than with DSP and digital mixing, since these are the areas in which the most operational experience has been gained to date.

At the end of 1990, this book is something of a celebration of 10 years of widespread use of digital recording. It was 1980 when the first stereo PCM adaptors began to appear, and only the year after that when the revolutionary Sony PCM-F1 was introduced (a device which probably did more to further the cause of digital recording than any after it). Ten years later the user is faced with a bewildering selection of formats: disk systems, tape systems, and other media, with little in terms of compatibility. This book is intended to help find a way through that maze, and to help those whose business is audio to be as comfortable working with digital audio as they are with analogue.

Francis Rumsey, November 1990

Contents

Fact Files

Chapter 1

Introduction

1.1 What is digital audio?

Digital audio is the term used to describe sound or audio information which has been converted into a time-discrete numerical format, this being distinct from analogue audio which relies on the representation of sound by a time-continuous waveform whose characteristics vary in direct relationship to those of the original acoustic sound pressure. An analogue audio waveform may be represented either electrically (such as might be found in the variation of current flowing in piece of wire), magnetically (such as might be found in the pattern of magnetisation of particles on a piece of audio tape), optically (such as in the pattern of light and dark areas on a film sound track) or physically (such as in the deviation of the groove of an LP record).

Humans receive sound in an analogue manner, since sound is carried through the air in the form of a time-continuous variation in atmospheric pressure which is translated into a time-continuous movement of the ear drum. Interestingly, though, the means by which frequency information is carried to the brain from the inner ear is in some ways more digital than analogue, since, at least at low-to-mid frequencies, frequency information is represented by bursts of nervous discharge synchronous with the peaks of the analogue waveform, rather than in any time-continuous manner. Because the hearing mechanism expects to be presented with an analogue waveform the transducers which convert sound from an electrical form into an acoustic form and vice versa (loudspeakers and microphones) will always be fundamentally analogue devices, since they must emit or receive a time-continuous acoustic waveform.

Although there is often discussion about so-called 'digital microphones' and 'digital loudspeakers', what is meant in these cases is that the conversion from analogue to digital or vice versa takes place at the transducer itself, rather than at another stage in the signal chain, allowing the microphone to offer a digital output, and the loudspeaker to accept a digital input. Such a technique would represent the closest possible approach to a fully digital signal chain from microphone to loudspeaker, and as such would be capable of preserving the highest sound quality, since many of the system components which are currently interposed between microphone and loudspeaker, such as recording, transmission and processing devices, are already available in digital form. Furthermore, it might finally lay to rest any arguments about the effect of loudspeaker cables on sound quality, which so plague analogue audio (although unfortunately there is already evidence of arguments concerning the effects of cables on digital audio sound quality; see Chapter 2).

Digital audio represents, without a doubt, the future direction of audio technology, since there will come a time when it is cheaper and simpler to achieve a particular function digitally than it is to use an analogue method.

1.2 Practical benefits

The use of a digital form for audio has many practical benefits and it has some disadvantages. Digital audio is ideal for the complex processing of sounds without the level of sonic degradation which normally results from many generations of analogue processing. The data which represent a sound signal may be operated upon at high speed by a computer (a process known as *digital signal processing*) to achieve effects which are impossible in analogue systems. Indeed the time-discrete binary nature of digital audio makes it suitable for many forms of storage and handling which are commonly used for other computer data. The various diverse strands of information technology (and sound is indeed a form of information) are moving closer together, and it is clear that computers will soon handle sound, pictures, text and numbers in one seamless operation (see section 1.3).

Digital processing allows for errors in a sound signal to be corrected, whether arising out of interference in a broadcast transmission, a piece of dirt on a Compact Disc, or a clogged head on a tape recorder. The result of this is that even if the information retrieved by a digital audio decoder is not completely intact it may be made numerically correct, within limits, using powerful error-correction techniques. The result of this is that a corrupted signal may be made indistinguishable from its original form. Such error correction is impossible in analogue audio, since it is not possible for an analogue replay or receiving device to know the original form of a signal. Furthermore, digital audio is inherently more immune to interference than analogue audio, and its sound quality is independent of the medium on which it is stored or through which it is transmitted, provided that errors in timing and logical state are corrected. Digital audio does not suffer in copying, provided that copying is achieved digitally (that is by copying the data, rather than by copying the analogue output of a digital system), and it may be stored or transmitted in discontinuous bursts if required, provided that it is reconstructed in continuous form before conversion back to analogue.

The fact that digital audio may be held in computer storage devices means that items of audio information may be accessed almost instantaneously, and in virtually any order. This makes for fast operation in such environments as editing and post-production, and makes it possible to rearrange an original audio sequence in a very short time without physically rearranging the recorded material (see Chapter 3).

With the benefits of digital audio come the problems that accompany all systems, audio or otherwise, based on digital data, namely the numerous formats in which that data may be stored, many of which will be incompatible. Furthermore, the future of audio will become ever more technology dependent, especially because it will be related to developments in the computer industry over which audio engineers have little control, resulting in a greater built-in redundancy of products, and shorter lifetimes of formats.

1.3 Digital audio and computer technology

As previously suggested, digital audio data is not very different from digital data of any other kind so far as a computer is concerned. There are certain specific requirements for audio data handling, such as the need for unbroken audio inputs and outputs to a system, but this can be overcome by the use of FIFO buffering (see Fact File 1). Because of this, audio data may be handled by digital computers, and mass storage components of a similar type to those used for micro-computers, a situation exemplified by the recent spread of desktop computers with integrated high-quality audio, such as the 'NeXT' computer. Computers such as these have built-in hardware and software for handling audio in real time, and are intended to serve the growing market for so-called 'interactive multi-media'. This developing branch of information technology (IT) draws together aspects of audio, video, text and interactive control in a manner which blurs the distinction between these previously different areas of technology. Pictures, sound and text, for example, may all be stored on the same disk as each other, the computer accessing the information in an appropriate order and combination, according to a path determined partly by the user and partly by pre-written software.

Now that all the different branches of audio-visual media are able to make use of the same computer facilities it can be seen that each will feed off and supply the others with the fruits of technological advance. For example, the high data-storage capacities required by digital audio and video have resulted in the development of storage devices such as the Compact Disc and the R-DAT recorder, which are capable of storing between 600–1000 Mbytes of data in a small space. Both of these devices have since proved attractive to the computer industry for mass data storage, and are now also used for purposes other than audio storage. Similarly, the rotary-head recording process used initially for video recorders has proved useful for high-density recording in digital audio. The disk drives required for digital audio editing systems (see section 3.10) must have fast access times, preferably faster than those available now with computer optical drives, and demand from the audio market may result in the development of a drive which then gets snapped up by the computer industry. The point is that these areas of technological development are now inextricably linked.

The computer industry has become used to a greater degree of natural redundancy in its products, since the power of a computer product, in respect of tasks which can be realistically achieved, is almost entirely related to the speed with which software instructions and data can be processed, and the number of data bits which can be handled at once. Manufacturers of microprocessors (the principle processing 'engine' in a computer system) bring out a more powerful processor practically every other year, and this brings with it the next generation of computers, able to perform a range of new tasks previously thought impossible.

To look back over 10 years, it can be seen that the desktop computer has come from a device capable of handling small amounts of text, games and basic programs to a device now capable of processing video images in full colour at broadcast resolution, capable of editing digital audio at CD quality in real time, and capable of producing the finished typeset pages for a book. The audio industry is going to find itself faced with the same potential rate of change and development, and this will put new pressures on people whose job it is to make decisions over product purchases. More important than ever will be the potential for upgrading a system as technology advances, whilst also retaining compatibility with recorded material made on the earlier system. To some extent this has been achieved in the computer industry, since although the two major personal computer systems, MS-DOS (based on the IBM PC) and Apple Macintosh, have changed and become vastly more powerful over the years, there is still compatibility with most older programs and data. It has been in the interests of the manufacturers of computer systems to ensure this, since no major user of computers wishes to find himself or herself unable to make use of data created only a few years ago. Over and over again it has been shown that it is standardisation and compatibility, rather than technical excellence alone, which have had the greatest success in establishing systems of all kinds as leaders in the world market.

1.4 Digital audio and MIDI

MIDI, the Musical Instrument Digital Interface, should be clearly distinguished from digital audio. Although MIDI is a digital interface with a defined protocol, it is not a digital *audio* interface, and should be contrasted with MADI (see Fact File 22), which *is* an audio interface.

MIDI exists for the interconnection of electronic musical instruments and associated peripherals (such as effects devices, mixers and synchronisers), in order that they may be remotely controlled. In other words, MIDI is an interface which carries control information and not audio information. The data sent over MIDI to an electronic keyboard, for example, consists mainly of commands to turn notes on and off. The data rate of MIDI (that is the rate at which binary information may be transferred) is only 31 250 bits per second, and, as will be seen in section 3.1, high-quality digital audio requires about 750 000 bits per second per channel in uncompressed linear form. MIDI, therefore, is unsuitable for the transfer of real-time audio data, although it may be used in certain instances for the non-real-time transfer of digital audio samples for the purposes of sound sample editing in electronic music.

The reader is referred to the book *MIDI Systems and Control* by this author (see the Bibliography at the end of this book) for a detailed study of the subject.

1.5 Digital audio and video

Video signals may also be represented in digital form, and a number of professional digital video recording formats exist (see section 4.17). Such formats also incorporate digital audio tracks, since once the mechanism has been devised for recording video it is a relatively simple matter to add a number of audio tracks (video requires considerable greater bandwidth than audio, and thus four audio tracks represent a relatively minor addition). Some analogue video formats also include digital audio tracks (e.g.: the consumer Video-8 format, and the professional M-II format).

Digital audio is found increasingly in broadcast television transmissions, both terrestrial and satellite, sometimes using data compression techniques to reduce the bandwidth (see Chapter 6), and this allows for high-quality audio in difficult reception conditions, as well as the possibility, in the case of some satellite systems, for the broadcasting of additional digital *radio* channels. Fully-digital picture signals are not easy to broadcast, because of the extremely high bandwidth required, and it is unlikely that we shall encounter the widespread adoption of digital video transmissions in the foreseeable future.

1.6 Professional or consumer?

A final point, which should not go unmentioned, is the difference between professional and consumer digital audio. There are both benefits and curses concerned with the fact that consumer digital audio can sound as good as professional digital audio, if not better in some cases. Because of this fact it is tempting for professionals to make use of consumer equipment, and the distinction between the two product areas becomes blurred. Certainly consumer equipment may be adequate for many professional needs, but professionals may find that they need more than such machines can provide in terms of ruggedness or reliability in some applications.

It is enough to state at this point that digital audio has, to a large extent, pushed the question of sound quality into the background when it comes to comparing consumer and professional equipment, whereas in analogue audio it was a more important factor. In the case of digital audio, it is features such as confidence replay, rugged error correction, error indication, varispeed facilities, reliability, editing facilities and interchangeability of recordings that will be paramount considerations.

Chapter 2

Digital versus analogue

2.1 The sound quality debate

Many have commented, and will continue to comment, on the relative merits of digital and analogue audio, and it is important in this area to separate facts from fallacy. There may be subjective preferences for one over the other, and these cannot be denied, but subjective preference should not be confused with the question of fidelity to the original sound. In the following section the factors which are capable of affecting sound quality in digital audio are described, comparing the situation with that which prevails in analogue audio.

2.1.1 Introduction

Firstly, although digital audio has been defined earlier as a representation of sound in a numerical time-discrete form, it is to be stressed that the process of digital-to-analogue (D/A) conversion, which is necessary at the final stage of any digital system if it is to be monitored aurally, involves the conversion of the sequence of binary numbers into a *truly analogue waveform*, which is not made up of tiny steps, and does not look like a staircase if examined closely. The fallacy that digital audio somehow can never be as good as analogue because it is made up of small steps is entirely false, since the last stage of a D/A convertor (DAC) involves an analogue reconstruction filter which converts electrical impulses of varying amplitude into a continuous analogue waveform, ideally removing any components of the signal above half the sampling frequency, and thus making it impossible for a step-like waveform to remain (see Appendix 1).

A simple analogue example may help to illustrate the above, as shown in Figure 2.1. A square wave may be shown (by Fourier analysis) to consist of a set of harmonic sine wave components which comprise a fundamental, third harmonic, fifth harmonic, and all odd harmonics above this. If this square wave is filtered so as to remove all harmonics above the fundamental the resulting waveform is a sine wave, and no sharp edges remain. Analogously (although there are some minor differences), if the train of pulses of varying amplitude which are produced by a DAC is filtered so as to remove any harmonics, the result is a smooth output waveform with no step-like edges. The harmonics are responsible for the sharp edges of the square wave.

Preferences exist among audio engineers for both analogue and digital recording and processing. There has been a tendency to confuse *preference* for a particular

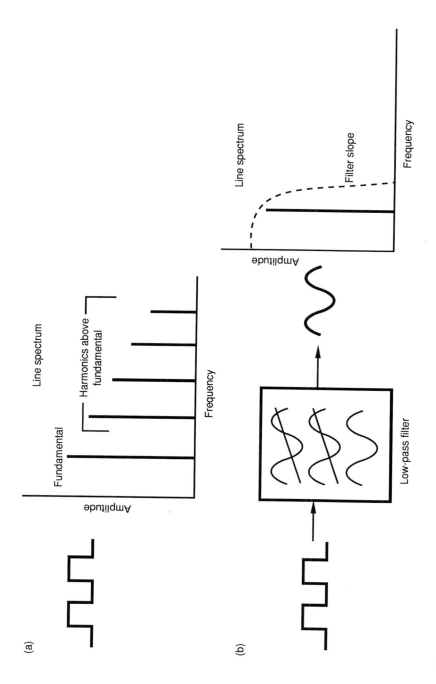

Figure 2.1 Spectral content of waveforms. At (a) a square wave's spectrum is shown to consist of a fundamental and a number of odd harmonics. At (b) the harmonics are filtered out, and the result is a sine wave at the fundamental frequency. The harmonics are thus seen to be responsible for the square wave's sharp edges

sound with *fidelity*, fidelity being the 'closeness', for example, of a reproduced sound from a tape recorder to that originally presented to that tape recorder by a mixing console (in other words, the 'transparency' with which a recording system handles a signal). In A/B double-blind tests using standard professional digital audio recording equipment it is rare for experienced listeners to be able to tell conclusively which is the sound coming directly from a microphone via a mixer, and which is the sound which has passed additionally via a linear digital encoding and decoding process, whereas it is usually possible to tell the difference when an analogue recording system has been interposed. The reader is left to draw his or her own conclusions from this. It may be that listeners do not *like* hearing the true sound as it was presented to the tape recorder, but this should not be interpreted as the digital recording system sounding 'cold', 'hard' or 'unreal'. Modern recording studios have very low noise floors and the lack of noise in silent passages during a recording may be uncanny to those used to a little hiss or rumble, but in most cases the digital recorder reproduces the input signal with minimal distortions of all kinds. This concept carries forward to the Compact Disc which is a direct digital copy of a master tape, thus suffering no degradation in sound quality when compared with the master tape. The CD mastering process introduces nothing that was not recorded in the first place, it being only the D/A convertors of the CD player which can affect the resulting sound quality, provided that replay errors are corrected and timing jitter is controlled (see below).

2.1.2 The signal chain

Looking at the diagram of a typical analogue signal chain in Figure 2.2(a), it will be seen that there are a number of stages at which degradation of a signal can occur. Degradations of the signal path in an analogue system are usually directly reflected in degradations in sound quality, since the system cannot distinguish between what are wanted and what are unwanted components of the signal. This statement must be slightly modified for an analogue system which has used a modulation method, such as frequency modulation (FM), but we shall consider unmodulated baseband systems for the time being. To be correct, one should point out that A/D conversion is just another form of modulation (PCM stands for Pulse Code Modulation). It pays to examine the types of signal degradation which may occur in the analogue signal path shown above, and to compare these with the artefacts of the digital signal path shown in Figure 2.2(b).

Firstly, non-linearities in the two transducers (microphone and loudspeaker) will introduce a number of distortions. Non-linearity in a device means that the output waveform will not be exactly the same shape as the input waveform, having been modified either in amplitude, phase or frequency. The result of this is both harmonic and intermodulation (IM) distortion (that is the production of harmonic overtones of a simple input signal, and the production of sum-and-difference tones between two input signals). Viewed on a spectrum analyser this would show that the output of a non-linear device contained signal components at frequencies other than those which had been input (see Figure 2.3). Phase distortion also features in the characteristics of transducers, as do distortions in the amplitude–frequency response. Perfectly linear microphones and loudspeakers are impossible to manufacture. It is possible that a means might be found by which the motion of a microphone diaphragm might be converted directly into a digital signal, and this process could be made more linear than the analogue process. Similarly a means may be found of using the output of a D/A convertor to move the diaphragm of a loudspeaker with sufficient excursion to produce a sound of high volume, but this technology is not available at the time of writing. It may be assumed, though, that transducers, because of their mechanical nature, will always be the most non-linear devices in an audio

(a)

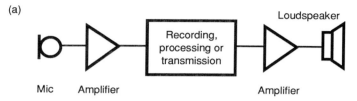

Mic   Amplifier   Amplifier

(b)

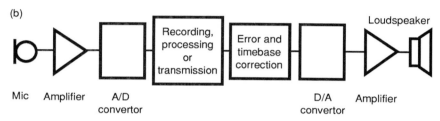

Mic   Amplifier   A/D   D/A   Amplifier
                    convertor   convertor

Figure 2.2 The signal chain. At (a) is shown a typical analogue signal chain, whilst at (b) is shown the digital equivalent. The digital version allows for error and timebase correction which is impossible in the analogue domain

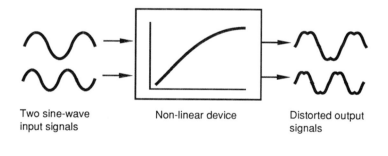

Two sine-wave   Non-linear device   Distorted output
input signals   signals

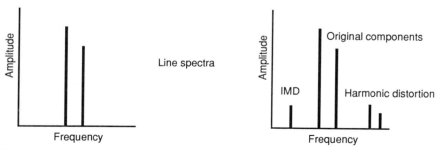

Figure 2.3 If pure sine tones are passed through a device with a non-linear transfer response the result is both intermodulation and harmonic distortion

system, whether digitally driven or driven from an analogue source.

The amplifiers shown in the analogue system (Figure 2.2(a)) are likely to be the most linear devices in the signal path, exhibiting minimal distortions of every kind. The largest problem with power amplifier design is that of interfacing a power amplifier to a loudspeaker, since variations in the load presented by the loudspeaker will vary with the frequency of the signal. For this reason, integrated amplifier–loudspeaker systems are often more satisfactory, since the amplifier can be designed correctly to match just one loudspeaker system. Some pre-amplifiers now incorporate 'digital inputs', which allow digital devices to be connected directly to the amplifier, the pre-amplifier housing its own D/A convertor. This simply removes the possibly degrading influence of any analogue cable which might otherwise have been used to connect the device. The question of whether or not an amplifier may truly be termed a 'digital amplifier' is difficult, since many so-called devices simply contain a D/A convertor on the input, and are otherwise analogue. Some amplifiers employ pulse width modulation techniques (PWM), which might more reasonably be called 'digital'.

Apart from in the transducers, which both analogue and digital systems require, it is in the recording or transmission process that the greatest potential for degradation of the signal lies in an analogue system. In the case of AC-biased magnetic tape recording there is potential for harmonic distortion, IM distortion, phase distortion, amplitude–frequency response errors, variations in speed (wow and flutter), hum, noise, compression, drop-out, and modulation noise. The sound quality of the signal chain is affected by all of these artefacts of the recorder, and will depend on the state of alignment of the tape machine, as well as the cleanliness and state of the heads, type of tape and age of the machine. Despite these points, the analogue tape recording process, like the internal combustion engine, has been developed to a point where it is capable of high performance, due to careful optimisation.

Considering the case of an LP record as the recording medium, it is clear that similar comments apply. A piece of dirt in the groove directly affects the sound that comes out of the loudspeakers, since the reproducing stylus and subsequent amplifier cannot distinguish between a movement of the stylus due to a genuine deviation of the groove and a movement caused by the piece of dirt. Similarly, any slight roughness in the plastic of the record will be turned into noise on the audio output, and any vibrations of the turntable will be heard by mechanical transfer via the stylus to the output. Any speed variations in the turntable will be translated into variations in the pitch of the output.

The point of listing the artefacts of the storage device which affect sound quality in an analogue system is to contrast the situation with that of the digital system, where the artefacts of the storage or transmission process may not necessarily be directly reflected in the sound output. Firstly, it is the role of the digital storage device or transmission/reception process to ensure that the binary data which is recorded may be recovered with reasonably low error rate on replay or reception. The system has only to distinguish between two states (one and zero), and these states might be represented, for example, by either a high or low voltage at a point, a bump or lack-of-bump on a Compact Disc, or a reversal of magnetic flux direction on a tape. It is also important for the system to be able to tell *when* the transitions between states occurred, and thus the audio data must be combined with a regular clock signal. Any noise, distortion or interference in the recording or replay process will be ignored by the decision-making circuits unless it is of sufficient amplitude to cause the system to believe that a binary one is a zero or vice versa, and this gives the system greatly increased immunity to the types of noise and distortion which are features of recording and transmission processes.

2.1.3 The effect of data errors

There is no 'half-way house' in the decision between a one and a zero on replay or reception, and a digital system will not work at all if it cannot decide between these states for the majority of the time; thus it follows that if a digital decoder can recognise the recorded or transmitted data correctly, and at the correct time, then the recording or transmission process will not have affected the accuracy of the information, and thus will not have affected the sound quality. Error correction (see Chapter 9) may be used to correct the occasional replay error, such that erroneous data may be perfectly restored, and it is only when this error-correction system is overwhelmed that the sound quality will be affected, either resulting in the system output muting for extreme errors, or, in some systems, switching to a process known as interpolation (see Fact File 14) which may result in the replay bandwidth being halved if it is prolonged. Some systems allow for muting to be turned off, thus allowing the user to hear the effect of an uncorrected bad error. Some professional systems never resort to interpolation, either correcting perfectly or muting, so as not to allow the situation in which the system still produces sound, but with reduced quality.

The diagram in Figure 2.4 shows conceptually how typical digital and analogue recording systems compare in the face of increasing noise and distortion in the signal path. The digital system's sound quality remains unaffected as the quality of

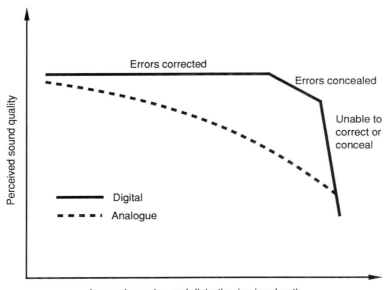

Figure 2.4 As noise and distortion increase in the signal path, the sound quality of an analogue system gets gradually worse, whereas the sound quality of a digital system remains unaffected until the error-correction system is overwhelmed

the signal path gets worse, up to a point where the error-correction system becomes unable to cope with the number of random errors which result. At this point systems may do different things depending on their design. Some will mute the system output in order that audio is either replayed correctly or not at all, some will resort to interpolation whilst there is still enough accurate data, and some will continue to replay the signal with errors. The first situation is probably most appropriate in professional mastering systems, where the operator wishes to know if uncorrectable errors exist, whilst the other two may be used more in consumer systems.

2.1.4 The effect of timing errors

Concerning timing errors in replayed or received data, it is important to show that these need not be reflected in timing errors in the resulting audio (which would indeed affect sound quality). In Fact File 1 the concepts of buffering and timebase correction are introduced, and it will be clear from this that it is possible to use a

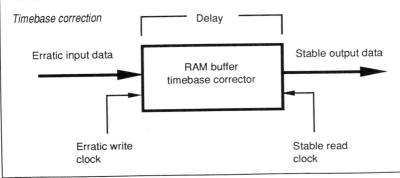

FACT FILE 1   Timebase correction

The sound quality of digital audio data is affected by errors in its timing, and thus a means is required for re-timing such data with reference to a stable clock. Furthermore, many digital audio systems process or handle data in a time-segmented form, requiring that such segments of data be reassembled into a continuous stream prior to conversion, or be split into segments from a continuous stream. Buffering is a means of effecting digital timebase correction, and may be used for either of the above applications.

As shown in the diagram audio data is written into a short-term memory which operates in the FIFO (First-In–First-Out) mode. In other words, the order in which data enters the store is the same as that in which it leaves. The timing of data entering the store may be erratic, perhaps having gaps in it or having other timing irregularities, but the timing of data leaving the store may be made steady by using a reference clock to control the reading process. Provided that the capacity of the store is adequate to cope with the irregularities in incoming data, and provided that the average rate of data entering the store is the same as the average rate of data leaving the store, the buffer will be able to supply a steady stream of data to the next stage of the system. Buffering introduces a delay equivalent to the difference in the number of samples between the reading-out point and the writing-in point.

Audio sample clocks may be 'cleaned up' by other means, without involving the need for significant delay, and this is discussed further in section 13.3.

Timebase correction

Delay

Erratic input data

RAM buffer timebase corrector

Stable output data

Erratic write clock

Stable read clock

short-term memory store to 'iron out' any speed variations in the replay or reception of digital audio data by re-clocking the data according to a stable reference. Even if, for example, the audio data replayed from a tape or CD has speed variations, it may be written temporarily into such a short-term store and read out a fraction of a second later at a steady rate, controlled by a crystal oscillator whose stability can be measured as a few parts per million (in other words, wow and flutter can be made undetectable). Provided that the order in which the data is read out of the store is the same as the original order of the audio samples, and the timing of those samples is as steady as that used in the original conversion process, the sound will not have been affected. Other methods for the stabilising of audio data also exist. This concept of re-clocking or timebase correction of digital audio is vital to the maintenance of high sound quality, and is discussed further in section 11.3.3.

As digital audio conversion becomes more sophisticated and gains higher resolution, the criteria for stable clock sources will become more rigorous. Digital audio can suffer as much from errors in the time domain as it can from errors in the amplitude domain, and this is often ignored.

2.1.5 The role of convertors

It is in the convertors of a digital audio system that much of the responsibility for sound quality lies. Here, and only here, provided that the rest of the system has faithfully carried through the audio data without corrupting it or modifying it, is it possible for the 'sound' of a digital audio system to be adversely affected. Naturally, the sound can be *intentionally* modified between the convertors, but here we are discussing the problems of unwanted and unintentional degradation of the signal. The A/D convertors (ADC's) which first 'digitise' the analogue signal are responsible for the 'sound quality' of the data which is to be subsequently recorded, processed or transmitted, and the D/A convertors which finally return this signal to the analogue world are responsible for the eventual quality of what is replayed. Since it is not possible to extract information from a signal which was never there in the first place, it follows that the replayed sound quality can only ever be as good as that which was initially converted at the A/D stage of the chain. This suggests that the quality of A/D conversion is paramount to good system performance, since nothing can be done at the D/A stage to make up for deficiencies in a preceding ADC.

Digital signal processing between the A/D and D/A convertors, such as often exists in digital audio systems, may intentionally modify the audio data samples due to such operations as mixing, filtering, equalisation and effects, and in such cases it is possible for sound quality to be adversely affected if the processing operation does not preserve the accuracy and integrity of the audio signal. Similarly, data compression between A/D and D/A convertors, in order to reduce the bandwidth required by an audio signal (see section 6.4), may have subtle audible effects (although these will naturally be kept to a minimum in good designs), but this may be considered as intentional degradation of the signal since designers will always be trading-off the degree of bandwidth reduction against perceived effects on audio quality, in order to make use of lower-cost storage or transmission.

There is a current trend in the hi-fi world to attach expensive D/A convertors to CD players and DAT machines in an attempt to improve sound quality, and it may be possible to achieve this improvement in some cases. It is also claimed that with the same high-quality D/A convertor, different CD players sound different, or even that different digital interfaces between CD player and convertor sound different, yet this would appear to be impossible given the above argument unless uncorrectable errors were being carried through, or timing jitter in the digital signal was being passed on to the convertor. It has been shown in some such cases that the error rates are not markedly different between CD players, but that expensive outboard D/A convertors do not all re-clock or de-jitterise the digital signal before conversion, preferring to use the clock derived directly from the digital input of the convertor to control the conversion process. It is not surprising in this case that differences are apparent between sources, since the degree of jitter which each produces will vary depending on the type of interface and the state of the source itself. Digital data should always be timebase corrected before conversion to preserve sound quality, and it is properly the role of the convertor to achieve this, since it is reasonable to expect a convertor to furnish itself with a clock of suitable stability for the resolution claimed. A convertor claiming to be 18 bit accurate will only be so if the clock is stable within certain limits (see section 13.3).

2.1.6 Further factors

Cables and other interconnections carrying digital signals need have no effect on digital audio sound quality, provided again that timing and data errors are corrected. This contrasts with the situation in an analogue system in which interconnections may have a noticeable effect on sound quality, there being a considerable market for highly priced pieces of wire which lay claim to improved audio fidelity.

The results of the above discussion are important, since they show that factors which typically affect sound quality in analogue systems, such as the type of tape used on a recorder and the type of cable used in connections, are not normally relevant to sound quality in a digital system. This is because data errors and timing errors which may result from a poor signal path may be perfectly corrected. There may be good reasons for choosing a particular tape, such as drop-out performance, but 'sound quality' should not be one of them.

There is a danger when discussing sound quality in digital audio to attribute the cause of degradation to the wrong part of the system. For example, a user may replay two different DAT recorders via an external D/A convertor, connecting them to the convertor using SPDIF (see Fact File 17). The user may say that they sound different, and thus that DAT machine A is better than DAT machine B, when in fact the sound quality difference was actually due to the lack of re-timing in the convertor, and that DAT machine A's SPDIF output had some jitter on it. Conversely, the user may compare interconnecting just one DAT machine to the convertor with both SPDIF and AES/EBU interfaces in turn (see Fact File 16), and say that the AES/EBU interconnect sounds better. Again this would most likely be due to the convertor not re-timing the data, since the consumer SPDIF might suffer worse clock degradation than the professional AES/EBU. Clearly it is difficult to decide exactly what is at fault, since the interface should incur as little degradation as possible, but perhaps, as suggested above, it is the job of the convertor to correct such things prior to conversion, since timing and data errors *are* normally correctable in digital audio, whereas they are not in analogue audio.

A further discussion of sound quality in digital systems, related specifically to operational conditions in recording, is contained in Chapter 8.

2.2 Practical considerations

Digital recording is inherently greedy in terms of storage space (see section 3.1), and digital transmission is inherently greedy in terms of radio frequency bandwidth (see Chapter 6), thus being potentially more expensive to store and transmit than analogue audio of the same bandwidth and resolution. Telecommunications links, for example, are costed according to the bandwidth required. It will soon become more expensive to use an analogue link for many purposes than it will a digital link, at which time the challenge will be to reduce the data rate required for one channel of digital audio. Nonetheless, data storage densities of recording media, both magnetic and optical, are ever being increased, making it possible to store a given amount of data in an increasingly small space, and data compression techniques are available which allow high-quality audio to be coded at a fraction of the normal rate, thus reducing the bandwidth required for transmission (see section 6.4).

Digital audio tape recordings are normally more fragile than analogue recordings, since the tape on which they are made is thinner and the frequencies involved are higher, making it possible to affect the integrity of the recording with simple fingerprints or edge damage. Conversely, digital audio disk recordings (especially optical ones) are more robust than analogue disk recordings, since in optical systems (see section 3.12.2) the protective layer and pickup methods used mean that dirt or scratches on the surface are not always turned into errors on replay, since the laser is not focused at the surface and the data surface cannot easily be damaged. Magnetic hard disks (see section 3.12.1) are sealed, and thus the data stored on them cannot easily be corrupted. Magnetic disks, though, have a filing and directory structure which, if corrupted due to a possible head crash, may prevent the replay of the complete contents of the disk.

Editing of digital audio tapes is generally more difficult and more expensive than editing of analogue tapes, since analogue editing has traditionally only required one tape machine, a razor blade and sticky tape, whereas digital tape editing normally requires at least two machines and an edit controller, requiring that the material to be edited is copied between the machines in real time. It has been made possible to splice digital tape recordings in some formats (see section 5.7), but it is widely acknowledged that this is a less-reliable and more-delicate operation than the splicing of analogue tape. On the other hand, the editing of digital audio *disks* is possible (see section 5.11), whereas the editing of analogue audio disks is virtually impossible. There is greater creative flexibility to be had in digital editing systems than in analogue systems, since editing may be performed electronically and may be made absolutely seamless. It is not possible to control an analogue tape machine's bias and erase voltage ramps with sufficient accuracy to achieve the same sort of performance in electronic editing as is possible with digital recording, since bias and erase must be turned on fairly slowly to avoid noises on the tape, and thus may mitigate against accurate edits with carefully controlled crossfades. There are also other editing operations which work better in digital systems, and these are covered in more detail in the chapters on editing technology and editing operations (see Chapters 5 and 11).

Digital signals are not as straightforward to handle in operational situations as analogue signals. First of all there are many different formats for data interconnection, for storage, and for transmission, making it difficult to interchange audio signals between systems. In the analogue environment a quarter-inch stereo tape may be replayed on virtually any quarter-inch tape machine in the world, with only minor problems of speed and equalisation to contend with (most machines are switchable). Similarly there is the familiar XLR-terminated balanced line for audio interconnection in professional systems, which may be plugged into virtually any sound system in the world, again with only minor problems such as the phase convention of the cable and the electrical level of the signal. In the digital domain one is faced with many different interface formats (see Chapter 10), and the fact that any signal must be decoded before it can be monitored. If digital tie-lines become the norm in broadcast establishments, then it will no longer be a straightforward matter to plug a pair of headphones into a jack socket on a patchfield to hear what is coming down a particular line. A new generation of digital monitoring devices will be required (e.g.: headphones with a built-in decoder and convertor).

Concerning the cost of digital audio, it is still true in many cases that digital audio is more expensive than analogue audio when comparing like with like as closely as possible, although it is often difficult to compare like with like since with the increased cost of digital audio may come increased operational flexibility and higher sound quality. This is unlikely to remain the case for ever, since digital devices will eventually become cheaper to produce than analogue devices, and electronics manufacturers are investing huge amounts of money in this aspect of the future. Even so, it is true that recording systems such as R-DAT are already available at prices similar to those of quarter-inch tape machines, and computer mass-storage-based digital editing systems are now available at competitive prices.

Professional digital *recording* (as opposed to communications) has only been in general commercial usage since the early 1980s (although that is not to say that digital recording had not taken place before this), and thus it is relatively 'young' as new systems and technologies go. The phenomenal rise of the Compact Disc as a replacement for the LP in domestic sound reproduction has had a large influence on the proliferation of digital music recording, and the rise of digital broadcasting systems (see Chapter 6) and digital video recording has encouraged the use of digital audio in television and radio. Much has been learned by those who were prepared to pioneer the commercial introduction of digital audio recording, and one may expect to see a consolidation of the field with a wider degree of usage, hopefully with an emphasis on standardisation, as the industry moves towards the turn of the next century. The wider usage will result in reduced prices.

Certain product areas are easier to 'turn digital' than others, and it may be some time before operations such as digital sound mixing are possible at a reasonable cost and with equivalent quality to their analogue counterparts. Digital recording and transmission have already proved themselves as viable propositions, as have digital interfaces and some aspects of digital signal processing (DSP) such as those used in effects processing and filtering, but at the time of writing it is still necessary to conquer the areas of large-scale digital mixing and digital transducer design. Digital mixers have been produced successfully, but they have tended to be either very expensive or quite small. A/D convertor performance limitations have been one of the principal limiting factors in the sound quality of digital mixers, but recent designs have been made capable of up to 20 bit resolution, which may remove the original hurdle presented. The architectural design of large digital mixers is also problematical, and delays between audio inputs and outputs may result. Further-more, most users of mixers find that they are perfectly satisfied with the perform-ance and facilities of current analogue systems, requiring that digital consoles offer something new for the money that they will cost. Digital recording, on the other hand, offered considerably increased sound quality over analogue recording, which was an immediate reason for its adoption, as well as the possibility for infinite generations of copying without sonic degradation.

2.3 Digital versus analogue – summary

Digital audio makes sound quality independent of the storage or transmission medium, *provided that any data errors and timing errors are corrected*. The primary influence on sound quality lies with the design of A/D and D/A convertors, whilst secondary influences are those of any data compression or digital signal processing which may be involved between the convertors. Thus the ultimate limiting factor on digital audio sound quality is the performance of A/D convertors, since information cannot be extracted from a signal which was never there in the first place. All other degradations may be seen as predictable and controllable within the design of a system, since if the data from an A/D convertor is carried through a digital signal chain to the D/A convertors entirely unmodified in timing and numerical accuracy then no degradation of audio quality will have resulted. This is not to say that it is impossible to affect the sound quality of digital audio between convertors, but that the normal operational processes of copying, recording, transmitting, and passing-of-signals-through-cables may be made transparent processes in a digital system. This is due to the robustness of a binary signal in the face of a poor signal chain, the possibility for re-timing of the data, and the ability of a digital system to correct errors perfectly.

The sound quality of an unmodulated analogue signal can be affected at any stage in the programme chain. It is not possible to error-correct analogue audio signals or correct for timing errors because there is normally no way of knowing what the 'correct' state of the signal should be. Analogue audio normally requires a smaller bandwidth for the same comparative sound quality than digital audio, and thus it may be cheaper to store or transmit, although this may not remain the case when digital systems become the norm rather than the exception. Digital audio allows for great flexibility in signal processing, due to the possibility for the computer manipulation of audio data, and allows the use of computer mass storage media for sound recording, thus facilitating fast random access and powerful editing facilities.

Digital audio suffers from a plethora of different data and storage formats, making interchange of material difficult, whereas analogue storage and interchange is largely standardised. An exception to this is the Compact Disc, which represents one of the few world standards in digital audio, and possibly DAT, which may form the stereo tape interchange format of the future. Digital tape recordings may be more fragile than their analogue equivalents, and more difficult to edit, although electronic digital tape editing may be achieved with greater accuracy and flexibility than analogue splicing. Digital disk recordings are robust and allow rapid random access which is useful in electronic editing systems. There are instances in which the digital implementation of a particular operation proves to be more expensive than the equivalent analogue implementation, although this is simply a result of the relative newness of the technology and is not a situation which may be expected to last for very long. Certain product areas may take longer to 'go digital' than others.

Chapter 3

An overview of digital disk recording

In the following two chapters digital audio recording technology will be introduced. The operational implications of using one recording format in preference to another are set out in detail in Chapter 7, and will not be covered here. It is intended to present in these chapters a summary of the currently available recording systems from a technical point-of view, looking at the 'how-it-works' aspects of both tape recording and disk recording, as well as the use of other media such as RAM (Random Access Memory).

3.1 How much storage space is required?

Although audio engineers are not used to considering the storage space required for recordings in computer terms, this approach will become more relevant as the use of mass storage media designed for computers becomes widespread in audio. An analogue recording engineer is used to purchasing a 10 inch NAB reel of quarter-inch analogue tape and knowing that it will last just over half an hour at a tape speed of 15 ips (38 cm/s). Digital *tape* recording may remain in this happy state (although see section 4.2), but digital recording on disks (or 'tapeless recording', as it is sometimes known) will tend to involve the quotation of storage capacity in terms of megabytes (Mbytes): 1 Mbyte is 1024 kbytes, and 1 kbyte is 1024 bytes. Because of the flexibility of such systems in terms of the assignment of storage capacity to 'tracks' (see section 3.11) it is not easy to equate a given number of megabytes to a given number of minutes of playing time. Furthermore, in digital audio it is possible for there to be a wide range of different sampling rates and recorded resolutions, which will affect the amount of data produced per second, and thus the amount of storage space required for a given length of recording. It would be as well, therefore, to learn to consider the storage capacity of a digital recording system in computer terms, in order to be able to calculate the amount of recording time available given a set of recording conditions. This will also help in the understanding of the requirements for multitrack recording.

Assuming for the moment that we are considering a conventional linear PCM system (see Glossary) operating without any form of data compression, the data rate in bits per second resulting from one channel of digital audio will depend on the sampling rate and the number of bits per sample. To take a typical example of a system operating at the professional rate of 48 kHz, using 16 bits per sample, the resulting data rate per channel would be $48\,000 \times 16 = 768\,000$ bits per second, ignoring for a moment the addition of any overhead for error correction and the possibility for varispeed recording. Storage capacities are normally quoted in bytes, kbytes or Mbytes, and 768 000 bits per second is equivalent to a storage requirement of 5.5 Mbytes per minute per channel. There is a direct relationship between the number of bits per sample, the sampling rate, the number of channels and the amount of storage required per minute of recording. Since professional sampling rates range from 32 kHz up to 48 kHz, with some systems operating at non-standard rates up to 100 kHz, and with typical sample resolutions ranging from 16 bits per sample up to 24 bits per sample, the amount of storage required per minute will vary enormously between systems. Tables 3.1(a) and (b) show a number of examples, giving both the amount of recording time available from 10 Mbytes of storage and the number of megabytes required per minute for one channel of audio at a number of recording rates.

For multi-channel recording the storage requirement will rise pro rata; thus stereo will need twice the space of the equivalent mono recording, and 24 channels will require 24 times the space. Thus for a given storage capacity, the available number of minutes 'programme time' will fall if the number of channels is raised. It will also fall if the recorded resolution is raised. For example, a format which allowed space for 24 bits per sample, even if it did not convert to that accuracy (as is the case in some systems which allow for future developments), would consume over 8 Mbytes per minute compared with the 5.5 Mbytes per minute of the 16 bit system. There is a case, therefore, for only using recorded resolution which is adequate for the purpose (hopefully with some reserve for the future), since the use of excessive resolution will consume storage space unnecessarily. Recorded resolution is directly related to sound quality, but there comes a point above which increases in sampling rate and resolution give diminishing returns in this respect (see Appendix 1).

Table 3.1(a) Total recording time for 10 Mbytes of storage

Sampling rate (kHz)	Bits per sample	Recording time (approx. min)
44.1	16	2
48	16	1.8
96	16	0.9
44.1	18	1.8
48	18	1.6
48	20	1.5

Table 3.1(b) Number of megabytes required per minute at a selection of sampling rates and resolutions

Sampling rate (kHz)	Bits per sample	Mbytes/min
44.1	16	5.1
48	16	5.5
96	16	11
44.1	18	5.7
48	18	6.2
48	20	6.9

3.2 Usage of storage capacity on disk and tape

The way in which storage capacity is used differs enormously between disk- and tape-based systems, especially when considering multi-channel operation. The important point here is that a multitrack stationary-head tape machine usually records each channel on a separate physical track, there being a number of tracks recorded in parallel across the tape. These tracks are fixed in their physical and temporal relationship and thus each point on the length of the tape represents a particular point in time. A 24 track tape machine has 24 monophonic tracks all recording in parallel, and thus the storage capacity is 24 times that of a single track of the same length. Each physical track is dedicated to a particular channel, and offers the same storage capacity as each of the others, even if that capacity is not required for that channel. More tracks might be added by widening the tape, or by increasing the number of tracks on the same width of tape.

If we suppose that the reel of tape lasts 30 minutes at normal speed, then the storage capacity, based on the example of 48 kHz, 16 bit conversion, is 5.5 (Mbytes per minute) × 30 (minutes) × 24 (tracks) = 3960 Mbytes. The full 3960 Mbytes will only be used when all 24 tracks are recorded for the full 30 minutes, but if there are gaps in some of the tracks, as there will be if tracks have been dropped in and dropped out of record mode, only a part of that capacity will be used. The problem is that the spare capacity left in the gaps is not available for use by anything other than the track concerned at the particular time of the gap, whereas in a random access system, such as one using a disk drive, the total storage capacity can be distributed in virtually any way between channels, such that spare capacity on one 'track' can be used to increase capacity elsewhere. This is why it is not so easy to talk of 'tracks' as such in random access systems, since there may simply be one central reservoir of storage serving a number of channel outputs when they are required (see section 3.11).

If the recorded resolution is increased in a tape-based system then more tape will be consumed per minute, provided that other factors such as recording density are not changed. For example, if the sampling rate of a DASH-format tape machine (see section 4.9) is increased from 44.1 kHz to 48 kHz, the tape speed increases pro rata and the recording time available on a given length of tape is reduced. That is why it is not always safe to refer to a reel of, say, DASH-format digital tape as being 'a half-hour tape', since the playing time will depend on the sampling rate. If the recorded resolution is increased in a disk-based system then the total storage time available will be reduced pro rata. In disk-based systems storage capacity tends to be purchased in units of so many megabytes at a time, corresponding to a number of single-channel minutes at a standard resolution. The system may allow, say, an hour of storage time to be divided between four channel outputs, but the total 'programme time' to which this would correspond would depend on the amount of time for which each channel output was being fed with data. If all four outputs were to be continuously and simultaneously fed then the total *programme* time would be 15 minutes.

3.3 Effects of data compression on storage requirements

It is possible to obtain a greater recording time from a given amount of storage by using one of the proprietary audio data compression systems, such as Audio Processing Technology *apt-X 100*, Dolby *Adaptive Transform Coding*, or the IRT

MUSICAM system, to name three current examples. The systems in question are designed to provide high quality audio from a reduced number of bits per second compared with that required for linear PCM. For example apt-X 100 reduces the data rate required by a factor of four, with minimal effects on the perceived sound quality. Such systems involve a coding and a decoding delay, and not all of them work well when sound is played backwards or varispeeded, and thus they may not always be appropriate for systems which require real-time manipulation of audio such as in editing systems, but they allow much more audio data to be stored per megabyte of capacity. This may be the only way in which large-scale multitrack recording can be achieved with disk-based systems, given the amount of data produced by 24 tracks over half an hour as shown in the example in section 3.2. The 3960 Mbytes required in the example for linear PCM could be reduced to 990 Mbytes by 4:1 data compression, and this brings it within the capacity of today's large disk drives. Data compression systems are described in further detail in section 6.4.

3.4 Background to disk storage of digital audio

There is something of a historical precedent for the storage of sound on disks. Edison and Berliner brought sound reproduction to the home, in the early part of this century, in the form of random access storage media (a cylinder in the case of the former, and a disk in the case of the latter). It was not until wartime (1940s) that AC-biased tape recording became a viable proposition, although some experimental work had been going on prior to this. The advent of tape recording brought with it two distinct advantages over disk recording: firstly the possibility for higher sound quality, and secondly the possibility for editing.

Editing facilities and high sound quality had remained the prime advantages of tape over disk until recent years. Now digital audio allows sound to be stored in numerical form, as binary data, on media other than tape. Disk drives and solid-state RAM form the basis of data storage in today's computers, and they have the advantages of fast access to stored data, especially when compared with tape which has very slow access to stored material, due to the need for serial spooling to distant material. With sound quality now being independent of the medium on which the data is stored (see section 2.1.2), it is possible to concentrate on the operational advantages of random-access disk storage over serial-access tape storage.

A number of disk types exist, some of which are more suitable for digital audio use than others, and a résumé is given of the characteristics of a number of drives which may be used in professional recording systems in section 3.12 . All computer mass storage devices are block structured, that is they involve the delineation of the storage space into blocks of fixed size, each of which may be separately addressed by a controller. In this way, information may be accessed quickly, by reference to a directory of the contents of the disk which contains information about the location of blocks of data relating to particular files. In the case of a sound recording system, these files contain digital audio data (see section 3.7, below). In the following section an overview of the principles of digital audio storage on disks is given, but for a comprehensive study the reader is referred to the book *Tapeless Sound Recording* (see the Bibliography at the back of this book). It is not intended to cover the subject of consumer replay-only media, such as the Compact Disc, in any detail.

3.5 Digital audio requirements

Digital audio samples, since they are time-discrete, may be processed and stored either contiguously or non-contiguously (that is adjacent to each other, or physically separated), provided that they are reassembled into their original order before they are converted back into the analogue domain at a fixed sampling rate. This attribute makes digital audio ideal for storage on block-structured media such as disks, provided that buffering is employed at the inputs and outputs to such a system in order to smooth the transfer of data to and from the disk (see section 3.9). Audio editing may be accomplished in the digital domain by the joining of one recording to another in RAM, using the buffer to provide a continuous output (see section 5.11), and the fast access time of the disk drive makes it possible to locate recordings (sound files) made at different times in a fraction of a second. Multi-channel recording may be accomplished by dividing the store capacity between the channels, provided that the transfer rate of the store is adequate for the purpose (see below).

3.6 Block diagram of a digital audio disk recorder

Figure 3.1 shows a conceptual block diagram of a digital recording system which uses disk storage. The system consists of a user interface, a central processor (CPU) to handle the overall control of operations, a digital signal processor (DSP) to handle the real-time processing of audio data, a block of solid-state RAM (random-access

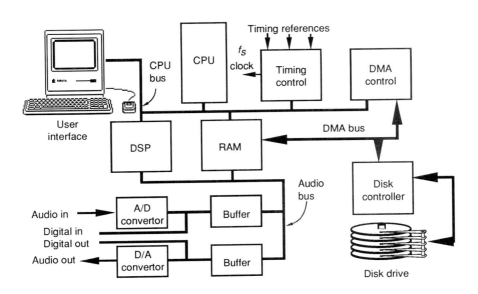

Figure 3.1 Generalised block diagram of a disk-based digital audio recorder

memory) to act as a temporary store for audio data, a direct memory access (DMA) controller, and a storage device which is likely to be at least one disk drive with its associated controller. There are also audio interfaces, both analogue and digital, connected to the system via further memory to act as a buffer (see below), as well as interfaces for timing information, such as SMPTE/EBU timecode, which communicate with the timing controller.

During the operation of the system, audio data is transferred to and from the disk via RAM, usually using a technique known as direct memory access, whereby data may be transferred directly from the disk to the RAM or vice versa without having to pass via the central processor. This assists in speeding up transfer. Data is transferred between RAM and the audio interfaces via the buffers, under control of the central processor which takes commands from the user interface. During editing, and any other audio processing operations such as fading or mixing, data is written from the disk to the digital signal processor, via RAM, which in turn passes it to the buffered audio outputs.

The following sections describe the specific concepts involved in digital audio disk recording and replay.

3.7 The sound file

It is important to grasp the concept of the 'sound file' as an individual sound recording of any length. With tape recording there is the distinct possibility that parts of a reel will have been recorded at different times, and in such a situation there may be sections of the tape, perhaps separated by leader tape, which represent distinctly separate periods of time: they may be 'tracks' for an album, 'takes' of a recording session, or short individual sounds such as sound effects. This is the closest that tape recording gets to the concept of the 'sound file': that is, a unit of recorded audio, of fixed size once it has been recorded, the size of the unit being anything which fits into the available space.

In the tapeless system, one must consider the disk as a 'sound store' in which no one part has any specific time relationship to any other part: no one section can be said to be 'before' another or 'after' another, since a disk recording does not 'start' at one place and 'finish' at another. This is the nature of random- or direct-access storage, although the proviso should be made that some forms of optical disk, such as the WORM cartridge and CD-R or CD-E (see below), record contiguously for all or part of their capacity, whilst retaining random accessibility. In this store may be kept a number of 'sound files' of different lengths, and containing different material. It is possible that one file might be a 10 minute music track whilst another might be a 1 second sound effect. Essentially, one may keep as many sound files in the store as will fit in the space available.

3.8 Sound file storage on disk

Just as in any well-organised filing system, it is necessary to know where items have been stored so that they can be retrieved again. In a computerised filing system, which is really what the tapeless audio system is, a 'directory' is used as an index to the store. The directory contains entries specifying what has been stored, the size of each file and also its location. By referring to the directory the system can retrieve previously stored files by looking in the indicated place. Every time a new file is stored, an entry must be made by the system into the directory specifying the location of the file. In the case of large files, the directory entry may refer to an 'index' or look-up table in which is stored a list of locations which must be read sequentially to reassemble a file. Within the directory or its sub-indexes, the locations of all the pieces of the sound file will be registered, and when the particular file is requested by the user the system will reassemble the pieces by retrieving them in sequence from the various storage locations.

3.9 Buffering

Buffering is the key to the process of ensuring that time-continuous data may be broken up, and that broken-up data may be made continuous again. A buffer is a short-term store which holds only a small portion of audio data at any one time (often less than a second's duration), and it is normally made up of RAM. The buffer may be imagined as analogous to a bucket of water with holes in it, because this neatly demonstrates the processes involved. A bucket, having a small hole in the bottom, may be filled intermittently, but the water will flow out of the hole continuously. Provided that the average flow rate of water entering the bucket is the same as the average rate at which it flows out of the hole, then the bucket will remain at the same average state of fullness. If water flows out of the hole faster than it is coming into the bucket then the bucket will eventually become empty. Alternatively, the water could enter the bucket continuously and could be let out of the hole in bursts, the important point being that the reservoir of water makes possible the translation from continuous to burst flow or vice versa (see Figure 3.2).

In digital audio terms, the bucket is a RAM buffer and the water is audio data. Disk media require that audio is split into blocks for storage (typically 512 or 1024 bytes), and this is achieved by filling the RAM to a given point from the continuous audio input, and then reading out of the RAM in bursts to the disk blocks. On replay the RAM is filled in bursts from the disk, and read out in an unbroken form at a constant

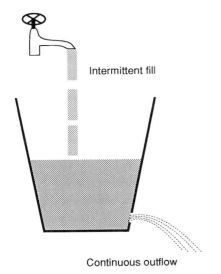

Intermittent fill

Continuous outflow

Figure 3.2 A bucket filled intermittently may give a continuous outflow, provided that the average rate of fill equals the average rate of emptying, and provided the bucket is large enough to contain the amount of water produced in one burst from the tap

rate to give an audio output. Provided that the average rate of data flow into and out of the buffer is the same, the buffer will not become empty. If data is read out faster than it is written in then eventually the reservoir will run dry, and the result will be either no audio at the output (on replay) or nothing written to the disk (while recording). In order to preserve the original order of samples, the buffer must operate in the FIFO (First-In–First-Out) mode.

The analogy could be taken further, as it may be appreciated that there might be more than one hole in the bucket (more channel outputs), larger holes in the bucket (higher data rates) or a tap with low water pressure (a slow storage device). It should be pointed out that the bucket analogy does not hold water if examined too closely, as in the real situation water will flow faster out of the holes in the bucket the fuller the bucket is: this does not hold true for memory buffers in tapeless recording systems!

The buffering of digital audio has a number of other useful possibilities. Firstly, it can be used to ensure that any short-term timing irregularities in the data coming from the storage device will be ironed out and will not be allowed to affect audio quality. Secondly, the buffer may be used for synchronisation purposes. If audio data being read from a storage device is required to be synchronised with an external reference such as timecode, then the rate at which data is read out of the buffer can be finely adjusted to ensure that lock is maintained. Thirdly, buffering is vital to the process of editing in tapeless recording. Since sections of audio which may be stored in a variety of different locations are to be joined together, there may well be short breaks between the acquisition of one section and the acquisition of another from the store. It will be the job of a buffer to smooth out the effect of the discontinuity, and to ensure a continuous output at the join. The only penalty of buffering (which may not be noticeable, depending on the mode of operation) is that it introduces a small delay between the input to and the output from the buffer, the extent of which depends on the delay between the writing of samples to the RAM and the reading of them out again. The maximum delay is limited by the size of the buffer, as with a small buffer there will come a point where the memory is filled and must be emptied to some extent before any new samples can be written in.

In a simple disk-based system, whilst recording, continuous audio data from the system's A/D convertors, or from a digital input, will be written into an area of the buffer, and from here it will be written to the appropriate parts of the disk as and when the disk is ready, making up a sound file whose details and locations are written into the directory. On replay, a file may be read from the disk into the buffer, and from there in continuous form to the D/A convertor or digital output (see

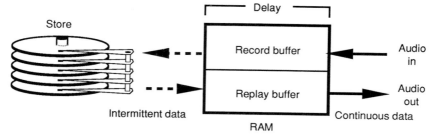

Figure 3.3 A RAM buffer is used in a disk-based recorder to convert the continuous flow of audio data required at the inputs and outputs into the burst flow required by the disk drive

Figure 3.3). There might be more than one audio input to or output from the buffer, in which case certain parts of the buffer would be reserved for individual channels.

3.10 Performance requirements of storage devices

The system, under the user's direction, will regularly request the transfer of sound files from the disk in normal operation. It may also be organising the writing of sound files to the disk. *Access time* is that time taken between the system requesting a file from the disk and the first byte of that file being accessed by the disk controller. It may also refer to the average time taken for the storage device to jump between one block of a file and another block which may be located in a different place, as the file may not be stored in contiguous blocks (see below). In a disk drive, access time is governed largely by the speed at which the read/write heads can move accurately from one place to another, and to a smaller extent it is governed by the physical size of the disk and the speed at which it rotates. If the head is directed by the controller to move to a particular location then there will be two delays to consider: one while the head moves radially across the disk to the required position (*seek latency*), and one while the disk rotates until the desired block passes under the head (*rotational latency*). Figure 3.4 illustrates this concept.

Transfer rate is the rate at which data can be transferred to and from the disk once the relevant location has been found. It will be measured in bits (or more usually megabits) per second. Transfer rate, in conjunction with access time, limits the number of audio channels which can successfully be recorded into or replayed from the disk simultaneously, and these two factors also limit the freedom with which long crossfades and other operational features may be implemented. Going back to

---

FACT FILE 2   The allocation unit (AU)

A disk block is very small in relation to the size of a digital audio file of even moderate length, and if a file were to be split up into blocks of 512 bytes spread all over the disk then transfer efficiency would be impossibly reduced due to the large number of accesses required to different parts of the disk. For this reason a minimum allocation unit (AU) is often defined, which is a contiguous sequence of blocks that are always used together, in order to improve efficiency (this has also been called a transfer unit). It might be that an AU would contain 8 kbytes of audio data, which in the case of 512 byte blocks would correspond to 16 blocks. The size of the AU must be small enough to engender efficient use of the disk space in cases of fragmentation, and large enough to engender efficient data transfer.

Physical placement of AUs corresponding to the same sound file on the disk surface or surfaces should be as carefully arranged as possible to allow the shortest access time between them, but effort spent in ensuring this is often negated when a store becomes badly fragmented or nearly full as there is then no option but to store data where there is space available. These factors depend considerably on the performance of the disk drive, whether it is able to transfer all the data on one track in one revolution, and what its access time is. The placement of AUs becomes further complicated in the case of multi-channel operation, and when sound files for different channels may be accessed with virtually any time relationship between them. SCSI drives may allow little or no external control over block or AU location.

FACT FILE
3

Fragmentation of disk stores

As files are stored by a system they will be assigned to blocks on the disk, and the blocks' locations will be entered in the directory. If the file is subsequently required by the system it will read each of the appropriate blocks in sequence to re-assemble the file. Since the size of a block on a disk drive is typically 512 bytes, most real files will span a number of blocks.

It may be that the store has already been used many times and that old files have been erased to make room for new ones. Unless a new file is exactly the same size as the space left behind by an old one the new file will be required to use a variety of locations, some of which belonged to the old file and some of which did not. If every new file were to use only brand new storage space which had never been used before the store would soon become full. The more a store is used, the more 'fragmented' it will become: that is, the more little spaces there will be dotted around which are no longer being used, as the file to which they related has ceased to exist. These 'fragments' will be used up in the storage of new files, although it will mean that newer files will possibly be more fragmented than old ones.

Fragmentation may not be a bad thing for tapeless sound recording, indeed it may in fact be desirable to fragment sound files for multi-channel operations where there is no fixed relationship in time between the sound files to be sent to different outputs. The whole approach to the design of a successful tapeless sound storage system is a perpetual trade-off between efficiency, number of output channels, size of memory buffer, length of cross-fade allowed, and so on. Fragmentation is good for efficiency in some cases, yet bad for it in others, to some extent depending on the application, and in any case it cannot usually be avoided.

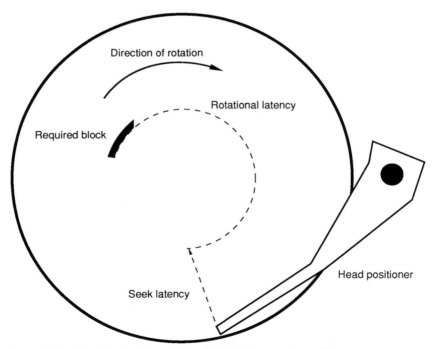

Figure 3.4 The delays involved in accessing a block of data stored on a disk

the bucket/buffer analogy, the transfer rate corresponds roughly to the rate at which water comes out of the tap into the bucket, and the access time corresponds to the gaps between times when the tap is turned on. If it is assumed for the moment that a hole exists in the bucket out of which water can flow at a constant rate (it would not in the real world, but let us assume that there is a valve in the hole which keeps the flow rate constant), then water will continue to flow out of the hole while there is water in the bucket. The water flowing out of the hole corresponds to the audio output of a tapeless recording system. The bucket will become empty only (a) if the bucket is filled too slowly while the tap is turned on (too low a flow rate), (b) if the gaps between fills are too long, or (c) if the rate of flow out of the hole is too great.

If the store were made up of solid state RAM which has a negligible access time (of the order of tens or hundreds of nanoseconds) then a transfer rate of 0.75 Mbit s^{-1} would be adequate for the replay or recording of a single high-quality channel at 48 kHz, 16 bits (see section 3.1). With a disk drive, the access time (which is likely to be of the order of milliseconds) will severely limit the average transfer rate to and from the buffer. Although the *instantaneous* transfer rate from the disk to the buffer may be high, the gaps between transfers as the drive searches for new blocks of data will reduce the *effective* rate. This is not to say that fast transfer rates are not desirable, because it is the combination of access time and transfer rate that go to make up the effective transfer rate. What is needed is fast transfer rates *and* fast access times.

To take an example, assume a disk drive with an average access time of 30 milliseconds and a transfer rate of 10 Mbit s^{-1}. If the access time had been near zero then the transfer rate of 10 Mbit s^{-1} would have allowed the audio data for some 13 channels to be transferred at the rates given above, but the effective transfer rate in real operation will bring this number down to perhaps six channels or less for safe, reliable operation in a wide variety of operational circumstances. It may be clear by now that the optimisation of efficiency of data transfer to and from a storage device will depend on keeping the number of accesses to a minimum for any given file, and this requires careful optimisation of the size and position of the audio data blocks.

3.11 Multi-channel considerations with disk systems

The terms 'track' and 'channel' may not necessarily mean the same thing in a disk-based system. In a multitrack tape recorder each physical track is dedicated to a numbered audio channel. In the tapeless system, the 'track' and 'channel' may be separated from each other, in that a sound recorded on any track may be replayed on any audio channel, it simply being a matter of re-routing the data to a different audio output (rather like re-patching an analogue signal on a jackfield). It may even be that the concept of the track is done away with altogether, but this depends on the user interface of the particular system, and some manufacturers have chosen to retain the concept of tracks so as to make the new technology approachable.

In many recording situations it is unlikely, for example, that a half hour programme utilising eight channels of output will use anything like eight times half an hour (4 hours) of storage space, because many 'tracks' may be blank for large amounts of the time. The total storage time will depend on the total duration of the monophonic sound files used in the programme, whatever channels they are assigned to. It is often said that tapeless systems do not record the silences on tracks, and therefore will use less than the predicted amount of storage space for a given number of track hours, but this may be misleading as space *will* be used if a silent passage is actually recorded as part of a file. The only time when silences save storage time is when they exist as blank spaces between the output of sound files, where no sound file is assigned to play (see Figure 3.5).

Multi-channel disk recording systems often use more than one disk drive, since there is a limit to the number of channels which can be serviced by a single drive. It is necessary, therefore, to determine firstly how many channels a storage device may handle realistically, and then to work out how many of these must be utilised to give the total storage capacity required. With multiple drives it is difficult to decide which files should be written to which storage device. To take an example, assume that each storage device handles four channels of audio, and that there are two storage devices, allowing a total of eight channels to be replayed together. What happens if the user decides that he or she wants eight files simultaneously replayed, all of which reside on only one of the storage devices? It is unlikely that the transfer rate of one device on its own is going to be able to cope with an eight channel replay. If truly-expandable multitrack recording is to be allowed, then it appears necessary to decide in advance which files shall be assigned to which storage devices, or perhaps less restrictively, to prevent in software the replay of more than a certain number of files simultaneously if they all reside in one store. Whether or not this is a problem depends rather on whether or not one is trying to imitate the functions of a multitrack tape recorder.

It is somewhat more acceptable in a music recorder to allow certain limitations on sound-file-to-audio-channel allocation, and to treat 'tracks' and 'channels' as the same thing. In this case, for example, two channels might be assigned to each disk drive and each drive could be constrained only ever to handling these channels. If sound files were to be copied from track to track, then true copying between storage devices would be required, rather than simple 'soft' reallocation of a file to a different output. This can be rather more wasteful on storage space than the soft assignment approach. Figure 3.6 illustrates an example of the two approaches.

One of the principal features of the tapeless system is its ability to replay files to

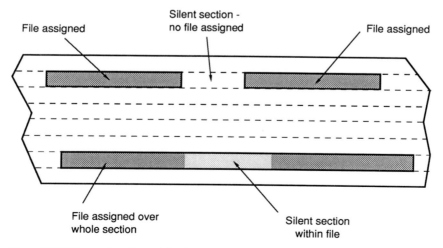

Figure 3.5 Disk space is only used for the storage of silent passages when the silence has actually been recorded. To save disk space, do not record silent passages

(a)

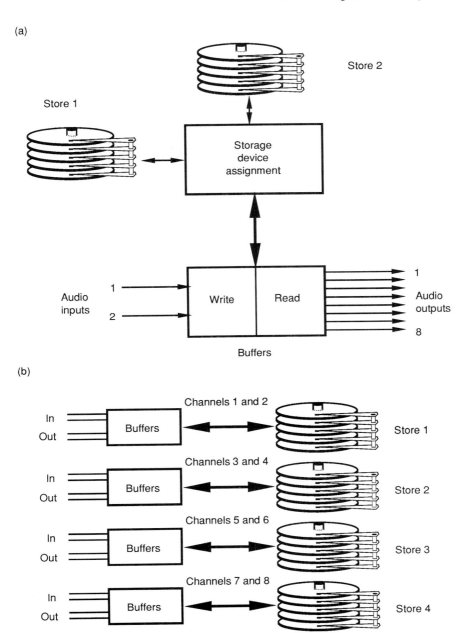

(b)

Figure 3.6 Two approaches to multi-channel disk recording. At (a) two drives are used for all eight audio outputs, and files are recorded from the stereo inputs to whichever drive is assigned by the controller. At (b) a drive is permanently assigned to a pair of audio inputs and outputs

any output channel at any time, because any preconceptions about fixed time relationships between files no longer hold true. If files which had once been close in time were to be placed physically close on the storage device this would favour a particular timing relationship between them, as it would give an access time advantage in the case where these files were required together, but a disadvantage if one of them was needed at the same time as one which was physically far away. Because of this it might be suggested that a storage strategy which places one file physically closer to another than it is to the rest of the files in the store will favour a particular relationship between those files. If there is the possibility for true random access to any file at any time then the only viable strategy is for files to be randomly distributed throughout the store, in which case no one relationship is favoured over any other.

The technique of pseudo-random storage described above maximises transfer efficiency in the case of true random access, but in the case of a system attempting to imitate a multitrack tape machine it may be that a strategy is adopted in which audio data is written to disk in a physically sequential order, such that a serial time relationship is established, assuming that files will be played throughout their lengths in a manner akin to tape replay. It must be said here, though, that in many modern disk-based recorders the system has only limited control over the storage strategy to be used on the disk, since so-called SCSI (Small Computer Systems Interface) drives are used because of their low cost. Such drives may allow little or no control over the allocation of blocks to sound files, preferring to manage this internally.

3.12 Disk storage media

In the sections below some examples are given of typical disk drive types (magnetic, optical and magneto-optical) which are suitable for use in tapeless recording systems.

3.12.1 The Winchester drive

The Winchester magnetic disk drive has been used in personal computers for quite some time now, as it provides space for the storage of a large amount of data in a relatively small space, is reliable, fast, and the cost is reasonable. The Winchester drive is a sealed unit, and the physical disks inside it cannot be removed to make way for others. It is not like the floppy disk drive that is present on most microcomputers which allows the user to insert and remove disks at liberty. The drive is a combination of physical disk surfaces on which data is stored, heads which read and write data, a positioner to move the heads to the right place, a motor which rotates the surfaces, a servo mechanism which controls the moving parts, and a controller which looks after the data flow to and from the surfaces, and interfaces to the rest of the computer system, an exploded diagram of which is shown in Figure 3.7.

The Winchester drive must be sealed (except sometimes for a small pressure-relief vent) in order to prevent the surfaces of the disks from becoming contaminated. The lack of contamination and the fact that the disks will never be removed means that fine tolerances can be used in manufacture, allowing a larger amount of data to be stored in a smaller space than is possible with removable magnetic disks. It also results in a very low error rate. More than one disk resides inside a Winchester

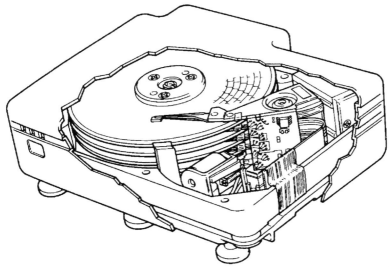

Figure 3.7 Inside a Winchester drive, a number of platters revolve on a common spindle, and heads are positioned over the surfaces by means of a rotary positioner. (Courtesy of MacUser magazine)

drive. These disks are rigid, not floppy, and all rotate on a common spindle. Each surface has its own 'pickup', or read/write head, which can be moved across the disk surface to access data stored in different places. The heads do not touch the surface of the disks during operation: they float just a small distance above the surface, lifted by the aerodynamic effect of the air on the head carrier due to the rotation of the disk. A small area of the disk surface is set aside for the heads to land on when the power is turned off, and this area does not contain data.

Data is stored in a series of concentric rings (*tracks*), each divided up into sections called *blocks*. Each block is separated by a small gap and preceded by an address mark which uniquely identifies the block's location. The term *cylinder* relates to all the tracks which reside physically in line with each other in the vertical plane through the different surfaces, and the term *sector* refers to a block projected on to the multiple layers of the cylinder (see Figure 3.8). A block typically contains 512 bytes.

Winchester drives chosen for audio applications tend to have the characteristic of allowing the transfer of data at 'disk rate', that is at a rate fast enough for all the data contained in one track to be transferred in one rotation of the drive. Typical performance parameters for the modern Winchester drive are:

Storage capacity:	~ 1200 Mbytes max.
Access time:	10–50 ms
Transfer rate:	<15 Mbit s^{-1}

These parameters, although not met by all drives, make the drive highly suitable as an audio storage device. Its access-time and transfer-rate combination makes it suitable for the recording or replay of a number of audio channels at professional rates in real time, and the storage capacity makes it possible to store up to around 3 hours of monophonic audio, although typical drives used in commercial audio

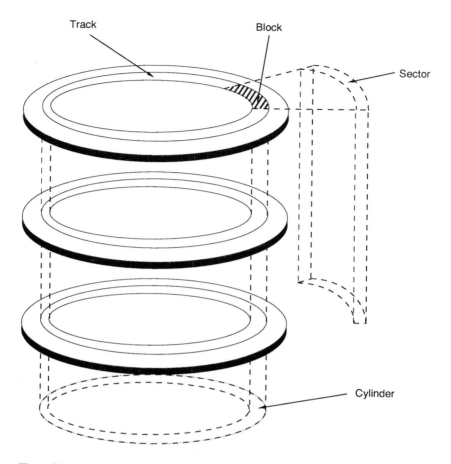

Track

Block

Sector

Cylinder

Figure 3.8 The data surfaces of a Winchester are divided into tracks, blocks, cylinders and sectors

systems have a capacity of around 360 Mbytes. The disk is of the 'write-many-times' format which means that old data may be overwritten many times in order to reuse the storage. Archiving is performed by downloading data from the drive to a removable medium such as a tape cartridge or optical disk.

The size of a Winchester drive makes it easy to install in a compact system, as the disk surfaces tend to be either 3.5 or 5.25 inches in diameter. A quiet drive is important for audio operations, especially if the drive is to be installed in the same room as the operator, for drives vary considerably as to their noisiness.

3.12.2 Optical disks - general

There are a number of families of optical disk drive, which have differing operational and technical characteristics. The question of whether or not disks may be interchanged between them requires some discussion, since the method of formatting and the method of data pickup may differ. Furthermore, each family differs from the other in its suitability for tapeless audio recording. The most obvious difference lies in the erasable or non-erasable nature of the disks. Non-erasable disks are called WORMs, for Write-Once-Read-Many, since the disk may only be written once by the user, after which the recording is permanent. The Compact Disc is not even Write-Once (at least from the user's point of view), since it is stamped at the factory and acts as a replay-only medium, although the CD-R, or recordable CD, is now available, being a CD-compatible disk which may be recorded once but not erased. This will have some applications in tapeless recording, but is unlikely to be appropriate for real-time editing, as discussed below. WORM cartridges enclose the optical disk in a plastic case, rather like a large floppy disk, which protects the disk from damage. CDs are single sided, whereas WORM cartridges may be double or single sided.

One major difference between the WORM cartridge and the CD format is that most WORMs use CAV (Constant Angular Velocity) recording, whereas CD's use CLV (Constant Linear Velocity) recording. Thus the CD drive changes rotational speed depending on the position of the pickup, whereas the WORM usually rotates at a constant speed (although one or two drives use CLV recording). This has a number of effects on performance, notably a longer access time for the CLV system, partly because of the extra servo action required to change the disk speed, and partly because the CD rotates more slowly than the WORM (between 200 and 500 rpm as opposed to around 1000 rpm), which increases rotational latency (the time taken to access a block of data once the head has moved to the right radius).

The erasable optical disk is similar in appearance to the WORM, but uses different technology which allows data to be erased and the surface re-recorded. Magneto-optical techniques are used for this purpose (see below). The speed of magneto-optical disks is beginning to approach the speed of a slow Winchester drive, which opens up possibilities for using them as a direct replacement for the Winchester. One of the major hurdles which had to be overcome in the design of such optical drives was that of making the access time suitably fast, since the optical pickup head is much more massive than the head positioner in the magnetic drive (it weighs around 100 g as opposed to around 10 g). Techniques are being developed to rectify this situation, since it is the primary limiting factor in the onward advance of optical storage (see Fact File 4).

3.12.3 The WORM drive

The WORM writing process involves the one-time modification of the disk's recording surface, such that the reflectivity of the surface is altered. The disk is made up of a sandwich of protective layer, reflective layer, recording layer and polycarbonate substrate (see Figure 3.9). In the Sony WORM cartridge, the recording layer is itself a sandwich of bismuth–tellurium and antimony selenide, which is claimed to offer a storage life of over 100 years, an important consideration since WORMs are ideal as an archival medium. In order to write data to the disk, the laser power is increased considerably above the power required to read data, such that the recording layer becomes heated and forms an alloy which has a different reflectivity pattern to the unheated areas. The surface of a WORM disk is 'pre-grooved' and formatted, to provide a guide track for the drive to follow when writing data. On replay, the lower-powered laser light is reflected back from the surface with a varying intensity which depends on the existence or lack of recorded areas. A WORM drive and disk are shown in Figure 3.10.

A number of different formats for WORMs exist, and not all disks are compatible

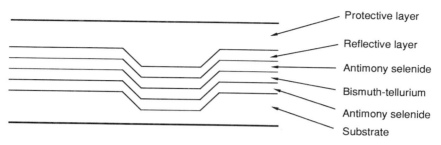

Protective layer

Reflective layer

Antimony selenide

Bismuth-tellurium

Antimony selenide

Substrate

Figure 3.9 Cross-section through a typical WORM disk

Figure 3.10 A WORM disk and drive. (Courtesy of Panasonic UK)

between different manufacturers' systems. Panasonic, for example, currently offers two drives which differ considerably in performance and capacity. Each requires a differently-formatted optical disk. Their LF-5200 drive uses disks which hold 200 Mbytes per side, using conventional sectors of 512 bytes with fixed angle of arc no matter what the radius, whereas the LF-5010 drive offers greater storage capacity by operating in a non-standard mode which increases the number of sectors in outer tracks compared with the number in inner tracks. The disks for this drive have 1024 byte sectors and hold 470 Mbytes per side. The rotation speeds are also different, being 875 rpm in the former and 1200 rpm in the latter. The performance of the latter drive is much more spectacular than the former, offering an instantaneous data transfer rate at the optical head of 5.55 Mbit s^{-1} (average) compared with 2.5 Mbit s^{-1}. From this it may be seen that the world of WORMs is not a straightforward one.

A WORM disk may be written-to until its capacity is filled, the directory of contents being added to as the number of files increases. Since the WORM disk may not be erased, data is very secure, and sound recordings committed to WORM would be free from the danger of accidental erasure. Files are stored sequentially, that is blocks of data are recorded one after the other in numerical sequence, with new files being recorded immediately after the end of the last file on the disk. There is no danger of the disk becoming fragmented since old data is never erased. These factors add up to making the WORM quite suitable for the storage of mono or stereo sound files, but perhaps less suitable for multi-channel operation. Whether or not real-time editing is possible from a WORM depends on the performance of the drive: an average transfer rate of at least 4 Mbit s^{-1} is sensible as a minimum for flexible stereo operation.

3.12.4 The magneto-optical (M-O) drive

M-O drives use optical disks which may be erased and re-recorded, and the principle of recording and replay is different to that used in the WORM drive, although still making use of the principle of laser pickup from a reflective surface. In order to write data, the laser is used at a higher power to that used in the reading process, again to heat spots in the recording layer which is made up of rare earth elements (typically gadolinium and terbium). A biasing magnet is used to create a weak magnetic field in the vicinity of the heated spot on the disk, whose recording layer then takes on this prevailing magnetic polarisation, although under normal conditions the recording layer cannot be magnetised (see Figure 3.11). When the spot cools it retains this magnetisation. Although the data is recorded by a combination of optical heating

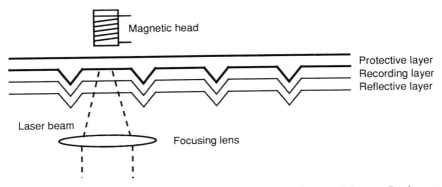

Figure 3.11 The magneto-optical disk is recorded by exposing small areas of the recording layer to high-power laser light, whereupon they take on the magnetic polarity provided by the polarising magnet. On replay, the magnetic polarisation affects the polarisation of reflected laser light

Normal CAV sectors

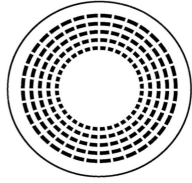

FACT FILE	Improving
4	optical drive performance

Improvements in optical drive performance appear to require both deviations from the ISO draft standard formatting of the disk in order to increase the capacity, and modifications to the pickup mechanism in order to speed up access time. Maxtor achieves shorter access times in M-O drives using a combination of two methods. Firstly it separates the optical head into two parts, one fixed and one movable, such that the heavier part containing the laser is moved for long seeks whilst a lighter mirror may be electromagnetically turned to skew the laser beam across a small number of tracks ($\pm$100 tracks). Secondly, it uses a method of track location which cuts a further 10 ms off the access time by cutting the seek down to a single-stage process, rather than the dual-stage process used in other drives. This leads the company to claim an average 43.5 ms access time. The same drive also sports an instantaneous transfer rate of 13.7 Mbit s^{-1}, although it is hard to tell how this is achieved, since the rotation rate is only 2200 rpm, slower than the Sony drive which rotates at 2400 rpm and offers 7.4 Mbit s^{-1}. Improvements in the speed of read/write electronics are claimed to help in this area.

Canon achieves an instantaneous transfer rate of 9.1 Mbit s^{-1} from its drive, owing to the fast rotational speed of 3000 rpm. Its access time, though, is only 92 ms (one-third full stroke), 130 ms (full stroke), and 10 ms average latency. Preliminary data shows that the drive is slightly different from the ISO standard, offering 256 Mbytes per side capacity, with 1024 byte sectors, 16 sectors per track (there are 17 sectors per track in the ISO standard for 1024 byte sectors).

Companies aiming to increase the capacity of optical disks are doing so by

Zoned CAV sectors

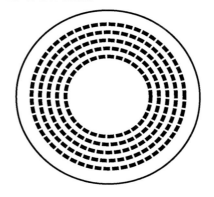

using a method known as 'zoned' or 'modified' CAV recording, in which outer tracks are made to carry more sectors than inner tracks (as shown in the diagram). There is more linear space in the outer tracks, which in normal operation leads to a lower recording density. In doing so, the disk becomes non-standard, but the capacity is increased to nearly 1 gigabyte (1000 Mbytes). This leads to a dilemma over whether one achieves greater capacity at the expense of standardisation. One company claims that its drive will operate in both ISO-standard and zoned-CAV modes, whereas others operate only in zoned-CAV mode.

and magnetisation, it is read by an entirely optical means which relies upon the fact that laser light reflected from the disk will be polarised depending on the *magnetic* polarisation of the recording layer. This is known as the Kerr effect, and the change in optical polarisation angle may be as small as a few degrees, depending on the material concerned. The reflected light passes through a polarisation analyser, resulting in changes in intensity of the light falling on a photodetector. The M-O disk is pre-grooved and sectored like the WORM drive.

The disk may be erased by heating the relevant area as it passes under the laser head, whilst biasing it with the opposite magnetic field direction to that used for recording, after which it may be rewritten by the same process as before. It is this erase cycle, required before rewriting, which makes M-O drives slower to write data than to read it, whereas Winchester drives erase old data simply by overwriting it with new data, and various techniques are being tried to circumvent the problem. In most drives, a permanent magnet is used to provide the biasing field which magnetises the spots on the disk when they are heated, the magnet being physically rotated between erase and write cycles to change the direction of the field (this can be achieved in a few milliseconds). Spots on the surface of the disk are magnetised or not by turning the laser on and off — only spots which are heated will have their magnetisation changed. Hitachi suggested a solution in late 1987 which appeared to allow rewriting without the primary erase revolution of the disk. It involved the use of an electromagnet rather than a permanent magnet, on the opposite side of the disk to the laser. In order to re-write, the laser heats the relevant areas of the disk and the magnetic field direction is switched electrically between −300 and +300 oersteds. It was said that this meant that recording could only take place on one side of the disk, and that oxidation of the disk surface would occur more quickly, shortening its life. 'Background erasure' has also been attempted by some designers trying to incorporate M-O drives into audio systems, which is a means of erasing old files 'in the background' whilst the drive is not being used for audio transfer, thus freeing up space for new files which may then be written without requiring the erase pass.

An ISO draft standard exists for M-O drives, to which most of the major manufacturers are adhering. This allows for two different sector sizes (512 bytes and 1024 bytes), giving 297 and 325 Mbytes per side of storage capacity respectively on a 5.25 inch disk (594 or 650 Mbytes in total). M-O drives rotate slightly faster than most WORM drives (Ricoh quotes 1800 rpm, Sony quotes 2400 rpm, and Canon quotes 3000 rpm), and again use CAV recording. Standards and interchange are discussed further below. The performance of M-O drives is good, with access times between 40 and 100 ms and a usable transfer rate of around 5 Mbit s^{-1}. Exactly how this relates to performance in an audio system depends considerably on the file storage strategy used. Some manufacturers have deviated from the ISO specification in order to achieve faster access and greater capacity, using techniques similar to those used in WORM drives, putting more sectors in outer tracks (see Fact File 4).

3.12.5 Phase-change drives

In phase-change recording data is written by a high-power laser, in much the same way as with a WORM, changing spots from a non-crystalline (amorphous) state to a crystalline state. In the crystalline state the reflectivity is increased considerably over that of the amorphous state. Data is again read back by a lower-power laser which detects changes in reflectivity. So the process is very WORM-like, but it is claimed that by careful selection of the recording material and laser beam control the process may be made reversible (and thus data may be overwritten). The only apparent drawback is the number of re-write cycles allowed (cycles of erasure and re-recording), which is quoted by Panasonic as being an order of ten lower than that of the M-O disk (between 10^5 and 10^6, as opposed to between 10^6 and 10^7).

3.12.6 CD-R and CD-E

The CD-R is a write-once Compact Disc which conforms with 'Red Book' CD standards, that is it will replay on any standard CD player. As such it has all the characteristics of the standard CD and uses CLV recording. The construction of the CD-R is similar to that of the WORM disk, in that it has a polycarbonate substrate, a recording layer (this time of organic dye), a gold reflective layer (although the gold may be changed in the future), and a protective layer (see Figure 3.12). As a CD it has a storage capacity of around 600 Mbytes, and data is recorded using the 8-to-14 modulation technique used for ordinary CDs. The CLV recording means that the rotational speed varies as the pickup moves from the centre to the outside, and the servo action required for this coupled with the relatively low rotational speed tends to limit access times to around 500 ms. Furthermore, the table of contents (TOC) must be written in a one-time operation, based on the PQ encoding of the data stored on the disk, making it difficult to use the CD-R for professional editing purposes in which files might be written to the disk at different times (the 'directory', in other words, may not easily be updated).

The CD-R is intended for purposes which require CD compatibility rather than fast access times and updatability. As such it is not immediately suitable for tapeless recording systems, but can be seen to have considerable value for the storage and archival of sound material which does not require real-time editing. Broadcasters see an immediate usage in sound effects libraries, since a professional CD player may be cued up and played-in manually, or under external control, with sufficient accuracy for this purpose. Studios and mastering facilities may use them for providing customers and record companies with 'acetates' or test pressings of a new recording.

The CD-E, or erasable CD, is not commercially available at the time of writing, but is widely expected to appear within the next few years. Its characteristics will be similar in many ways to those of the CD-R, except that it may be erased and recorded more than once.

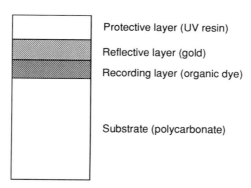

Protective layer (UV resin)

Reflective layer (gold)

Recording layer (organic dye)

Substrate (polycarbonate)

Figure 3.12 Cross-section through a typical CD-R

Interchange of optical disks

It might well be imagined that compatibility between optical disks will be virtually non-existent. There will certainly be incompatibilities, but there are a number of points to be made. The first point is that M-O disks which conform to the ISO standard should be able to be read by other drives which conform to the same standard. M-O drives do not all rotate at the same speed, although this should not affect interchange, since the data structure on the disks should be the same, but transfer rate will be better on faster drives. Whether or not this interchangeability applies to audio systems using M-O drives is rather another question, because the way in which sound files are stored on the disks will differ between each system. Some systems will store sound files contiguously, whilst others may 'scatter store' files to make for better random access performance. Some systems may store stereo sound files as a special entity with a single directory entry, whilst other systems may store each audio channel in a separate file. There is no agreement on the number of audio channels which should be served by one drive.

At the time of writing, progress has begun on the standardisation of an interchange file format for professional audio systems. The major difficulty is that the file storage strategy used by each manufacturer is a closely-guarded secret, since it is one of the main keys to successful and flexible operation. A universal interchange format will most likely be devised, and it is also possible that manufacturers may devise software which allows their systems to read a third-party's files, since only if interchange can be made easy will people consider disks as a universal alternative to tape. This situation already exists in desktop computing in other areas, since although a computer may be able to read disks from another drive of the same sort, it may not be able to read and write a particular word processor format, so translator software exists to allow for exchange of text files between word processors. From preliminary information it appears that the interchange format would be a unique format designed principally for making sound files transportable. It is unlikely that the full editing and manipulation features of a system would be available on interchange files, since this would require that they be converted into the system's native file format first. Limited edit list information may also be made the subject of an interchange format, although the extent of this is not yet clear.

3.12.7 Optical disks in tapeless recording

Most of the audio products which to date have incorporated either WORM drives or M-O drives have done so by making the optical drive a secondary store for audio data, with a Winchester drive as the main store. The optical drive has thus acted as a library or database of sounds which may be used by copying them to the Winchester hard disk. Now that reasonable speed can be achieved from M-O drives, it is possible that we may begin to see them becoming main storage devices in their own right, with no Winchester in sight. Indeed, Akai has a digital recorder, the DD-1000 (see Figure 3.13), which uses an M-O drive as its main storage, offering two stereo channels of recording and replay (four channels in total, but arranged as stereo pairs).

The performance of the optical drive, as already suggested, limits its potential in audio recording. If it can achieve similar performance to the hard disk there is no reason to consider continuing with the hard disk, unless there is an enormous price difference, since the optical disk has many advantages. Optical studio recorders may become more widespread in the next few years. A stereo recorder with no editing

Figure 3.13 The Akai DD-1000 optical disk recorder uses an magneto-optical erasable disk as the sole recording medium. (Courtesy of Akai UK)

facilities could be designed very easily (a suggested block diagram is shown in Figure 3.14), with the option for connecting the recorder to an editing system. Alternatively, the disk from the studio recorder could be edited elsewhere by taking the disk and inserting it into the drive of the editing system.

3.13 Use of RAM in digital audio storage

RAM is a form of solid state memory which may be written to and read many times, having almost instantaneous access time (~100 nanoseconds). It is normally volatile, that is it loses its memory when it loses power, although some types may be backed up using a battery supply. Typically, RAM is available in units of up to 4 Mbytes (although storage density is the subject of regular increases).

A number of audio products make use of RAM in conjunction with disk drives, as described in the preceding sections, and a few use it exclusively for audio data storage. One commercial example, pictured in Figure 3.15, uses RAM as the main working store, having a hard disk to 'shadow' the RAM storage, acting as a backup in case of power failure. RAM is not a block-structured store, and thus is not subject to the same divisions of the total capacity that must be made with disks. Even so, it is common for RAM to be divided up in software system architecture so as to make it appear to act as a disk drive in some applications, functioning as a so-called 'RAM disk'. In this way the operating system may treat the RAM as a very fast disk drive.

The principal problem with using RAM as the sole means of audio storage is the cost of providing adequate capacity. Currently, the retail cost of RAM is typically in the region of $50–100 per megabyte, putting the cost of a professional-quality track-hour of audio storage at around $18 000. This compares with a current cost of only a few thousand dollars for the equivalent Winchester or optical disk drive.

Nonetheless, RAM storage is used in systems where shorter storage times are required, such as in radio workstations which are used for the assembly and editing of 'trails', commercials and short programme items. As RAM becomes cheaper it

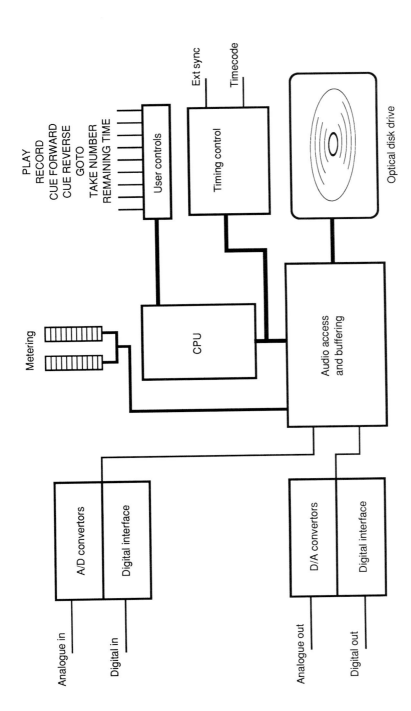

Figure 3.14 Conceptual block diagram of a proposed optical disk audio recorder

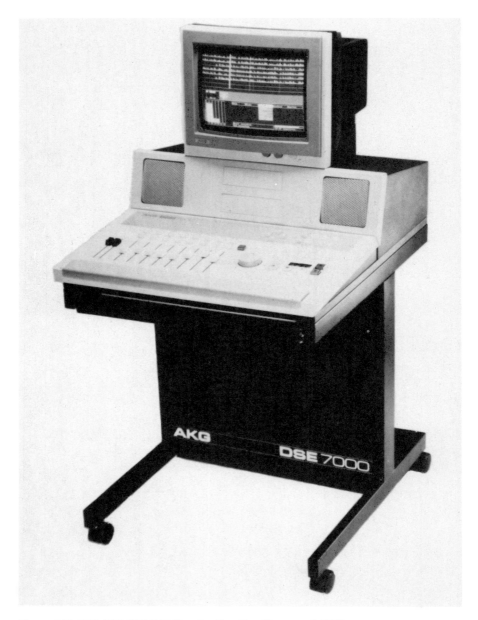

Figure 3.15 AKG DSE-7000 RAM-based audio editor (Courtesy of AKG)

is possible that it will be more widely used, since the very fast transfer rates and access times make it attractive for use in systems with multiple outputs. The volatility of RAM is likely to preclude its widespread use as a longer-term storage format.

Chapter 4

An overview of digital tape recording

In the preceding chapter the methods by which digital audio is stored on disks have been examined, together with a discussion of the differences between disk and tape recording from a point-of-view of usage of available storage capacity. In this chapter the principles of digital audio storage on tape will be examined in a similar overview fashion, together with a summary of the technical features of the different digital tape formats which are important to those who use them. The emphasis is placed on helping the reader to understand the merits of different formats and their implementations from a practical point of view, rather than examining the tape format *per se* as an abstract concept. Only the recording formats in wide use throughout the world will be examined in detail, and it is not intended to go into a detailed analysis of error correction strategies, channel codes and circuit design, since excellent coverage of these subjects is to be found elsewhere. Operational implications of choosing one recording format over another are discussed in Chapter 7, whilst the principles of digital editing are covered in Chapter 5.

4.1 Two-track and multitrack recording

In the following sections a clear distinction will be made between two-track (and stereo) recording and multitrack recording. Some recording formats cover both of these possibilities (such as the stationary-head DASH and ProDigi formats), but many are limited to two-channel operation only. There is a greater range of two-channel and stereo formats available than multitrack formats. The difference between 'two-channel' and 'stereo' is that a true two-channel format allows the independent recording of tracks 1 and 2, whilst the stereo format requires that both tracks are recorded simultaneously. The stereo format is therefore really suitable only for situations in which the two tracks are the left and right channels of a stereo pair, whereas the two-channel format allows for channel 2 to be recorded at a different time to the channel 1 recording. Multitrack is taken to mean four tracks and upwards, the current maximum number of digital audio tracks available being 48 on one machine.

4.2 Background to tape storage of digital audio

Stereo digital recording systems have been commercially available since the early

1980s, although experimental systems existed before that. At that time it was necessary to make use of a so-called PCM adaptor and a video recorder, since the bandwidth required for two channels of digital audio was more akin to that required for analogue video than analogue audio. Sony produced PCM adaptors for professional usage, such as the PCM-100, pictured in Figure 4.1 (see section 4.6), and the PCM-1600 which rapidly evolved into the PCM-1610, well known as the standard system for CD mastering during the early part of the 1980s (see section 4.8). Sony also produced consumer PCM adaptors, such as the PCM-F1 and PCM-701, which became more widely used by professionals than domestic users because of their low cost (in professional terms) and high sound quality. The record company Decca had also developed an in-house digital recording system, based on modified IVC open-reel video transports, and JVC had a pseudo-video system similar to Sony's PCM-1610. All of these systems were stereo rather than two channel, since the data for left and right channels was multiplexed in the same video signal, and no signal could be monitored 'off tape' with the early systems. Electronic copy editing of recordings was possible with the PCM-1610 format, the Decca system and the JVC format, using a special editing controller (see section 5.3), but was not normally possible with all of the so-called EIAJ-format systems (PCM-100, PCM-F1, PCM-701) because of the error correction structure and the tape format, although some third-party systems were developed which made possible limited electronic editing on such recordings. Splice editing was not possible.

Multitrack recording was not possible using the same approach, due to the high data rates involved and the need in multitrack systems for the traditionally expected facilities of punch-in and punch-out, independent channel recording, overdub modes, sync replay and off-tape monitoring. In short, a digital multitrack tape machine was expected to emulate all of the functions currently available on an

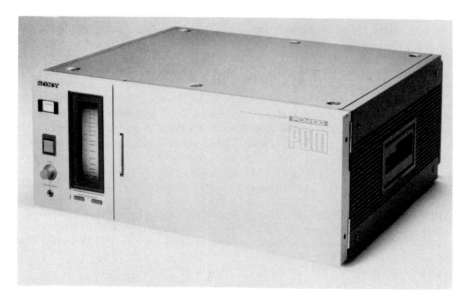

Figure 4.1 The Sony PCM-100 PCM adaptor was one of the first professional PCM adaptors to be available in the early 1980s, allowing two channels of 14-bit audio to be recorded on an NTSC video recorder. (Courtesy of Sony.)

analogue machine. Another facility deemed vital to the success of digital tape recording at the time, especially by broadcasters, was splice editing, that is the ability to edit the tape by cutting and sticking, just as in analogue recording. With hindsight this has proved to be a 'red herring', and may have resulted in a lot of development work for little return, since there is little evidence that splice editing is widely used in professional digital recording, and little evidence that broadcasters have actually purchased the splice-editing digital tape machines which resulted from their suggestions. There are perhaps two main reasons for this, one being that splice editing in digital recording is less reliable and less flexible than in analogue recording (see section 11.1), and the other being that the cost of the digital machines which offer this facility is around four times that of the equivalent analogue machine.

In order to implement splice-editing facilities and multitrack operations equivalent to those of analogue recorders, a number of stationary-head open-reel recording formats were developed (see section 4.3), the two commercially-surviving formats at the time of writing being the DASH (Digital Audio Stationary Head) and ProDigi formats. These formats catered for a whole family of recording options from two track up to 48 track (32 in the ProDigi format), and have found greater success in the digital multitrack market rather than the two-track mastering market. More recently, stationary-head recording has been used in digital cassette tape formats such as that used by Yamaha for eight-track systems (see section 4.16).

During the later 1980s, the PCM-adaptor-with-video-recorder approach became superseded for stereo recording by true rotary-head digital tape systems, the most well known and widely used of which is the R-DAT format (Rotary-head Digital Audio Tape). Like the PCM-F1 and PCM-701 before it, R-DAT was supposed to be a low-cost consumer format to replace the analogue Compact Cassette, but it was fraught with political problems due to fears in the record industry that it would allow 'perfect' copies of CDs and therefore threaten the CD market due to pirating. To date R-DAT has failed to establish itself as a consumer recording format, but has been adopted widely in professional circles because of its relatively low cost and high performance. Professional DAT recorders are now available which offer editing and synchronisation options, making them suitable for a wide range of applications in stereo recording.

By the end of the 1980s there have also appeared formats designed for low-cost cassette-based digital multitrack recording, specifically that used by Akai in its 12-track A-DAM (Akai Digital Audio Multitrack) and by Yamaha in its eight-track cassette system (see section 4.16). These formats are unique to these manufacturers, and are designed for use in dedicated multitrack recorders. The Akai is a rotary-head system, and the Yamaha is a stationary-head system.

4.3 Rotary- and stationary-head recording compared

There are two fundamental mechanisms for the recording of digital audio on tape, one which uses a relatively low linear tape speed and a quickly-rotating head, and one which uses a fast linear tape speed and a stationary head (see Figure 4.2). In the rotary-head system the head either describes tracks almost perpendicular to the direction of tape travel (such as the method used in early quadruplex video recorders), or it describes tracks which are almost in the same plane as the tape travel. The former is known as transverse scanning and the latter is known as helical

(a)

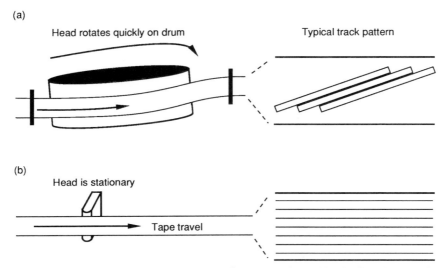

Head rotates quickly on drum   Typical track pattern

(b)

Head is stationary

Tape travel

Figure 4.2 Helical-scan and stationary-head recording compared. At (a) a head rotating on a fast-revolving drum describes angled tracks on a slow-moving tape, whilst at (b) a stationary head describes parallel, horizontal tracks on the tape

scanning, since in the latter the tape is wound helically around a head drum, whilst in the former the head drum scans the tape transversely as it passes. Transverse scanning uses more tape when compared with helical scanning. It is not common for digital tape recording to use the transverse scanning method.

The reason for using a rotary head is to achieve a high head-to-tape speed, since it is this which governs the available bandwidth. Although the tape itself travels quite slowly in such a system, the head rotates at high speed (often up to around 2000 rpm), which makes the *relative* speed between the head and the tape quite high. Many stereo recording systems make use of rotary-head technology, but it has not commonly been used for multitrack recording, and until recently it was difficult to achieve the required track capacity unless the recording time was made very short by using a high tape speed (this is the approach taken by Akai in the A-DAM system, see section 4.16). Recently, digital video has resulted in the development of rotary-head systems capable of recording very high bandwidths, and these allow the heads to be switched on and off for short portions of a helical scan, opening up the possibilities for flexible multitrack operation. Rotary-head recordings may not easily be splice edited (although see section 4.14 on the Nagra-D system), because of the track pattern. In rotary-head recording a large number of tracks would be destroyed by a splice edit, the tape is very easily damaged, and the recorded wavelengths are very short, all of which make it inadvisable to handle or cut the tape. Such recordings may, though, be electronically edited using at least two machines (see section 5.3).

Earlier rotary-head systems were based on video tape transports which recorded sloping tracks that did not overlap, in order to avoid crosstalk between tracks, but dedicated digital audio recorders such as R-DAT use a technique known as azimuth recording which lays down tracks which overlap each other (see Figure 4.3), by means of a pair of heads mounted opposite each other on the drum. In azimuth recording adjacent overlapping tracks are recorded with heads wider than the

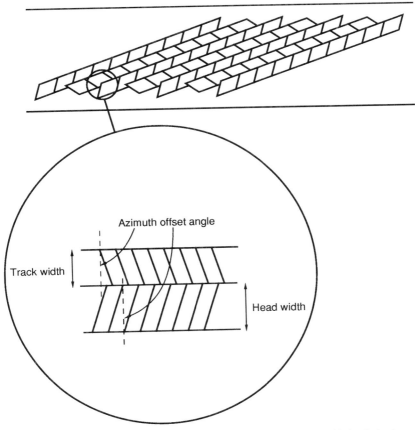

Figure 4.3 Azimuth recording involves the recording of overlapping tracks with heads having opposing azimuth angles. The resulting track is narrower than the head, once the overlap has been taken into account. Tracks are replayed with two heads of the appropriate azimuth, each experiencing considerable high-frequency attenuation of the adjacent track due to the azimuth error

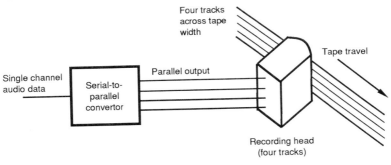

Figure 4.4 A single channel of audio data may be converted into a parallel form for recording across a number of tracks on tape. In this example the incoming audio data is spread across four tape tracks, thus reducing the data rate per track to one quarter of what it would have been if using only one track per channel

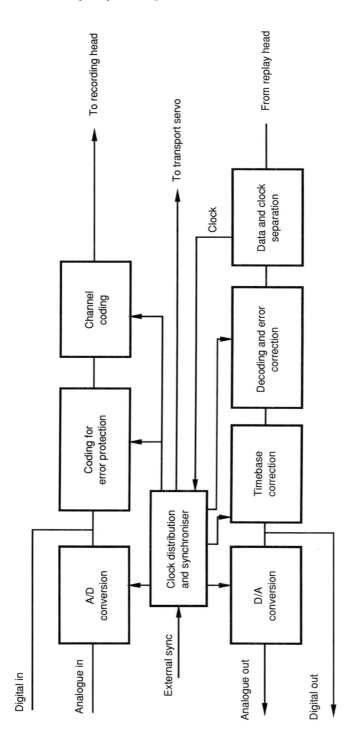

Figure 4.5 A generalised block diagram of a digital audio tape recorder

Channel coding

Since 'raw' binary data is normally unsuitable for recording directly onto tape, a 'channel code' is used which matches the data to the characteristics of the recording system, uses storage space efficiently, and makes the data easy to recover on replay. A wide range of channel codes exists, each with characteristics designed for a specific purpose. The channel code converts a pattern of binary data into a different pattern of transitions in the recording or transmission medium. It is another stage of modulation, in effect. Thus the pattern of bumps in the optical surface of a CD bears little resemblance to the original audio data, and the pattern of flux transitions on a DAT cassette would be similarly different. Given the correct code book, one could work out what audio data was represented by a given pattern from either of these systems.

Many channel codes are designed for a low DC content (in other words, the data is coded so as to spend, on average, half of the time in one state and half in the other) in cases where signals must be coupled by transformers, and others may be designed for narrow bandwidth or a limited high-frequency content. Certain codes are designed specifically for very-high-density recording, and may have a low clock content with the possibility for long runs in one binary state or the other without a transition. Channel coding involves the incorporation of data to be recorded with a clock signal, such that there is a sufficient clock content to allow the data and clock to be recovered on replay. Channel codes vary as to their robustness in the face of distortion, noise and timing errors.

Some examples of channel codes used in audio systems are shown in the diagram. FM is the simplest, being an example of binary frequency modulation. It is otherwise known as 'bi-phase mark', one of the Manchester codes, and is the channel code used in the AES/EBU interface and in

SMPTE/EBU timecode, as well as in any VCR-based digital recording format. MFM and Miller-squared are more efficient in terms of recording density, Miller^2 being used in the D2 digital video format. MFM is more efficient than FM because it eliminates the transitions between successive ones, only leaving them between successive zeros. Miller^2 eliminates the DC content present in MFM by removing the transition for the last one in an even number of successive ones.

Group codes, such as that used in the Compact Disc and R-DAT, involve the coding of patterns of bits from the original audio data into new codes with more suitable characteristics, using a look-up table or 'code book' to keep track of the relationship between recorded and original codes. This has clear parallels with coding as used in intelligence operations, in which the recipient of a message requires the code book to be able to understand the message. CD uses a method known as 8-to-14 modulation, in which original 16 bit words are each split into two 8 bit words, after which a code book is used to generate a new 14 bit word for each of the 256 possible combinations of 8 bits. Since there are many more words possible with 14 bits than with eight, it is possible to be choosy over which combinations of bits are selected, and those are chosen which have appropriate characteristics for the CD recording channel. In this case, it is those words which have no more than 11 consecutive bits in the same state, and no less than three. This limits the bandwidth of the recorded data, and makes it suitable for the optical pickup process, whilst retaining the necessary clock content.

Examples of channel codes

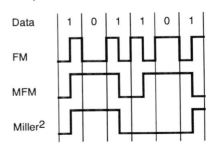

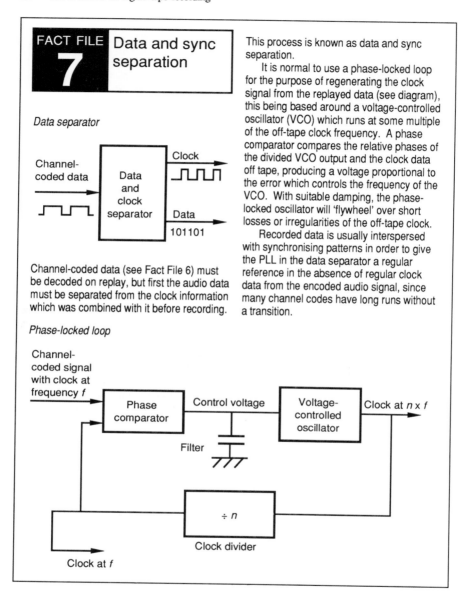

FACT FILE 7 Data and sync separation

This process is known as data and sync separation.

It is normal to use a phase-locked loop for the purpose of regenerating the clock signal from the replayed data (see diagram), this being based around a voltage-controlled oscillator (VCO) which runs at some multiple of the off-tape clock frequency. A phase comparator compares the relative phases of the divided VCO output and the clock data off tape, producing a voltage proportional to the error which controls the frequency of the VCO. With suitable damping, the phase-locked oscillator will 'flywheel' over short losses or irregularities of the off-tape clock.

Recorded data is usually interspersed with synchronising patterns in order to give the PLL in the data separator a regular reference in the absence of regular clock data from the encoded audio signal, since many channel codes have long runs without a transition.

Data separator

Channel-coded data → | Data and clock separator | → Clock

→ Data 101101

Channel-coded data (see Fact File 6) must be decoded on replay, but first the audio data must be separated from the clock information which was combined with it before recording.

Phase-locked loop

Channel-coded signal with clock at frequency *f* → Phase comparator → Control voltage → Voltage-controlled oscillator → Clock at *n* x *f*

Filter

÷ *n*

Clock divider

Clock at *f*

resulting track having different azimuth angles. On replay, the head with the correct azimuth for each track is controlled so as to follow the appropriate track, and the azimuth difference between tracks is such that signals from the adjacent track are attenuated considerably at high frequencies (just as high-frequency (HF) loss is experienced when an analogue replay head is out of azimuth). Crosstalk is thus avoided at high frequencies where the predominant spectral content of the digital audio signal lies. This technique is also used in D2-format video recording.

Stationary heads, on the other hand, have allowed the design of tape machines which are very similar in many respects to analogue transports. With stationary-head recording it is possible to record a number of narrow tracks in parallel across the width of the tape, perhaps with more than one tape track being used for each 'audio track'. It is already known that two channels of standard rate digital audio result in a data rate of around 1.5 Mbit s^{-1} (see section 3.1), and such a bandwidth initially seems impossible to record on a tape travelling at a similar speed to that of an analogue machine with an audio bandwidth of only 30 kHz.

Stationary-head systems manage to record and replay such a high bandwidth by a number of means. Firstly, the heads used are specially designed to have very narrow gaps and the tape is made very thin, to avoid the losses which would otherwise arise with short wavelength recording; secondly, a channel code (see Fact File 6) is used which restricts the bandwidth of the recorded signal; thirdly, the signal-to-noise ratio of the recording channel required by digital audio is much lower than that required by analogue audio because the system has only to be able to recognise the difference between two states on replay (see section 9.1); fourthly, it is possible to use 'saturation' recording in which the tape is magnetised to saturation, since it is the detection of transitions between polarity of magnetic domains which is important on replay; and fifthly, tape speed can be traded off against the number of parallel tracks used for each audio channel, since the required data rate can be made up by a combination of recordings made on, say, four separate tracks (see Figure 4.4). This approach is evident in the DASH format, where the tape speed may be 30 ips using one track-per-channel, 15 ips using two tracks per channel, or 7.5 ips using four tracks per channel (although see section 5.7 concerning 'twin DASH').

Although stationary- and rotary-head approaches differ in detail, it can be seen from looking at the generalised block diagram in Figure 4.5 that the principles are very similar. Both involve conversion, encoding and recording, followed by replay, data and sync separation (see Fact File 7), decoding and conversion. In this initial block diagram the additional heads and circuits needed for confidence replay, editing and overdub recording are not shown.

4.4 Confidence replay

It is common to find a facility for confidence replay in analogue tape machines, that is the facility for monitoring a signal 'off tape' whilst recording. In analogue systems confidence replay is achieved using a replay head mounted further down the tape than the record head, such that confidence replay is delayed by a fraction of a second (see Figure 4.6(a)). In a stationary-head digital recorder a similar approach can be taken. In a rotary-head system, confidence replay can be achieved by mounting a replay head at a different point on the head drum, such that it follows the record head by the delay taken for the head to rotate (see Figure 4.6(b)), reading the helically scanned track immediately after it has been recorded. This technique is also called 'read-after-write'.

4.5 Overdub, edit and 'read-after-read' operations

The incorporation of a second head or pair of heads into the rotating drum has other uses also, such as in editing and overdubbing. In these applications the function order of the heads must be reversed such that the replay head *leads* the record head,

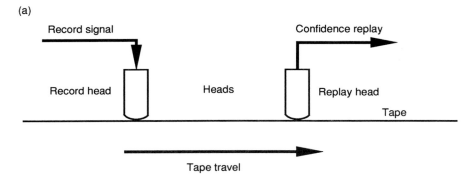

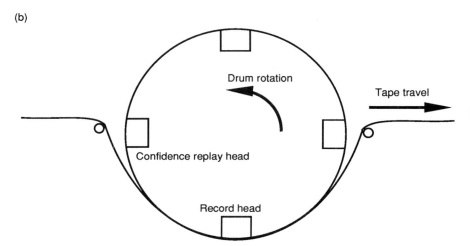

Figure 4.6 Confidence replay. At (a) the recorded signal is replayed by a head mounted further down the tape, as would be the case in a stationary-head system, whilst at (b) the confidence replay head is mounted in the rotating drum so as to follow the recorded track immediately after it has been written (rotary-head system)

in order that previously-recorded data may be read, modified, then written back to the tape by the trailing record heads (see Figure 4.7(a)). This approach, used for overdubbing and editing, is called 'read–modify–write'. In read–modify–write operation, the physical delay between the two heads must be the same as the digital delay which results from decoding and re-encoding the signal, allowing for a track to be re-recorded in its original location, but with modifications. These modifications might involve the crossfading of old material into new material at an edit point, or (in a multitrack system using rotary heads) might involve the replacement of a data block somewhere within the scan corresponding to a single overdubbed channel.

In stationary-head systems, the read–modify–write operation is achieved using a second replay head *before* the record head, possibly in addition to the confidence replay head which comes *after* the record head (see Figure 4.7(b)). Again the time taken for the tape to travel between the advanced replay head and the record head

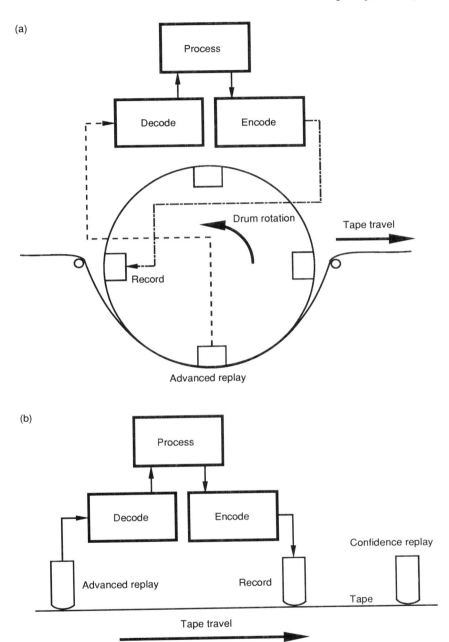

Figure 4.7 Read-modify-write recording. In the rotary-head system shown at (a) an advanced replay head reads previously-recorded data into the decoder, which is then processed (modified) and re-recorded by the trailing record head in exactly the same place. In the stationary-head system shown at (b) the advanced replay head is mounted further up the tape so as to read old data before it is re-recorded. In both cases the physical delay between the heads is equal to the decode–encode delay

must be equivalent to the decode/encode delay (which is electronically controlled so as to allow for varispeed operation). In a multitrack stationary-head recorder this head arrangement allows for overdubs on any track whilst monitoring others, an operation which, in analogue tape recording, would involve the 'sync replay' mode in which the record head is used for both recording and replay (since there is a negligible delay between the inputs and outputs of an analogue tape recorder), recording on the track to be overdubbed whilst replaying the other tracks. In analogue systems, sync replay from the record head may have a poorer frequency response than replay from the replay head, since the record head gap is often wider than the replay head gap, but in a digital system sync replay should be of exactly the same quality as normal replay.

In many systems, both rotary- and stationary-head, there are not enough heads to allow for both confidence replay *and* read–modify–write operation (editing, over-dubbing, etc.) at the same time. This is because either the leading head acts as the record head whilst the trailing head provides confidence replay ('normal' mode), or the leading head acts to provide advanced replay whilst the trailing head records ('edit' or 'overdub' mode). In such machines it is necessary to switch between modes depending on the application.

There is in fact another possible mode, used by Sony in its PCM-1630 system, called 'read-after-read', which allows for each helical track on the tape to be read twice (see Figure 4.8), using the read-after-read processor to determine which data to use. In this way, double error protection is provided, and may be useful if one head becomes clogged or faulty.

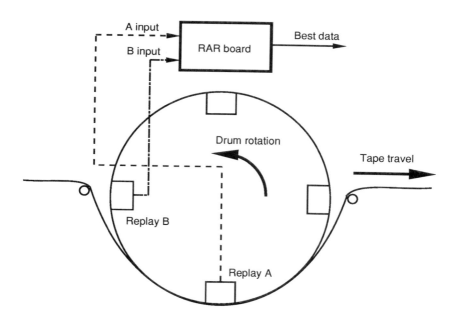

Figure 4.8 Read-after-read (RAR). Sony makes an optional board for the PCM-1630 which receives two video inputs from a special U-matic video machine having two replay heads. The board chooses the best data from the two heads, providing additional protection against head clogs

4.6 'Composite digital' encoding in PCM adaptors

As introduced in section 4.2, early stereo digital recording made use of ordinary video recorders. In such systems a PCM adaptor is used which takes an analogue or digital audio input and encodes it in such a way as to resemble a video signal, so that it can be recorded by a standard VTR (videotape recorder). This signal is sometimes labelled 'Composite Digital' on equipment, and should not be confused with other digital inputs and outputs (see section 10.2.1). All of the EIAJ-format processors are of this type (see section 4.7), as are the Sony PCM-1610 and 1630 CD mastering systems (see section 4.8) and the JVC VP-900 system (see section 4.13). These formats are described in more detail below, but it should be pointed out that in general the use of a PCM adaptor and separate VTR makes for less flexible operation than a dedicated rotary-head digital tape recorder, since VTRs were not originally built for handling digital audio.

PCM adaptors produce a pseudo-video output in either the 60 Hz/525 line format, the 59.94 Hz/525 line format or the 50 Hz/625 line format, depending on the system and the country. EIAJ-format processors are mostly designed for use with domestic VTRs of either the Betamax or VHS formats, and have error correction systems suitable for this purpose, whereas Sony CD-mastering PCM adaptors require U-matic VTRs, slightly modified for digital audio purposes. PCM adaptors are being gradually superseded by dedicated digital audio recorders, although there are a large number of systems world-wide which will remain in use, especially considering that the established CD-mastering format uses a PCM adaptor.

4.7 Specific considerations with EIAJ-format PCM adaptors

Systems based on the EIAJ format (devised by the Electronic Industries Association of Japan) are being superseded by R-DAT, although EIAJ-format processors formed the backbone of low-cost stereo digital audio recording for most of the 1980s. EIAJ-format PCM adaptors were produced by a variety of Japanese manufacturers, including Hitachi, but by far the most widely used have been those made by Sony. The PCM-10 and PCM-100 were the first commercial adaptors to appear, and these operated to the 59.94 Hz/525 line NTSC video standard used in Japan and the USA, among others. They were professional systems, intended for use with industrial Betamax VTRs which ran at twice the normal tape speed, the SLO-323 type being recommended. There was no 50 Hz/625 line (PAL) version of these adaptors, so European users were restricted to purchasing special VTRs for digital recording. The PCM-10 and 100 were 14 bit systems, using a sampling rate of 44.056 kHz, with pre-emphasis in the recording chain to 50/15 μs time constants (see Figure 4.9) and de-emphasis in the replay chain, in order to boost high frequencies on recording and cut them on replay in order to reduce the audibility of quantising noise.

Subsequently, Sony developed more reasonably priced consumer versions of the PCM adaptor, such as the PCM-F1 (a portable battery- or mains-powered device) and the PCM-701 (a mains-powered device), which revolutionised the world of digital recording (see Figure 4.10), since they allowed people to make recordings which did not differ in sound quality from those made on professional systems costing many times the price. The PCM-F1 and 701 both offered 16 bit resolution, having replay compatibility with the 14 bit version of the format used in the

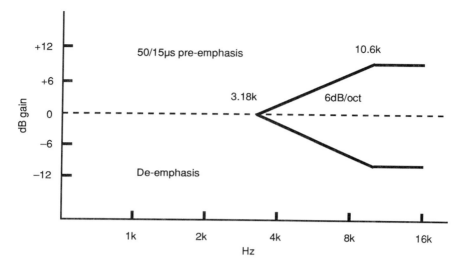

Figure 4.9 50/15 μs pre-emphasis and de-emphasis curves as used in a number of digital recording devices. High frequencies are boosted on record and cut on replay to reduce the effects of quantising noise

Figure 4.10 The Sony PCM-F1 was one of the first PCM adaptors to make digital stereo recording available widely, due to its low cost, high quality, and portability. (Courtesy of HHB)

PCM–100. The 16 bit version of the EIAJ-format is somewhat non-standard, since it relies on the removal of one of the error-correction words from the 14 bit format and its replacement by the extra data needed for 16 bit recording, but the advantages of 16 bit recording have been seen as of greater value than the increased error protection offered by the 14 bit version, mainly due to the fact that 16 bit, 44.1 kHz recordings can be used for CD masters. Consequently, 16 bit EIAJ recordings are more prone to catastrophic drop-out than 14 bit recordings, since the level of errors which can be tolerated before the system mutes or the audio output breaks up is lower.

These more recent EIAJ processors were available in either the PAL or NTSC video formats, and would work with ordinary domestic VTRs, although significant differences existed between the performance of VTRs in this respect, some exhibiting greater error rates than others. NTSC-format systems ran at a sampling rate of 44.056 kHz, whilst PAL-format adaptors ran at 44.1 kHz. PCM-F1s and 701s (and later 501s and 601s) could only record in one or other of the video formats, but any adaptor could *replay* either format, provided that the appropriate VTR was used. A number of third parties modified these systems to give them professional inputs and outputs, digital interfaces for copying recordings to professional formats for editing, and switchable PAL/NTSC outputs (PAL versions only). They also added what has become known as CTC (Coincident Time Correction) to correct for the fact that A/D conversion was performed by a single convertor shared between left and right channels, resulting in a half-sample delay (11.33 µs) between the timing of the channels. This did not matter if the recording was played back on a similar system, since the D/A convertor worked in the same way, thus reinstating the correct relationship, but was important if the signal was copied digitally to a system (such as Sony's PCM-1610) which used dual synchronous convertors. Without CTC in such a situation, a small phase difference would have resulted between the channels which was particularly noticeable when CDs made from PCM-1610 or 1630 tapes were replayed in mono, since the phase difference resulted in a reduction of HF signal level.

The EIAJ-format involved 'convolutional interleaving' of the audio data in such a way that data blocks were not complete within one field of video (corresponding to one helically-scanned track on tape), and this made it very difficult to edit recordings, since errors were created if a video edit was performed at a frame boundary, resulting in an audible 'spit' or 'click'. Sony's DAE-1100 editor was able to handle correctly EIAJ-format recordings made using a PCM-100 and a U-matic recorder, but very few people used this method of recording. Without this system, if a video edit was performed in a silent passage (such as between tracks) then sometimes it was acceptable, but even then a sound could often be heard. Consequently a number of people attempted to develop systems which 'hid' the sound of the edit, one (the audio dealer HHB's 'CLUE' system) using the error flag from the PCM adaptor to trigger a short HF attenuation for a few milliseconds over the edit point, and this was moderately successful commercially.

The recording time of these systems was essentially that of the VTRs with which they were associated, namely around 3 hours maximum with VHS and Beta, but experience showed that the use of 2 hour tapes was a safer option, since 3 hour tapes are very thin and more prone to drop-out.

4.8 Sony CD-mastering format

Sony's PCM-1610 and -1630 PCM adaptors have dominated the CD-mastering market for a number of years, although by today's standards they use a fairly basic recording format and rely on U-matic VTRs. The system operates at a sampling rate of 44.1 kHz and uses 16 bit quantisation, being designed specifically for the making of tapes to be turned into CDs. It requires the use of a 60 Hz/525 line U-matic machine with minor modifications for digital audio use, including the disabling of the internal video drop-out compensator which would normally replace drop-outs with video black, and the shifting of the head switching point. Originally Sony recommended the use of U-matics such as the BVU-200 or VO-5850 machines, but subsequently they have sold U-matic machines dedicated to digital audio use, having internal timecode generators and being ready modified, namely the DMR-2000 and DMR-4000 systems. The DMR-4000 is based on the BVU-800 professional U-matic machine, having confidence replay designed for use with the optional read-after-write and read-after-read facilities of the PCM-1630 (see sections 4.4 and 4.5).

Recordings made in this format may be electronically edited using either the DAE-1100 or DAE-3000 editing systems, and the playing time of tapes runs up to 75 minutes using a tape specially developed for digital audio use.

Because the system is based around a 60 Hz/525 line video standard, it is not easy to synchronise recordings with European-standard video recordings, although means have been devised to achieve this end (see section 14.5).

4.9 DASH, PD and X-80 formats

The DASH format preceded the ProDigi (or PD) format by a number of years, and consists of a whole family of open-reel stationary-head recording formats from two tracks up to 48 tracks. There is commonality between the formats used for different track capacities (see Table 7.3). DASH-format machines may operate at 44.1 kHz or 48 kHz (and sometimes optionally at 44.056 kHz), and they allow varispeed ±12.5%. They are designed to allow gapless punch-in and punch-out, splice editing, electronic editing and easy synchronisation. Twin DASH was developed for two-track recording to make tape-cut editing more robust (see section 5.7). Currently the format is supported by more than one manufacturer, these being Sony, Studer and TEAC. Existing machines at the time of writing include the Sony PCM-3102, 3202, 3402, and the Studer D820X (two track); Sony PCM-3324, 3324A, Studer D820X, TEAC (24 track); and Studer D820X and Sony PCM-3348 (48 track).

The ProDigi format was introduced by Mitsubishi in the mid 1980s to supersede the earlier X-80 format used in Mitsubishi's first two-track stationary-head machine. There is less commonality between the two-track and multitrack versions of the PD format than there is between the equivalent versions of the DASH format, but this commonality has little practical benefit to the user in any case, it being simply an elegant way of approaching the design of a family of formats. PD-format machines offer similar operational facilities to DASH-format machines. Existing machines at the time of writing are the Mitsubishi X-86 (two track), X-400 (16 track), X-800, X-850 and X-880 (32 track), and the Otari DTR-900 (32 track).

4.10 R-DAT

This format was agreed upon by a large number of manufacturers, most of them Japanese. It is a small rotary-head cassette-based format offering a range of sampling rates and recording times, including the professional rates of 44.1 and 48 kHz. It is normally a stereo recording format, although an optional four-track mode is available in theory (see Table 7.2). To date, consumer machines have operated at 48 kHz to avoid the possibility for digital copying of CDs (see sections

FACT FILE 8 — Subcode recording

In dedicated digital audio recorders it is valuable to be able to store non-audio data alongside audio data. Such data might take the form of cueing information, take numbers, timecode (see section 14.2), AES/EBU channel status (see section 10.2.4), CD subcode (see section 12.1) or other user data. It might even include text and slow-speed graphic information, depending on the data rate available. Earlier digital formats did not include any capacity for this type of information, but the more recent R-DAT format and the digital video formats have set aside an area for subcode information. In the R-DAT format, subcode is stored in an area at both ends of the helical scan, and is able to be independently recorded by turning the record current on for just that short segment of the scan (as shown below). In the D1 and D2 video formats the important channel-status and user-bit information from the AES/EBU interface is stored as part of the audio block.

The stationary-head formats include a linear auxiliary track on which may be recorded user data, suitably modulated so as to fit within the audio bandwidth. There is no standard convention for the use of these tracks at the time of writing.

Subcode blocks in R-DAT scan

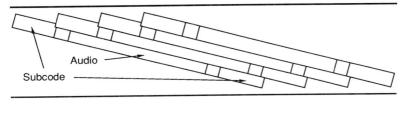

Audio

Subcode

10.2 and 10.6), but professional versions are available which will record at either 44.1 or 48 kHz. There are a fairly large number of consumer machines available, although there are only a few truly professional designs at the time of writing, offering read–modify–write editing facilities (see sections 4.5 and 5.4), external sync and IEC-standard timecode.

The IEC timecode standard for R-DAT was devised in 1990 as a common format for the insertion of timecode into the subcode area of the helically-scanned track (see Fact File 29). In practice it will allow for SMPTE/EBU timecode of any frame rate (see section 14.2) to be converted into the internal DAT 'running-time' code, and then converted back into any SMPTE/EBU frame rate on replay. This will involve the installation of an intelligent timecode reader/generator into the DAT machine. Fostex introduced its own timecode standard prior to the standardisation of IEC timecode, and this is not compatible with IEC machines. Fostex intends to modify its D-20 DAT machine to allow the recording and replay of both types of timecode.

4.11 Stationary-head consumer formats

The S-DAT format was devised as a stationary-head contender for the consumer digital audio cassette market, although it still only really exists in prototype form.

It is possible that S-DAT recorders may eventually find a place in the professional recording world, but there is no evidence of this to date.

Philips has announced its intention to introduce a digital compact cassette format (DCC) in 1992, using the same shell dimensions as the analogue compact cassette and intended for replay in dual-standard (analogue and digital) cassette recorders. This proposed format uses data compression techniques (see section 6.4) to record at either 32, 44.1 or 48 kHz sampling rate using stationary heads. Data compression is achieved through the use of a proprietary coding technique known as PASC (Precision Adaptive Sub-band Coding) which has some similarities with *apt-X 100* as described in section 6.4.2, being a technique which relies on preferential coding of dominant signals and less-accurate coding of signals which are effectively masked. Philips claims a dynamic range equivalent to 18 bit linear PCM.

Little further information is available on this format at the time of writing, but the development signals a possible move towards the use of data compression in consumer formats, and the reader is reminded that such techniques may not always be appropriate in professional recording. Although a first-generation data-compressed recording may sound adequate, signals may not stand up satisfactorily to repeated copying via the analogue domain and to varispeed operation, amongst other possibilities. Furthermore, data compression techniques involve a coding and decoding delay which may perhaps be unacceptable in some professional applications. It will be some time before the professional recording world has had sufficient time to research the possible side-effects of data compression, even though such techniques may become widely adopted in broadcast communications and in consumer equipment in the mean-time. For an enlightening insight into audio data compression the reader is referred to Michael Gerzon's article, *The Gentle Art of Digital Squashing* (see Bibliography).

4.12 Decca rotary-head format

Decca developed an in-house rotary-head recording format using modified IVC 1 inch open-reel videotape recorders. Decca has used these machines for all its CD master tapes, converting the edited master to the Sony format before sending the tapes to a CD pressing plant. The recorders have been designed to offer confidence replay (see section 4.4), and Decca also designed in-house editors and digital mixers to complement the recorders. Since machines of this format are not available to the industry in general they will not be covered further in this book.

4.13 JVC VP-900

This system involved the use of a PCM adaptor operating in the NTSC video format, having similar facilities and features to the Sony PCM-1610. Recordings could be made on to NTSC VHS or U-matic recorders, and sampling rates of 44.056 and 44.1 kHz were available. An editor, mixer and synchroniser were developed to complement the system. The JVC format became established more widely in the USA than it did in Europe, there being very few systems in the UK. It suffered from a lack of compatibility with the Sony format which had established itself as the format of choice for CD mastering.

4.14 Nagra-D format

The Nagra digital tape recorder, although not available at the time of writing, is designed as a digital replacement for the world-famous Nagra analogue recorders, and as such is intended for professional use in field recording and studios. A portable machine is intended, as well as synchronisable studio machines.

The format has been designed to have considerable commonality with the audio format used in D1- and D2-format digital VTRs, having rotary heads, although it uses open reels for operational convenience. Allowing for 20–24 bits of audio resolution, the Nagra-D format is suitable for recording the entire contents of the AES/EBU interface audio sample, and would be appropriate for use with recent 18 and 20 bit convertors. The tape may be roughly splice edited, but it is intended that editing will mainly be electronic. A proposal exists for the use of a large RAM buffer (see Fact File 1) to allow disposal editing without cutting of the tape (see section 5.8).

The error correction and recording density used in this format are designed to make recordings exceptionally robust, and recording time may be up to 6 hours on a 7 inch reel, in two-track mode. The format is also designed for operation in a four-track mode at twice the stereo tape speed, such that in stereo the tape travels at 4.75 cm s^{-1}, and in four track at 9.5 cm s^{-1}.

4.15 3M format

3M manufactured a digital multitrack recorder in the early 1980s which is no longer available. It had 32 tracks and a 30 minute recording time. Splice editing was not possible, but an electronic editing system could be purchased. A number of systems were sold in the USA, but not many exist in the UK and Europe. Owing to the non-current nature of this format it will not be discussed further.

4.16 Miscellaneous multitrack formats

A small number of unique multitrack formats exist, designed by companies such as Yamaha and Akai. Yamaha introduced its DMR-8 recorder in 1990, it being an eight-track cassette-based system using stationary heads and offering full read–modify–write facilities on all tracks (see section 4.5). It is possible to punch-in and punch-out with a crossfade, and the format allows 20 bit resolution, which is not currently available in any other multitrack tape format, professional or otherwise (see Table 7.7). The tapes cannot be splice edited, and are not compatible with any other system. The recording time is 20 minutes at 48 kHz, and pro rata at 44.1 kHz and 32 kHz (the tape speed changes with sampling rate). The Yamaha recorder is incorporated within a digital mixer and effects unit, aiming to offer high-quality digital audio recording and mixing at a much lower price than most professional systems. A stand-alone eight-track transport is also available for track expansion or as a separate recorder. The limitations are in the low recording time and lack of compatibility with major formats, but this may not be important in private studio applications. The recorder can be synchronised using timecode and video sync, and interfaces are available to a range of common standards (see Chapter 10).

Akai's A-DAM (Akai Digital Audio Multitrack) is a 12 track format based around a Video-8 cassette, and uses rotary-head recording. Recording is 16 bit linear at 44.1 or 48 kHz, and again tapes are not compatible with any other format. Recording time is 16.5 minutes. Other facilities are very similar to those of the Yamaha system described above. Both formats are aimed at the 'private' studio, for low-cost digital multitrack recording, possibly synchronised with video.

4.17 Digital audio in videotape recording

There are considerable advantages in the incorporation of digital sound tracks within a professional videotape recorder. Audio may be copied through many generations during the video editing process, and the analogue sound tracks of older VTRs were notoriously poor, partly because the machine and tape were not optimised for audio recording, and partly because there has been a traditional tendency to ignore sound in television production so long as it can be heard. Recently, with the rise of higher-quality sound transmission and distribution systems, such as NICAM-728 (see section 6.2) and DSIS (see section 6.1), the need has arisen for better performance from VTR sound tracks.

4.17.1 Background

All modern VTRs use rotary-head recording (see section 4.3), and the analogue audio tracks which have traditionally accompanied the helically recorded picture have been in the form of narrow linear tracks along the edges of the tape (see Figure 4.11). Two, or sometimes three tracks were offered, along with a linear timecode track. In semi-professional or industrial video formats often one of the two audio tracks had to be used for timecode. The frequency response of such tracks was not good (often extending only just above 10 kHz), and the signal-to-noise ratio lay around the 50 dB mark. Dolby noise reduction of the 'A' type was incorporated as something of a standard in C-format video recorders, and this had the effect of improving the S/N ratio by between 10 and 15 dB. Dolby 'C' noise reduction was later incorporated into the U-matic SP, M-II and Betacam formats, and this also offered a useful degree of noise reduction but was susceptible to alignment errors.

A first attempt at higher-quality sound tracks on professional VTRs came in the form of frequency-modulated (FM) 'tracks' in addition to the conventional linear

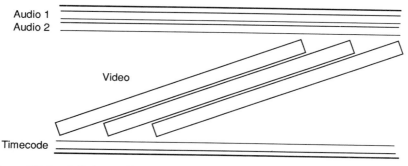

Figure 4.11 In a helical-scan video recorder, analogue audio tracks and the timecode track were normally recorded linearly along the edges of the tape

FACT FILE 9 — Time compression

In analogue recording, one is used to the concept of a continuous audio track, but digital audio may be broken up into segments for recording or processing, provided that it is reconstructed in a continuous form for replay. Disk-based systems rely on this attribute of digital audio, as described in Chapter 3. The possibility for segmented recording is useful in many tape formats, especially those using rotary heads, since it makes possible the recording of audio in segments, separated by gaps or other data such as subcode. The principle involved is the same as the buffering technique used in disk-based recording (see section 3.9), and is otherwise known as time compression, since it involves the recording of a given duration of 'real time' in a shorter time. To take an example, a hundred samples may be recorded in a quarter of the time it took to acquire them,

followed by a gap in which more samples are acquired, followed by another burst at four-times speed, and so on. As with disk recording this involves the use of a temporary memory into which samples are written at one rate and read out at another. Provided that the average input rate is the same as the average output rate, and the buffer size is adequate to accommodate at least the number of samples recorded in one burst, the system will work.

Such a technique is used in R-DAT recording, the Akai A-DAM format, and in D1 and D2 video recording, because only a portion of each helical scan is set aside for audio recording, or the helical scan is divided into segments for each audio channel. This concept is shown diagrammatically below, using an example from the D2 format. It may be appreciated that this technique makes possible the storage of many channels of audio in one helical scan, since the recording head may be turned on for only a short portion of the scan corresponding to a particular audio channel, recording a time-compressed burst of data.

Buffered time compression

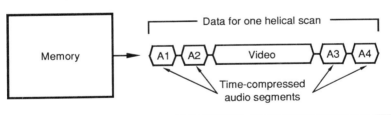

analogue tracks, and these involved the addition of two FM sound carriers mixed with the video signal and recorded in the same helically scanned track as the picture. These tracks were used in both the Betacam and M-II formats, and a similar implementation may be found in the consumer Beta and VHS 'Hi-Fi' formats. The frequency response of the FM tracks was much better than that of the linear tracks (up to 20 kHz), and the S/N ratio lay at around 80 dB. The major limitation lay in the fact that the FM audio tracks could not be edited separately from the picture, requiring that they be cut with the picture. This made them suitable for origination purposes, but not for use in the editing suite except as source material, unless very simple audio editing was required. Some users have claimed that the FM tracks suffer small clicks and spits due to tape drop-outs, and thus they are not used by people who experience this problem. FM tracks may not be recorded separately to the picture, and thus post-produced sound may not be 'laid back' to an edited picture, except to the linear analogue tracks.

Digital audio tracks first appeared in Panasonic's M-II format, as an optional feature, and subsequently such tracks have appeared in both the major digital video formats (D1 and D2), as well as in the analogue C format as an option. They are now also offered with the Betacam format. Such tracks have the advantage that they may be recorded and edited independently, as well as having the high sound quality of digital audio, avoiding such artefacts as wow and flutter so common in VTRs. If copied digitally, these sound tracks will not suffer over the many video generations involved in post-production.

4.17.2 M-II and Betacam formats

In the M-II and Betacam formats, which are cassette-based component video systems, two digital audio tracks are offered as an option, being recorded by the rotary head at the end of the helical scan occupied by the video, in a time-compressed segment (see Fact File 9). Because of this it overwrites one of the linear audio tracks (see Figure 4.12). Without the digital audio option, these formats include two linear analogue tracks (independent) and two FM tracks (combined with video), and with the digital audio option they have two digital tracks (independent), one linear analogue track and the two FM tracks. Thus the digital audio option increases by one the number of independent audio tracks, and makes available higher-quality sound recording. Such machines are normally equipped with AES/EBU interfaces (see section 10.2.4) and operate at a 48 kHz audio sampling rate with 20 bit capacity.

4.17.3 C format

The C format is now over 10 years old and is being replaced by more recent video formats. It was the mainstay of professional video recording during the 1980s. Sony introduced a digital audio version of its BVH-2000 range of C-format recorders, called the BVH-2800, and this offered two digital audio tracks in addition to the three existing linear analogue tracks. The audio was recorded with the rotary head, again at the end of the helical scan, in place of the video vertical sync sector which is not a mandatory requirement and was often replaced by a fourth audio track (see Figure 4.13). As can be seen, the PCM audio is laid down in time-compressed form (see Fact File 9) in three narrow adjacent tracks, by three heads which occupy the same width as one video track. This allows adequate time-compressed data to be stored in the space available.

Independent audio editing and confidence replay is possible using the read–modify–write and read-after-write processes described in sections 4.4 and 4.5, and a second replay head is located on the head drum for this purpose. Separate recording of either audio channel requires that the data is read by the advanced replay heads and then rewritten with the data for one channel modified, since the two audio channels are multiplexed into one data stream as opposed to being recorded in separate segments as they are in the D1 and D2 formats (see below). 16 bit quantisation and a 48 kHz sampling rate are used.

4.17.4 D1 format

The D1 format is a component digital video format, and thus the incorporation of digital audio tracks was inherent in the design from the start. The data rate required for component digital video (around 180 Mbit s^{-1}) is such that the additional data

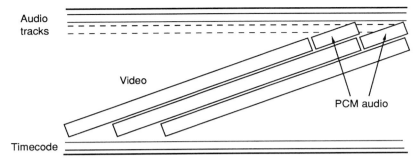

Figure 4.12 In the M-II format, two channels of PCM audio are recorded in a segment of the helical scan, over-writing one of the linear analogue audio tracks

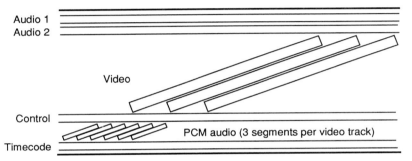

Figure 4.13 In the C format, two channels of PCM audio are recorded in three segments per helical scan, using three small heads to write in the segment normally reserved for recording either an additional linear audio track or the video vertical sync interval

rate required for four channels of digital audio (around 4 Mbit s^{-1}) represents a very small percentage of the total. In the D1 format the four audio channels are recorded in separate time-compressed segments in the centre of the helical scan, as shown in Figure 4.14. The heads may be switched on and off in order to record any of these segments independently.

Confidence replay and independent editing are made possible in many machines by the use of read-after-write and read–modify–write processes. The audio is sampled at 48 kHz and is stored at up to 20 bit accuracy, and there is space for subcode data, allowing for AES/EBU interface signals to be stored without loss of auxiliary information. The format allows for both synchronous and non-synchronous audio recording (see section 14.8). A linear analogue cue track is provided for cue audio at non-normal replay speeds.

4.17.5 D2 format

The D2 format is a composite digital video format and, like the D1 format, incorporates four digital audio tracks, the main difference being the location within the helical scan where these tracks are recorded. In the D2 format the audio track segments are located at the ends of the scan, as opposed to being in the middle, and are double-recorded (see Figure 4.15). The use of azimuth recording (see section 4.3) makes this possible, since azimuth recording is more tolerant of tracking error

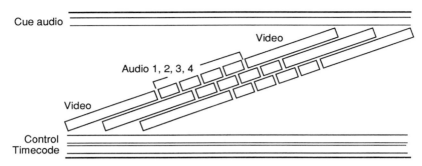

Cue audio

Video

Audio 1, 2, 3, 4

Video

Control
Timecode

Figure 4.14 In the D1 digital video format, four channels of PCM audio are recorded in four segments in the centre of the helical scan, where tracking errors are at a minimum. Each of these segments may be independently edited

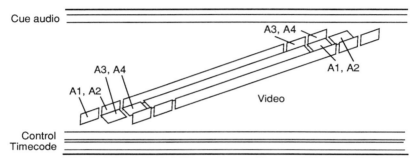

Cue audio

A3, A4

A1, A2

A3, A4

A1, A2

A1, A2

Video

Control
Timecode

Figure 4.15 In the D2 digital video format, four channels of PCM audio are recorded in four segments at the ends of the helical scan, since azimuth recording reduces the effects of tracking errors. Each segment is recorded twice (at opposite ends of the scan) to provide added redundancy

which is worst at the ends of a helically-scanned track.

In respect of audio functions and resolutions available in D2 machines, these are the same in most respects to those of D1, except that audio recording *must* be synchronous with video. The four independent digital audio tracks provided in both of these formats are a useful advance on the track capacity of earlier formats, and are valuable for stereo television operations in which the requirement for increased track capacity arises, although broadcast sound post-production operators would welcome further tracks since the need for more tracks existed even before stereo was adopted.

4.17.6 Half-inch composite digital format

The half-inch composite digital format is a recent development, having been dubbed variously 'D3' and 'DX', since it has no clear title at the time of writing. It is the result of collaborative work between the Japanese broadcaster NHK, and Matsushita (Panasonic). Using an audio segment layout similar to D2, four independent digital audio channels are made available, in addition to a linear cue track. Like D1 and D2, audio is sampled at 48 kHz, and to either 16 or 20 bit resolution.

4.17.7 Digital HDTV recording

To take a step even further into the realms of high-density digital recording it is interesting to take a passing look at Sony's high-definition digital video recorder, the current model being the HDD-1000. The number of picture lines is doubled (compared with conventional TV pictures) in a high-definition television picture, and the video bandwidth is increased, so the data rate required is even larger than that required for recording digital video in either the 525 or 625 line formats. Because of the high data rate required for the video in the Sony digital HDTV recorder, it is possible to include *eight* channels of digital audio within the helical scan, in a similar configuration to the digital VTRs described above. It was once said, not entirely in jest, that this was Sony's new multitrack audio machine which also had a cue video track!

Chapter 5

Editing technology

Unlike analogue recordings, a digital recording may not simply be cut at any point and joined to another for the purposes of adding or removing material from a programme. Analogue recordings contain a continuous unbroken magnetic analogy of the audio waveform, each physical point of which represents a point in recorded time. Digital recordings contain a carefully constructed sequence of binary data, the correct reconstruction of which is vital, it being normal for a time-contiguous sequence of data to be broken up and interleaved (see Fact File 13) for recording on to the tape, making it difficult to say exactly what physical tape position corresponds to a particular point in time. Any random joining of two digital recordings might result in a breaking of the correct binary sequence, the consequence of which would be errors in replay, possible loss of synchronisation, and corruption of the audio output. For this reason care must be taken in ensuring that either the effects of the resulting errors are hidden, or that an edit is never made in a place where it would destroy the binary sequence.

Digital audio editing involves the joining of recordings made at different times, in such a way that the join is made audibly seamless. This operation may be performed electronically, in order that the correct sequence of data is maintained at an edit point, or it may be performed mechanically (that is by cutting and splicing), with electronic assistance in 'hiding' the join. In this chapter the principles of digital editing, both in disk- and tape-based systems, will be described, preparing the ground for the discussion of operational matters in Chapter 11. Examples will be taken from key formats and systems which illustrate the different approaches to editing. It is not intended to describe every system available. The suitability of different formats for editing is covered in Chapter 7.

5.1 The effects of a splice on analogue recordings

It is worthwhile to look first at the nature of an analogue edit on quarter-inch tape, since this is what is to be imitated (at least initially) in digital editing. Much more flexibility than this is often possible in digital editing, in terms of crossfading, level correction and accuracy, but a simple splice is a good place to begin.

Typically, analogue tape is cut in a splicing block which has 45° and 60° cutting angles, as well as the perpendicular 90° cut which makes a butt join possible. Looking at Figure 5.1(a) it will be seen that a mono recording cut and spliced at 60°

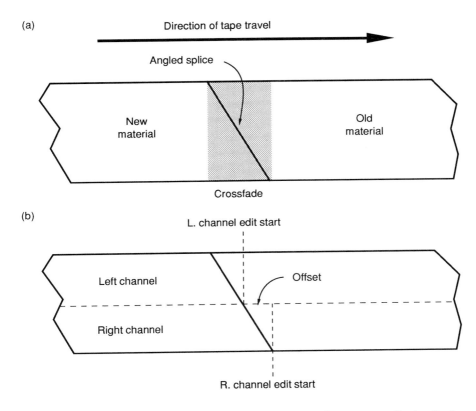

Figure 5.1 Crossfade at a manual splice in analogue recording. At (a) a mono recording is spliced at 60° and a crossfade between old and new material arises over the duration of the splice, since the replay head reads both old and new material simultaneously. At (b) a stereo recording similarly spliced results in a crossfade on each channel, offset by a small amount

is left with a short portion of tape over which both old and new recordings will pass the head (the duration of the splice), and the audible effect of this is a crossfade between old and new material. The exact length of crossfade depends on the speed of the tape and the angle of the splice, and it also depends on whether the recording is mono or stereo. Table 5.1 shows some examples of crossfade times which result from splices at 60° and 45° on quarter-inch tape using different tape speeds. It will be seen that the range of crossfade times is from around 5 to 20 ms.

If a stereo recording is spliced in the same way, the angled splice will cut across one track before the other, resulting in a staggered crossfade between old and new material (see Figure 5.1(b)). Thus the edit would be slightly delayed on one channel. The audible effect of this is not always noticeable, but sometimes shows up on sibilant or transient sounds as they cut-in slightly early on one channel and then jump to their correct positions in the stereo image as the other channel's signal comes in. In digital editing this phenomenon can be avoided by making both tracks cut at the same time.

Long crossfades are not impossible on analogue recordings, but they are more difficult, since they either involve the cutting of the tape at a very shallow angle (and

Table 5.1 Crossfade times and L/R offsets resulting from typical analogue edits

Angle of cut	Tape speed (cm/s)	Crossfade time per track ms (mono/stereo)	L/R offset (ms)
45°	19	33/17	17
60°	19	19/10	10
45°	38	17/8.5	8.5
60°	38	10/5	5
45°	76	8.5/4.3	4.3
60°	76	5/2.5	2.5

creating a matching cut on the tape to be joined), or the use of three tape machines (two players and a recorder) with a manual crossfade between player machines at the edit point, involving the synchronous replay of the source takes.

An analogue splice may normally be picked apart if it has been made in the wrong place, although there is a limit to the number of times that this is possible, owing to the potential for tape damage. Joins may be made in any location, and there is no theoretical limit on the distance between joins.

5.2 Imitating an analogue splice in digital editing

As described in Chapters 4 and 7, some digital tape recording formats have been designed to imitate analogue recorders very closely, having open reels and allowing manual splice editing. Even so, an angled cut of the type shown in Figure 5.1 would not have the same effect on a digital tape as it would on analogue tape (namely the introduction of a crossfade between the two recordings). In the digital recording a splice would simply destroy the sequence of replayed data, resulting in a join between two recordings which would be accompanied by major errors (see Chapter 9). The crossfade between recordings would have to be implemented electronically in the digital domain. Tape-cut editing of digital recordings is covered in more detail in section 5.7.

In order to create a smooth join between two recordings in any digital audio system it is necessary to implement a digital crossfade (see Fact File 10), and this may be made of either fixed or variable length depending on the format and the editing system. The crossfade may be made to start at the same point in each channel if required, avoiding the offset which results with analogue splices. Furthermore, there is no reason why the crossfade might not be of different duration on each channel, if such a thing was required. Such a process is inherent in all disk- and tape-based digital audio editing, it being most unusual to encounter a system which only allows butt joins to be made. The crossfade is vital in ensuring a smooth transition between old and new material.

5.3 Electronic copy editing of tapes

One of the most widely used processes for editing digital recordings involves the compilation of a master tape by copying from source tapes, with crossfades introduced at joins (see Figure 5.2). This process involves the use of at least two

FACT FILE 10   Digital crossfading

A crossfade between one audio signal and another is achieved digitally by adding time-coincident samples from both signals together, multiplying outgoing samples by gradually decreasing values over a period of time whilst multiplying incoming samples by gradually increasing values.

These multiplication values, or coefficients, are calculated so as to conform to a particular mathematical law which corresponds in turn to either, say, a constant-power or constant-voltage crossfade, or perhaps even a more unusual curve such as a cosine or root-linear function. Using the more unusual crossfade laws it is often possible to execute an inaudible join in material at a point where it would have been

Digital crossfader

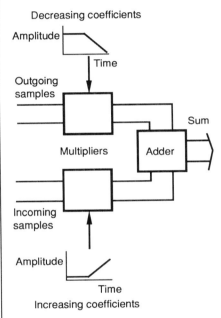

Gain profiling

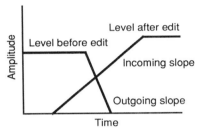

considered impossible in analogue recording.

Digital crossfaders allow for the fade-in time to be different from the fade-out time, such that one track of music could fade out slowly whilst another was brought in quickly. Furthermore, they may allow for the gain profiles of the signals at the crossfade point to be modified to suit the creative requirement. For example, the gain after the crossfade could be higher than that before.

machines (a player and a recorder), with three machines making for greater flexibility, not least because with three machines it is possible to have two source tapes 'on-line' at the same time, rather than having to swap tapes in one player. In many ways, this type of editing has similarities with video editing, especially in the systems based around a PCM adaptor and VTRs (e.g.: Sony PCM-1610/1630 and JVC) where the edit controller has its basis in the operation of a video edit controller, with added facilities for digital audio purposes.

Typically, an external edit controller is used with the player and recorder machines, its job being (a) to synchronise machines together using timecode, (b) to perform the crossfade between recordings, and (c) to provide a user interface with appropriate displays and controls. Additionally, an edit controller may be equipped with facilities for storing a short portion of sound to allow for 'memory preview' of an edit without requiring the tapes to play, and facilities for storing edit decision lists

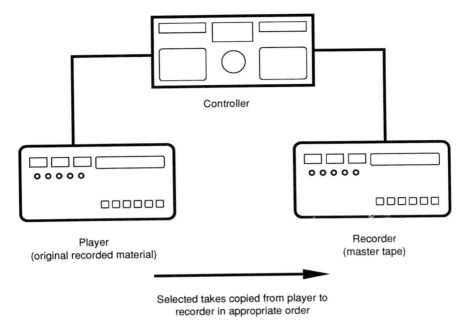

Selected takes copied from player to
recorder in appropriate order

Figure 5.2 In copy editing, selected takes are copied in sequence from a player or source tape to a recorder or master tape, under the command of an edit controller. Crossfades are implemented electronically at joins

(EDLs) in which the locations and characteristics of edits may be stored for later modification or execution. Various audio processing features may be provided, the most common of which is a fader for adjusting the gain of the player material so that it can be matched with that of the outgoing recording.

All of the above functions must reside in the edit controller in a system which uses VTRs as the main tape recorders, since VTRs do not contain any special features for handling digital audio, but in dedicated digital recorders, such as DASH, PD and R-DAT machines, it is possible that some or all of these functions will be integrated within the recorder. For example, DASH and PD machines both require an internal crossfader to allow for splice editing, and many also contain an internal synchroniser. Professional four-head DAT machines also have internal crossfaders to allow for punch-in and punch-out, as well as editing, and thus this function may not be required externally. In such cases the edit controller may simply take on the role of machine controller, with all audio processing and synchronisation being performed by the machines themselves. Some digital tape machines may even be connected together as an 'editing pair' without the intervention of an external controller, and this approach could be used for simple operations, but the user interface is normally limited in such circumstances to the front panel controls of the tape recorder concerned, having limited display capabilities.

Fact File 11 discusses the difference between the processes known as insert and assembly editing, and Fact File 12 describes the normal sequence of operations used in electronic copy editing.

FACT FILE

11

Insert and assembly editing

The terms 'insert' and 'assembly' stem from video terminology, and relate to the type of edit to be performed when copying from source tapes onto a master tape. The assembly edit involves copying source material from player to recorder in correct sequence, progressively building up a finished master by successively dropping the master machine into record with new material at the end of each previously dubbed section, introducing a crossfade at the join. The insert edit involves the insertion of a section from the player into an existing master recording, requiring that a crossfade be introduced both at the drop-in and drop-out points.

Assembly may often be carried out on recorder tapes which have not been 'pre-striped' in any way. If a videotape recorder is switched to assemble mode it normally records everything (video, audio and timecode), whereas if it is switched to insert mode it is normally necessary to select whether a particular audio track, video or

timecode will be inserted. In other words, insert mode expects a tape with something already recorded on it. Digital audio recorders seem to have inherited this terminology, since, for example, 'assemble' in some stationary-head machines refers to the recording of digital audio tracks, auxiliary tracks and the timecode track. The reader should be aware, therefore, that the use of assemble mode on a digital audio recorder will usually wipe out anything already recorded, including timecode, whereas insert mode is preferable if the tape is already striped with video (or digital audio) and timecode, unless it is truly desired to erase the tape and destroy any contiguity in synchronisation or timecode information.

With the Sony DAE-1100 and DAE-3000 systems operating in assemble mode, it is possible to use a 'virgin' tape in the recorder, with only the need to stripe a few minutes of video black (digital silence) and timecode at the start of the tape. At each subsequent drop-in the recorder timecode generator is jam-synced to the replayed timecode (in other words it is reset so as to start from exactly the same value as that replayed) and the video circuits ensure a seamless video join.

5.4 R-DAT: rotary heads with internal crossfader

Professional systems are now available which allow R-DAT tapes to be edited electronically. Professional DAT machines are likely to be equipped with four heads (two for record and two for replay), offset at 90° angles around the drum, and these allow for read–modify–write operation as described in section 4.5. Alternatively, without an advanced replay head, it is still possible to edit recordings by using a technique similar to that described in section 5.5. It will also be possible in the future to use R-DAT machines as players in larger editing systems such as Sony's DAE-3000.

Read–modify–write editing with DAT involves the use of two professional four-head machines and a synchroniser, with the optional addition of a controller to provide a flexible user interface (see Figure 5.3). Audio is transferred digitally between the player and the recorder over one of the standard digital interfaces, such as the AES/EBU, or it may be transferred over analogue links if necessary. Editing is not normally possible with consumer machines, although limited joins may be made with these machines in silent passages of a recording, by manual operation of record and pause functions.

In order to execute an edit the recorder's advanced replay head reads the audio

---

FACT FILE **12**   Tape copy editing

Copying from a source machine to a master machine is the only way in which digital recordings may be edited in many tape formats, since they may not be spliced and they may not make use of real-time play-lists as disk recorders may. In the following description, the term 'out-point' refers to the point on the recorder tape at which it begins to record new material (fading *out* of old material), whilst 'in-point' refers to the point on the player tape at which the source material to be copied to the recorder begins for the edit in question. Typically, the sequence of operations involved in such assembly-editing is as follows:

1. Master tape is pre-striped with digital silence and timecode for a short time at the start of the tape. Alternatively the whole tape may be pre-striped.

2. First out-point is marked on master (the start of the programme, normally about two minutes into the tape), first in-point is marked on player (the beginning of the correct take for the start of the programme), then first edit is executed by pre-rolling both machines, synchronising them at the correct offset and dropping the master into record at the edit point, executing a crossfade at this point between silence from the recorder and new player material. Recorder timecode generator is jammed to replayed recorder code, to ensure contiguous timecode track at edit point.

3. Recorder and player are stopped a short time after the first edit point is intended to occur within the programme.

4. First edit point is located on master ('out-point').

5. First edit point is located on player ('in-point').

6. Edit is rehearsed by pre-rolling both machines and simulating crossfade at edit point, or by memory replay with crossfade.

7. Edit parameters are trimmed if incorrect (in, out and crossfade).

8. Edit is executed by pre-rolling both machines, synchronising them at the correct offset and dropping the master into record at the edit point, executing a crossfade at the precise edit point between outgoing recorder material and incoming player material.

9. Recorder and player are stopped soon after the next edit point and process is repeated.

---

data from a particular tape track into one input of the machine's internal crossfader. The other input of the crossfader is fed from the audio input of the DAT machine, carrying the material from the player, and the output of the crossfader is fed to the lagging record head. The physical delay between the two heads is made to be exactly the same as the electronic delay involved in decoding the audio data from the replay head, passing it through the crossfader and re-encoding it (see Figure 5.4), so the record head can be made to re-record the track with exactly the same information as had originally been there, but with a crossfade to new material starting at some point during the track. At the beginning of the track in which the edit is to take place, the external controller (or synchroniser) drops the record machine into record mode, at which time the lagging record head begins to re-record the track which the advanced replay head has just read, crossfading to material from the player at the designated point, after which it continues to record player material until told to stop.

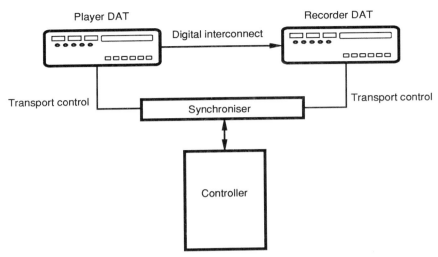

Figure 5.3 In a simple DAT editing system using four-head machines (example taken from Fostex) two transports are synchronised by means of an external synchroniser, under the command of an optional controller. An AES/EBU digital link carries audio from the player to the recorder. Crossfades are carried out using the internal crossfader of the recorder DAT machine

The same process can be made to work in reverse at an edit out-point, where new material fades back into old. At this point the advanced replay head is still reading old material ahead of the record head which is writing new material from the player, and thus it is possible at any time for the crossfader to be made to fade back into old material from the advanced replay head, dropping out of record at the next convenient frame boundary. At this point, where new recording ceases, a half-width track is created (due to the use of overlapped tracks in azimuth recording, see section 4.3), and this will result in a reduced signal level from tape when replayed. Normally the error correction system is adequate to cope with the increased random error rate which results, but due to variance in the mechanical tolerance of transports and tapes it is possible that repeated overwriting with punch-out at exactly the same point on the tape might result in the aforementioned overwritten track being too narrow to give a satisfactory signal level, or the overwriting of an old track with the same azimuth as the new data, possibly resulting in tracking problems and crosstalk. The likely result would be a brief period of interpolation (see section 9.3), and one solution would be to complete the crossfade electronically at the same point as before, but to continue re-recording old data for slightly longer so as to cease recording in a different place. Alternatively, a 'flying' full-width erase head could be mounted in the drum to create a narrow guard-band at the edit point, avoiding the possibility for either of the above scenarios.

The crossfade time in DAT editing is not theoretically limited, and it could be made infinitely long since the advanced replay head will continue to read old material ahead of the record head no matter what the duration of the fade to new material, but in practice it may be limited to that of the DAT machine's internal crossfader. In a current commercial design (the Fostex D-20) the crossfade time is 10 milliseconds, since the same internal crossfader is used for editing as for punch-in and punch-out operations. Theoretically, the edit point location may be defined

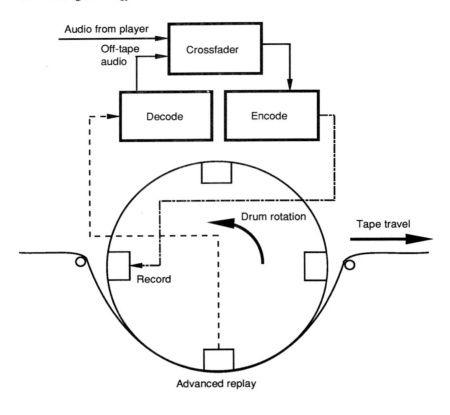

Viewed from oxide side

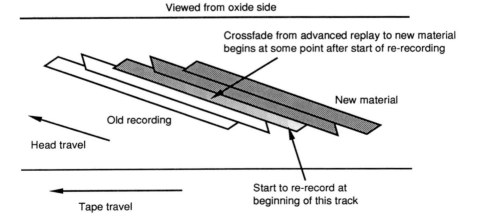

Figure 5.4 Read-modify-write editing in a four-head DAT machine. An advanced replay head reads audio off tape into one input of a crossfader. The other input to the crossfader is fed with the player audio. At the start of the scan in which the edit is to take place the record head is turned on and re-records old data from the advanced replay head until the start of the crossfade, at which time the crossfader fades out the signal from the advanced replay head and fades in the player audio

to sample accuracy, since, although the record head must be turned on at the beginning of a recorded block, the actual crossfade from old to new material (which is performed electronically) may start at any point within the block. In practice some DAT machines may have been equipped with software-limited edit-point accuracy.

Edits may be previewed, since most machines allow for a dummy crossfade to be instituted when switching from monitoring replay to monitoring the input.

The same process of rotary-head read–modify–write editing is used in other dedicated rotary-head recorders, and is apparent in the audio channels of many D1 and D2 digital video machines (see sections 4.17.4 and 4.17.5). The process of electronic editing in stationary-head systems is also very similar (see section 5.3.3).

5.5 Sony CD-mastering system: rotary heads with external crossfader

Sony has established its CD-mastering format as the international standard for submitting recordings to be turned into CDs, and its editing system is one of the most widely used for music purposes. The system is an example of one which involves the use of VTRs for digital audio recording (see section 4.6) and thus the edit

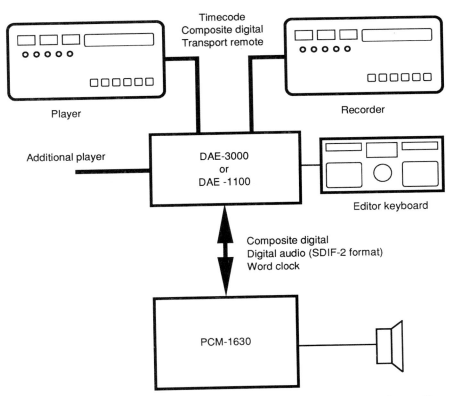

Figure 5.5 In the Sony CD-mastering system, the DAE-1100 or -3000 editor communicates with players and recorder, handling control, synchronisation and crossfading. The PCM-1630 is used for encoding and decoding the video signals and monitoring the output of the editor

controller must handle all of the audio processing required, as well as acting as a synchroniser and controller. The system does not make use of the same read–modify–write process as used in DAT editing (see above), although there are some similarities, since the VTRs used are standard U-matic machines which do not have the head arrangements required for this, nor are the delays between heads optimised with relation to the delay of the digital editor.

Sony has produced two editors to date, the DAE-1100 and the DAE-3000, both made to control U-matic machines in conjunction with either a PCM-1610 or a PCM-1630 PCM adaptor. The DAE handles synchronisation, crossfading and control, whilst the PCM handles encoding and decoding, conversion and monitoring of the audio signal (see Figure 5.5). The DAE-3000 is more sophisticated than the DAE-1100, having memory preview, full bandwidth search, and interfaces to a wider range of recorders (including DASH and DAT machines). The principles of editing, though, are similar, and will be described with relation to the rotary-head PCM-1630/DMR-2000 configuration.

As in the R-DAT editing system, this system involves the use of at least two machines, a player and a recorder, with additional players for increased flexibility. Material is copied from player to recorder, using either insert or assembly modes, with crossfading and gain correction being performed within the edit controller. Since the record VTR may only be dropped into record at the beginning of a helical scan, whereas the edit point may be required to be defined to greater accuracy than this, it is necessary for the editor to store a portion of audio in its internal memory, so that it can re-record the outgoing material from memory after it has dropped the recorder into record, up to the crossfade point where it crossfades to incoming material from the player (see Figure 5.6). This is similar to the read–modify–write process used in the four-head the DAT machine (see above) except that in the DAT machine the old material to be re-recorded could be derived from an advanced replay head, as opposed to the memory of the editor. It will be appreciated that the memory of the editor must be large enough to hold enough audio to re-record from the start of the helical scan to the end of the crossfade, and thus the crossfade time

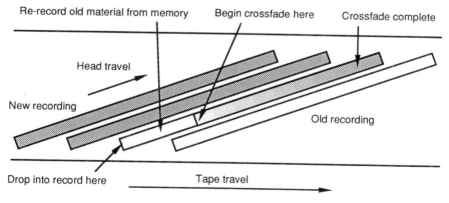

Figure 5.6 Crossfade editing without advanced replay. Where no real-time advanced replay is available, old material from the record drop-in to the end of the crossfade must be stored in temporary memory using an initial pass to load this material. At the start of the scan in which the edit is to take place the record head is turned on and re-records old data from the temporary memory, crossfading to new material from the player at the appropriate point

will be limited by the size of the memory.

In such a system, it is also possible to perform a crossfade at the out-point of an insert edit, provided that this is known in advance, since the internal memory of the editor can also be used to store a short period of incoming material around the intended punch-out point. At the end of an inserted recording the editor will fade out of material from the player and into material previously stored in memory, before ceasing to record at a frame boundary.

5.6 DASH and PD: stationary heads with internal crossfader

Electronic editing is possible with DASH- and PD-format machines, in addition to tape-cut editing (see below). The process is normally the stationary-head equivalent of the read–modify–write editing process described for R-DAT (see section 5.4), and again requires two machines to be synchronised together. Instead of the

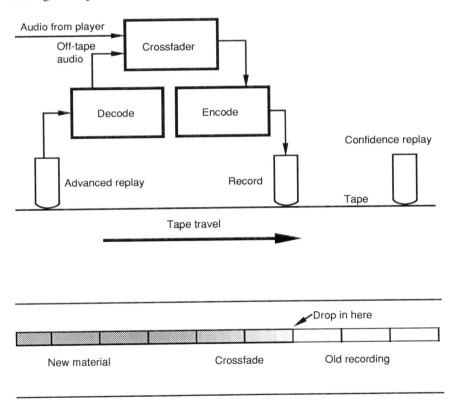

Figure 5.7 In stationary-head systems with advanced replay the approach to editing is similar to that described in Figure 5.4. The record head is turned on as close as possible to a block boundary on tape, after which it re-records old data from the advanced replay head and crossfades to new material from the player at the appropriate time. Where no advanced replay head is available, the memory technique used in Figure 5.6 may be used

recorder's advanced replay head being mounted at a different angle on the drum (as it would be in a rotary system) it is mounted further up the tape, reading audio in advance of the record head (see Figure 5.7). The advanced replay head is connected to one input of a crossfader, and the other input to the crossfader is fed from the audio input of the tape machine (digital or analogue) to which the player is connected. The output of the crossfader feeds the record head, and the gap between advanced replay and record heads is equivalent to the encode–decode delay.

In order to perform an edit, the machine is dropped into record as close as possible to a convenient block boundary prior to the edit point, then old material is re-recorded until a crossfade is instituted between the advanced replay and the incoming player material at the precise edit point. At the out point the reverse process takes place, whereby the crossfader fades back to old material from the advanced replay head and then stops recording at the next convenient block boundary. Replay errors will arise at punch-in and punch-out points due to the fact that blocks are destroyed at random, but these are designed to be within the capacity of the error-handling system.

It is worth noting that exactly the same process is used at a punch-in point and at a punch-out point, as might be used during an overdub session, except that in such a situation the input to the crossfader is derived from a normal audio input which might have come from a mixer instead of from a synchronised player machine.

5.7 Splice or 'tape-cut' editing

As indicated in the introduction to this chapter, the random joining of two digital recordings is likely to result in severe errors in replayed data. This is due partly to the joining of two unrelated numerical sequences which are not complete in themselves (resulting in replay errors), and partly to loss of signal which is created at a splice due to the join, any slight gap which might result, and the poor head contact which arises from such things as fingerprints and the thickness of the splicing tape. For these reasons a number of techniques are used to make splicing possible, the technique normally applying to stationary-head systems (although it is not impossible with rotary heads). From this point forward, the term 'splice editing' will refer to manual tape-cut editing, as opposed to electronic editing.

The simplest approach to splice editing takes the view that since it is unavoidable that a splice will destroy a large number of samples then the best that can be done is to hide the effects of the errors which will be created. In both DASH and PD formats the audio data is split up into odd and even samples to be recorded on to tape, with odd-numbered samples separated from adjacent even-numbered samples by an interleave delay (2448 samples in DASH). This places originally adjacent samples physically far apart on the tape, and means that a splice will destroy odd-numbered samples in one group and even-numbered samples in another group, separated by the interleave delay. The result of this is that there will always be either good odd samples or good even samples present at any one time, and the system is designed to interpolate (see Fact File 14) between good samples (either odd or even) to provide an audio output.

Such systems detect the occurrence of a splice either by looking for large burst errors, monitoring the control track which runs alongside the audio tracks and which carries an incrementing address (DASH format), or by looking for a large signal loss in all tracks simultaneously (PD format). Once it has detected the splice it will

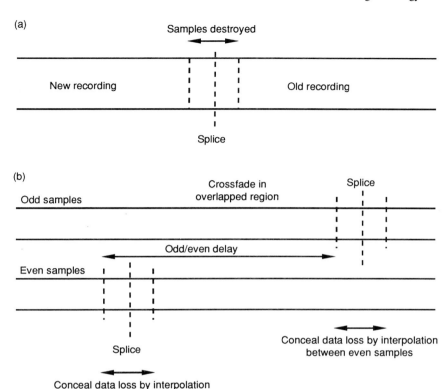

Figure 5.8 If a DASH tape is manually spliced there will be an area of errors in the replayed data as shown in (a). Because odd and even samples are separated by a delay on tape, the result after de-interleaving is a delay between the burst of errors in the odd and even samples, as shown in (b). During each burst interpolation can be used to conceal the error, and a crossfade can be made in the period in between, during which good samples exist from both streams

perform a crossfade between old and new material at a point where both even and odd samples are present (see Figure 5.8). The problem with this approach is that the audio output is not properly corrected, since interpolation is not true error *correction*: it is error *concealment*. The result is a reduction in audio bandwidth over the duration of the error, possibly leading to aliasing (see Appendix 1) in the case of high-frequency audio signals. What is needed is a means of allowing splicing with full *correction* of audio data.

The twin DASH format achieves full correction at splices by the use of large amounts of redundant data (redundant data is data which has been recorded more than once, only to be used when the original version has been affected by errors). Twin DASH records everything twice, using two sets of tracks, one with the odd–even interleave reversed so that even samples come first. In this format (used in Sony's PCM-3402 and Studer's D820X) there are always sufficient good samples at a splice, since where odd samples have been destroyed from one set of tracks they can be taken from the other set (from a point later or earlier on the tape), and the same for even samples, allowing a decision to be made by the error correction system over which data to use at any one time: thus no interpolation is required.

The crossfade time in tape-cut editing is limited by the period over which both incoming and outgoing samples are available simultaneously and is not normally variable for each edit (since this would require the recording of a message on the tape at each join to tell the crossfader what to do on replay), although it may be fixed over a certain range. The exact maximum duration of the crossfade depends on which speed and format is in use, but typically the maximum is between 5 and 20 ms.

5.8 Jump editing

Other methods have been suggested to avoid error concealment at splice-edit points, since interpolation introduces an unnecessary degradation in audio quality. The principle of jump editing is one which involves cutting the tape in a different place to the actual edit point, so that the outgoing material is cut after the edit point whilst the incoming material is cut before the edit point (see Figure 5.9). The two pieces of tape are then joined together, there being two real edit points separated by a piece of unwanted tape. On one of the auxiliary tracks the locations of the edit points are marked by recording a code, and the replay machine is programmed to jump over the unwanted section of audio in its memory, thus avoiding the replay of the spliced section. This necessarily results in audio replay which is then 'ahead' of tape replay, and requires the tape to be speeded up for a short time to compensate. Audio data is buffered (see Fact File 1) between tape and output, so the change in tape speed is not reflected in a change in speed of the audio output.

Such a process places limits on the closeness of splices, and the distance between the actual cut point and the edit point. The limits depend on the size of the buffer used to store audio either side of the edit point. To date jump editing has not been used in commercial products, although it has been proposed for a slightly different use in the Nagra-D format, this being a rotary-head system. The proposal for the Nagra–D is that a very large buffer would be used for broadcast disposal editing (the removal of erroneous sections from a single recording, such as coughs in an interview), such that editors could mark the starts and ends of sections to be disposed of, without cutting the tape. The system would then simply play through the tape jumping over the unwanted sections and relying on the buffer to continue the audio output whilst the transport moved quickly to a point just before the cut-back to

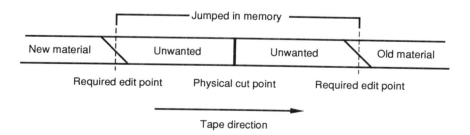

Figure 5.9 In 'jump editing', the tape is cut after the actual edit point in the outgoing material, and before the edit point in the incoming material. The tape is marked with a cue signal to show where the true edit point lies, and the unwanted section is skipped in memory. In this way, no errors are encountered in replayed data due to the splice

wanted material and began loading the buffer again. This would clearly require a considerable duration of advance playback or buffer pre-loading for instant replay, but provides a neat solution to the editing problem, does not require cutting or copying of the tape, and would be fast in operation. Such an approach would only be possible for disposal-type editing, and would not work for assembly-type editing.

5.9 Edit-point searching in tape-based systems

In analogue tape editing, the edit point is located first by playing the tape and then by moving the tape manually back and forth across the replay head in a process often known as 'rock-and-rolling'. Normally an analogue machine will produce an audio output in this mode, and editors are experienced at interpreting the sounds which are reproduced when tape is moved in this way, in order to find the correct edit point. In digital tape machines, audio is not normally reproduced when tape is moved at speeds widely different from the normal replay speed, and thus some other means of locating the edit point is required.

In basic digital editing systems it is not possible to imitate the rock-and-roll searching process, and edit-point location relies on accurate punching of a button at approximately the right point in the programme, followed by trimming of this

(a)

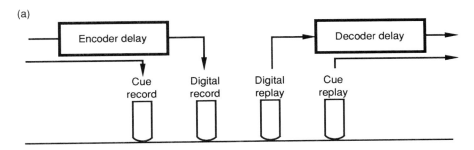

(b)

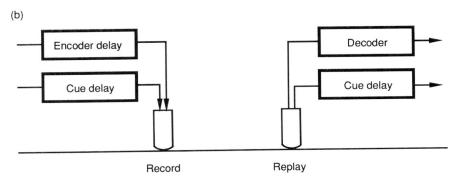

Figure 5.10 Cue-audio timing in stationary-head recorders. The cue tracks may either be handled by heads offset from the digital heads, to account for the encode and decode delays, as shown in (a), or the cue signals may be artificially delayed to match the digital signals, being handled by the same heads, as shown in (b)

point in small increments if required following a preview of the edit. In open-reel systems designed for splice editing, audible output is provided during rock-and-rolling from two cue tracks on which is normally recorded a version of what is on the digital tracks. In some systems the cue-track record and reproduce heads are mounted at a suitable distance from the digital heads to compensate for the encoding and decoding delay of the digital signal (see Figure 5.10), so that an edit point marked whilst listening to the cue tracks will be accurate with relation to the digital tracks. In other systems, the cue-track signals are recorded and replayed by the same heads as used for the digital audio, being delayed appropriately to match its timing.

In digital recorders which do not allow manual movement of the tape reels, a simulation of rock-and-rolling is often provided as an editing system function, using variable-speed replay of audio from solid-state memory (RAM). When playing a tape to locate the edit point audio is constantly being stored into a short portion of RAM, such that the RAM always holds the last so-many seconds of audio replay. When the edit-point is roughly located (by hitting a button) the system continues to store audio in RAM for a further few seconds and then stops the tape, leaving a few seconds of audio either side of the edit point available in RAM. The user may then use a wheel to simulate the movement of tape reels, which generates appropriate read addresses to the RAM resulting in audible replay. Various techniques are used to improve the quality of audio replayed from RAM at low speeds, including filtering to remove alias products. Once the edit point has been finely-trimmed a full preview may be made.

Depending on the amount of RAM available, audio may be stored at either full or reduced resolution. Since RAM is much cheaper than it used to be, there is a tendency for modern editing systems to store audio at full resolution, whereas older systems such as Sony's DAE-1100 combined two channels into mono and compressed the audio for temporary storage of this kind.

5.10 Edit preview

One of the beauties of electronic editing, as opposed to splice editing, is the non-destructive nature of it, and the ability to preview an edit before it is committed to tape. Previewing involves the simulation of the edit, either by synchronising both player and recorder at the right offsets and then switching over from monitoring recorder to monitoring player at the edit point (with a dummy crossfade), or by a simulation completely from memory (if the RAM store is large enough). A memory simulation is vastly preferable because it avoids the need for lengthy cueing and pre-rolling of tape machines, and can be performed instantaneously. Further operational aspects of edit previewing are discussed in Chapter 11.

5.11 Editing in tapeless systems

In the tapeless system, pre-recorded sound files (see section 3.7) are replayed in a predetermined sequence, in accordance with a replay schedule (see below). Memory is used to 'hide' the gap between the outgoing file and the incoming file, using a process similar to that used in 'jump editing' (see section 5.8) in which outgoing and incoming material are both present in different address areas at the same time and can be joined by controlling the read address of the memory so as to

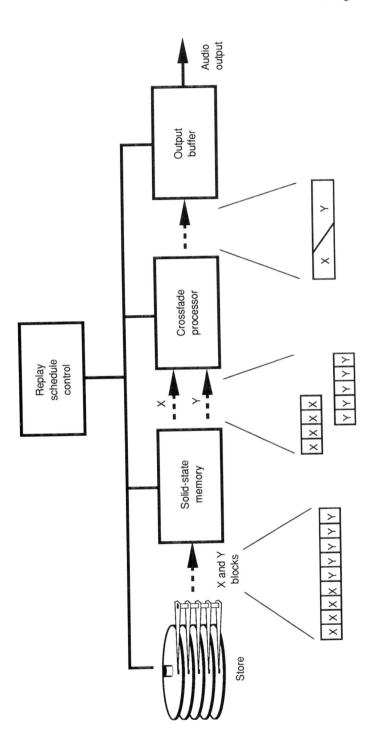

Figure 5.11 Real-time crossfade execution in a disk-based system. Blocks of incoming and outgoing files (Y and X) are read into memory in advance of being required. Time-coincident samples of X and Y are then routed to the crossfader at the appropriate time, whereupon the crossfader fades out X and fades in Y, feeding the combined result tot the output buffer

jump over unwanted material. By finely controlling the read addresses at which the jump takes place, it is possible to set an edit point which may not lie exactly on the boundary of one storage block and another. Most tapeless systems are extremely flexible in allowing any number of edited masters to be compiled from one set of source files or 'takes', simply by altering the replay schedule, such that edit points may be changed or new takes inserted without ever affecting the integrity of the original material.

To take an example, we will assume that a simple edit with a short crossfade is to be performed between file X (the outgoing) and file Y (the incoming). Once the edit points have been located, both in file X and file Y (see section 5.13), the system will adjust the replay schedule such that file Y is read from the disk until just after the edit point and file X begins to be read from just before the edit point. Both files are read out via memory, and at the time of the crossfade the system will ensure that data from both files exists simultaneously in different address areas by reading from the disk ahead of 'real time'. The exact overlap between old and new material will depend on what value of crossfade has been selected by the user. At the start of the crossfade the system will begin to read out samples of both file X and file Y into a crossfade processor. Time-coincident samples of X and Y will then be added together, and the result sent to the appropriate channel output (see Figure 5.11).

The demands on the transfer rate of the disk (see section 3.10) become greater during an edit, because the system requires access to more than one file at a time. The longer the crossfade, the longer this doubling in demand is made on the disk in order to feed a single audio output. A device which feeds four channels adequately during normal play may fail to satisfy demands if all four of those channels are performing crossfade edits at the same time, because in effect the system is asking for the store to serve eight channels temporarily during the crossfade. A number of things may help to alleviate this problem— primarily the utilisation of as large a temporary memory as possible. The larger memory will be able to continue outputting audio for longer periods than the small memory in cases of increased demand where the storage device would be temporarily unable to keep up, provided that the increased demand is not too prolonged and is followed by a period of recuperation. If the replay schedule is known in advance the system can ensure that the memory is kept as full as possible during periods of lower demand, loading it with portions of sound files for editing well in advance of the edit point.

The original water reservoir analogy, used in section 3.9, serves well here, because a large reservoir will be able to continue supplying water to a number of taps even if the number of taps turned on is increased temporarily above its intended load. The situation will result in the water level in the reservoir getting low, but this will not be a problem if the reservoir is allowed to fill up again after the increased demand has passed. Problems arise if another bout of increased demand arises too soon after the previous one, as the reservoir will eventually run out of water. This corresponds to the situation in tapeless editing when a number of edits are placed very close together.

Clearly there will be a limit on the number of edits which may be executed by the system in a given period, and also on the length of crossfade which can be accommodated. The fewer the audio channels assigned to each storage device, the greater will be the flexibility in editing for any given transfer rate, as although the store will be working well under capacity in normal play it will have plenty of performance to spare in cases of high demand such as those given in the above example.

5.12 Alternative crossfade techniques in tapeless systems

Although the method given in the previous section is perhaps the most flexible in a wide range of situations, and also the most elegant, it places considerable demands on the memory and limits the crossfade time or number of edits per second. Two further possibilities exist to help in the editing process, both of which involve the non-real-time calculation and separate storage of the crossfade.

The least elegant solution is that which involves the creation of a 'real' edited master recording from the assembled takes. Rather than the virtual assembly of a master recording using a replay schedule and real-time calculation of crossfades, this system would assemble a new recording as a separate sound file in the store, with the crossfades having been calculated and written into the file. The replay of the edited master is then a simple matter of replaying the assembled master file. Disadvantages of this approach are many, including the particular problem that the master file itself requires storage space which must be set aside before editing. Furthermore this approach takes away the flexibility which is the beauty of tapeless editing.

A second approach involves the storage of crossfade segments separately from the main sound files, allowing these to be inserted into the replayed data at edit points. Once the editor has auditioned and perfected the crossfade it can be written as a separate short file into a temporary store (perhaps just another partition of the main store) in order that it may be read out at the edit point using a 'butt join' to the outgoing and incoming files. If the edit in the example given in the preceding section were to be performed in such a system, the replay procedure would involve reading file X from the store into the buffer up until just before the edit, then reading the crossfade file from the store, followed by the reading of file Y from just after the crossfade (see Figure 5.12). In this way a crossfade could be of virtually any length, provided that the temporary store was large enough.

Some commercial systems have adopted the above approach to editing as it has the advantage that the user is not limited by the memory size or store speed in what can be achieved in terms of crossfade length or number of edits per second. The approach has the slight disadvantage that it is not a true real-time process, and the user may have to wait a few seconds while the system calculates a complicated crossfade. Some manufacturers have taken the approach that this is a small price to pay for greater flexibility. It may be appreciated that a change to any of the edit

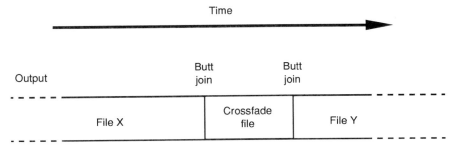

Figure 5.12 A separate, pre-calculated file may be used for storage of the crossfade area, in which case the replay of an edit is a simple matter of creating a butt join between outgoing file, crossfade file and incoming file

parameters after the calculation of the crossfade file will result in the need to rewrite the crossfade file. This approach is sometimes offered as an alternative to real-time crossfading in order to make possible the replay of edits on a number of tracks simultaneously which would not be possible in real time.

5.13 Edit-point searching in tapeless systems

During the recording of sound files it is probable that the system will have allowed the attachment of labels to these files, naming the file in such a way that it may be easily recalled. During the editing process the operator will call up appropriate files and audition them, both on their own and in a sequence with other files. The exact method of assembling the edited sequence depends very much on the user interface, but it is common to present the user with a visual analogy of moving tape, allowing him or her to 'cut and splice' or 'copy and paste' files into appropriate locations along the virtual tape. These files are then played out at the timecode locations corresponding to their virtual position on this 'tape'.

Variable speed replay in both directions to simulate 'reel-rocking' is usually controlled by a wheel which moves the 'tape' in either direction around the current play location. This wheel is used to control the rate at which samples are read out of the replay buffer (see section 3.9), and this replaces the fixed sampling rate clock as the controller of the replay rate. In normal circumstances this would result in a change in the replay sampling rate, but this is not always acceptable for a number of reasons (see section 10.3). In order to provide digital audio from the output of the system at a constant sampling rate it will be necessary to employ sampling rate conversion between the output of the buffer and the convertors or digital outputs, such that the output of the system remains at the nominal sampling rate no matter what the input rate.

5.14 Replay scheduling in tapeless systems

The heart of the real-time editing process in disk-based systems is the replay schedule, which is really a list of the sound files which are to be sent to particular audio outputs at specific times. This list, sometimes called the edit decision list or EDL, controls the replay process and is the result of the operator having chosen the sound files and the places in which they are to be joined. In order to arrive at the final EDL, the operator will have auditioned each sound file and determined the points at which one file is to be joined to another, as described in the examples above. The EDL may never be displayed as a list, but it must exist within the system memory even if it is displayed in graphic form.

The schedule of retrieval of sound files from the disk need not correspond absolutely with the edit list or replay schedule, although it is bound to be very similar to it. This is because of the need to maintain transfer efficiency, to which end the scheduler will determine which blocks of data should be moved to memory at which times, based on the replay schedule (see Figure 5.13). The schedule will be executed against a timing reference, which may be an internal measure, or it may be derived from external timecode.

In a system in which the crossfade calculations are performed in real time, a more complex scheduling procedure is required than for a system in which crossfades are

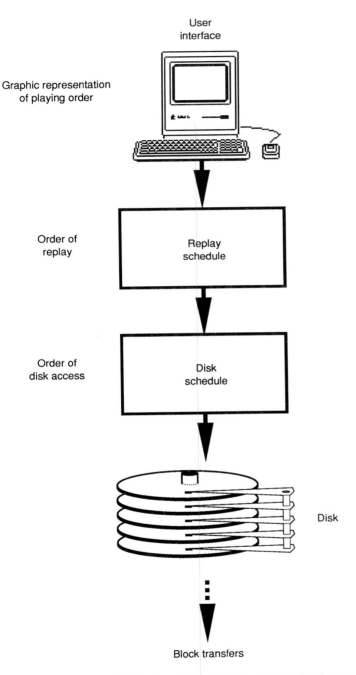

Figure 5.13 A replay schedule, determining which files will be replayed to certain outputs at certain times, is created under command of the user, and is subsequently translated into a disk schedule. For greatest transfer efficiency the disk schedule may need to be different from the actual playing order

pre-calculated and written to separate files (see above). The process in which the scheduling control software is constantly looking ahead at the replay schedule, measuring the state of emptiness of buffers and fetching data from the store, is often known as 'dynamic scheduling'. In order to perform its task efficiently the dynamic scheduler must know quite a lot about the nature of the store, such that it may predict accurately where problems are likely to occur, and when the periods of greatest demand will be. It would also be advantageous for it to know the physical locations of all the sound file blocks in the store so that it may arrange the most efficient retrieval of them for any given replay schedule, although this may not always be feasible since many SCSI-interfaced disk drives (see Chapter 3) do not make such information available externally.

Chapter 6

Broadcast distribution and transmission

As digital audio becomes more widely used in broadcast studio centres the need for various means of distributing that audio both around the studio centre and around the network will increase. Network links to other studio centres will become digital, up- and down-links to satellites will become digital, and feeds to terrestrial transmitters will become digital. This process is already well under way in parts of the world.

Analogue tie-lines and land lines cause degradation to the signal which cannot easily be corrected for, and matched stereo pairs of 'music circuits' are expensive to rent. Digital links preserve the integrity of audio signals, and will eventually become the norm rather than the exception. Digital audio data compression systems are becoming more widely used in both recording and broadcasting, and these offer ever greater reductions in the bit rate required for high-quality audio, offering savings in the costs of renting radio frequency bandwidth, and allowing more audio channels to be encoded within a given bandwidth.

6.1 Dual Sound-In-Syncs (DSIS)

A technique used in the UK for the transfer of stereo digital audio around TV networks is known as dual sound-in-syncs or DSIS. It is a development of the original mono SIS system which was used for many years, and allows for two channels of digital audio at a sampling rate of 32 kHz to be transferred within the horizontal sync pulses of the TV signal with which it is associated. This avoids the need for separate high-quality stereo sound circuits, and ensures that picture and sound are kept together.

In DSIS, digital audio data is NICAM-728 encoded (see section 6.2) and then time compressed (see Fact File 9), being inserted in short bursts into the horizontal line-sync period of the TV waveform (see Figure 6.1). Four voltage levels are used to represent the four possible states of a pair of bits (00, 01, 11, 10), and the NICAM data stream is split up into pairs of bits for this purpose. DSIS is decoded by separation of the data burst from the sync period, replacing it with a normal TV sync pulse, followed by recognition of the bit pairs based on the voltage level and then NICAM-728 decoding. A video signal incorporating DSIS may not be fed directly into a TV monitor or other video system without first stripping the DSIS burst and replacing it with a normal sync pulse. If the signal is being fed to a NICAM-728 transmitter it may not be necessary to decode the NICAM DSIS data, but simply to

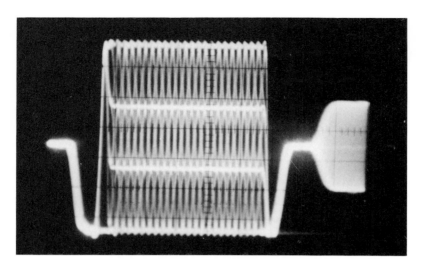

Figure 6.1 DSIS information within the TV line sync pulse

separate it from the vision signal. The states of the bit pairs in the DSIS signal may then be used directly to modulate the NICAM carrier for transmission (see below).

NICAM-728 DSIS is now used throughout the UK within the Independent Television network, and is being installed also by the BBC. It is used for programme interchange between studio centres and from remote sites, and for distribution to transmitters. DSIS has been shown to work well when used with good vision links, but occasional problems have been reported with audio drop-outs when used with poor vision links. The problem appears not so much to be related to amplitude errors caused by noise, but to timing jitter and distortion of the data.

6.2 NICAM-728

The NICAM 728 system was designed by the BBC in the UK during the 1980s, and is now used as the main terrestrial means of transmitting stereo sound with television programmes. The following is a brief résumé of the principles of NICAM-728.

As discussed in Chapter 3, two channels of digital audio at a sampling rate of 44.1 kHz, using 16 bit resolution per sample (Compact Disc resolution), demand a data rate of over 1.4 Mbit s^{-1}. Such a data rate simply cannot be accommodated within the bandwidth available for TV broadcasting (see Figure 6.2). The NICAM-728 system reduces the data rate necessary for two channels of digital audio to 728 kbit s^{-1}, which, when combined with the right modulation method and careful spectrum shaping, allows stereo sound to be transmitted on a carrier just above the FM mono sound carrier, at 6.552 MHz above the vision carrier. It achieves this reduction in data rate by a number of means.

Firstly, it is assumed that a 15 kHz audio bandwidth is acceptable for the purposes of TV sound transmission. This is towards the upper limit of most adults' hearing (and above that of many!), and is the same as that used for high-quality FM radio broadcasts on Band II VHF. This allows the use of a 32 kHz sampling rate, which

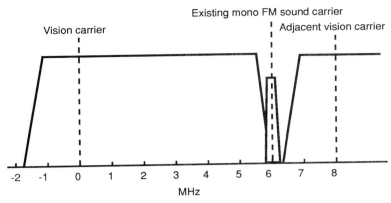

Figure 6.2 Bandwidth available for NICAM sound. Little space exists between the lower sideband of the adjacent vision carrier and the FM sound signal

offers a significant reduction in data rate over the sampling rates of 44.1 or 48 kHz used in professional recording. Secondly, audio samples are initially quantized to a resolution of 14 bits, as opposed to the 16 of the Compact Disc, giving rise to a theoretical dynamic range of around 80 dB. This is considered adequate for TV sound whose levels have already been controlled to be within an acceptable window for domestic listening purposes.

At 32 kHz sampling rate, 14 bits per sample, the data rate is still too high for the intended purpose, and thus a *compansion* (compression and expansion) technique is used in the digital domain to reduce it still further. It is in this compansion technique that the main ingenuity of the NICAM system lies. The system relies partially on a psycho-acoustic effect which most people will have noticed, that is the effect of *masking*, in which quiet sounds are made inaudible by a louder sound in the same frequency band.

In order to reduce the bit rate to 728 kbit s^{-1}, the original 14 bit audio samples are reduced to 10 bits for transmission, the missing 4 bits being re-constituted on decoding. In effect (and this is a slight simplification), a sliding window is used on the audio samples, selecting which 10 bits of the sample are to be transmitted, depending on the level of the audio signal. For low-level signals the least significant bits of the sample are transmitted, leaving off the MSBs which are not used anyway for a low level signal (they would be set to zero). On reception, the missing zeros are restored to the MSB positions, and the LSBs restored to their rightful places, and thus nothing is lost. The higher the level of the audio signal, the more MSBs will have been set, and thus some data will necessarily be lost in truncation to 10 bits per sample. At the highest level of signal, only the 10 MSBs are transmitted, omitting the LSBs, and this results in an increase of noise. Usefully, since this only happens with high-level audio signals, the increased noise is masked by the signal. Generally, the higher the level of the audio signal, the more resolution is lost in the truncation to 10 bits per sample, but the greater the masking effect and thus the less noticeable the increased quantisation noise. Pre-emphasis (see section 8.3) of the signal in the analogue domain prior to encoding (complemented by de-emphasis at the receiver) also helps to reduce the audible effects of noise.

The 'Near Instantaneous' part of the title of the system refers to the fact that

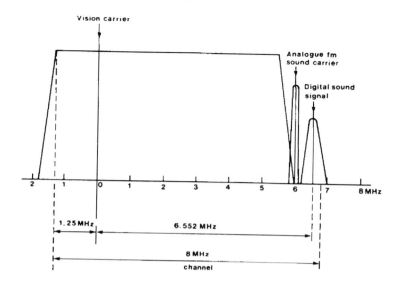

Figure 6.3 The NICAM 728 sound carrier within the transmitted spectrum. (Courtesy of BBC)

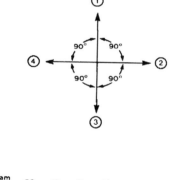

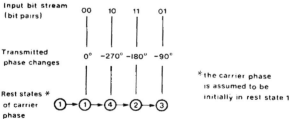

Figure 6.4 DQPSK modulation is used to transmit NICAM 728 data, such that each pair of bits causes a different change in carrier phase. (Courtesy of BBC)

samples are compressed in groups lasting 1 millisecond (32 samples), each group being accompanied by a range coding word which tells the receiver which of five gain ranges has been used at the encoding stage. The receiver uses this range coding word to restore the group of samples to its correct level. In order to set the range (effectively to set the position of the sliding window which dictates which bits are transmitted) the encoder looks at each group of 32 samples and bases the range on the highest-level sample within the group.

One 728 bit frame of NICAM data (representing 1 millisecond of stereo audio) is made up as follows:

32 samples of Channel A data	
(10 bits audio plus one parity bit per sample)	352 bits
32 samples of Channel B data	352 bits
8 bit frame alignment word	8 bits
5 bits of control information	5 bits
11 bits of auxiliary data	11 bits

The range coding words for each frame are cleverly incorporated into the parity bits of the audio samples, using a scheme by which parity bits are modified according to a table. On reception, majority-decision logic determines the gain range by investigation of the state of the parity bits.

In order to transmit the NICAM data created as shown above, samples are first interleaved to reduce the effects of burst errors (see Fact File 13), and then scrambled according to a pseudo-random data stream which has the effect of spectrally-shaping the signal, such that it appears almost noise-like in the radio frequency domain, causing any interference with the picture to be benign. The resulting data is then modulated on to the 6.552 MHz carrier (see Figure 6.3) using differential quadrature phase shift keying (DQPSK), whereby pairs of bits are used to modify the relative phase of the carrier in increments of 90°, depending on one of the four possible states of a pair of bits (00, 01, 11, 10) (see Figure 6.4). These pairs of bits are the same as those used to set the voltage levels within the TV sync pulse in DSIS (see previous section).

On reception, the receiver demodulates the DQPSK, detects the frame alignment word (which has not been scrambled), and subsequently de-scrambles, de-interleaves and decodes the compressed audio data, before passing it through a D/A convertor to feed the television's loudspeakers. NICAM-728 has been shown to be exceptionally robust in transmission, standing up to severe multipath reflections and poor signal-to-noise ratios. In many cases the digital sound may be picked up almost perfectly even if the picture is extremely noisy.

6.3 Dolby Adaptive Delta Modulation (ADM)

A contender for the UK stereo sound transmission standard, and adopted in Australia for stereo sound on direct broadcast satellites (DBS), Dolby Laboratories' adaptive delta modulation (ADM) system is a means of digitally encoding audio information using a high sampling rate but a small number of bits per sample. Such a method has certain advantages: principally that decoders may be relatively cheap, and that the traditional low-pass filter required in digital convertors need not be nearly as steep or precise as in conventional PCM systems because of the high sampling rate. Additionally, there is considerable flexibility in the transmitted data rate to suit a number of applications, having a minimal effect on perceived audio quality.

6.3.1 Principles of operation

The process of delta modulation is already well documented, being a means of using essentially a 1 bit code to indicate changes up or down in the level of the audio signal. Provided that such changes are signalled regularly enough, the perceived quality of such a system may be as good as that of linearly encoded PCM. The sampling rate required to accommodate high frequency, high-level audio signals at similar quality to linear PCM is considerably greater than that of a system like NICAM (see above). The high sampling rate has the benefit of allowing a shallow low-pass filter to roll off components above the audio baseband, as aliasing is much less likely to occur.

Adaptive delta modulation is used for broadcast purposes because it is difficult to get a wide enough dynamic range out of a simple delta modulation system whilst keeping the bit rate within reasonable limits. Effectively it is a non-linear system, in that the step size (change in audio level) represented by each bit can be altered using an additional control signal, this being adapted to suit the programme material such that programme-modulated noise is kept to a minimum. With ADM, the choice of step-size is always a compromise between it being too small (leading to distortion related to slew-rate limiting), and it being too large (leading to programme-modulated noise), and thus the key to the adaptive principle is in the effective prediction of the correct step size.

As the sampling rate is high, quantisation noise is spread over a wide frequency band, much of it outside the audible range, and thus it is possible to employ noise-shaping techniques to remove in-band noise at the expense of noise at higher frequencies (out of band). Complementary to this, variable pre-emphasis is used, based on the spectral content of the audio signal, to optimise the signal-to-quantising-noise ratio for a wide variety of different input signals and step sizes. A subsidiary data stream is generated to control the de-emphasis at the decoder.

The block diagram in Figure 6.5 indicates the main processing hardware of such an ADM system, and it may be seen that it is essentially a feed-forward system whereby the input audio signal is delayed to allow for forward-looking prediction of the correct step size and emphasis. The total delay in this particular system, amounting to some 20 milliseconds, might become significant if synchronisation with a picture was involved. Typically, it is possible to achieve good audio quality in a broadcast application with an audio data rate of between 200 and 350 kbit s^{-1} per channel, whilst the control signals for step size and emphasis are at a lower rate of around 8 kbit s^{-1} each. This matches closely with the data rate used in the NICAM-728 system, and thus would lend itself to adoption in similar situations where limited bandspace is a problem.

6.3.2 Transmitting ADM

Since the data rate is similar to NICAM-728, it is reasonable to assume that a similar modulation method might be used in order to transmit ADM sound alongside terrestrial TV signals, and this has been suggested by Dolby Labs. In the event, NICAM has been adopted by the EBU as its digital standard for stereo TV sound, although the ADM system has found favour in Australia for use with the B-MAC DBS system.

In the Australian DBS system, six channels of ADM-encoded sound are transmitted at an audio data rate of 204 kbit s^{-1} per channel, with 13 bit packets sent once

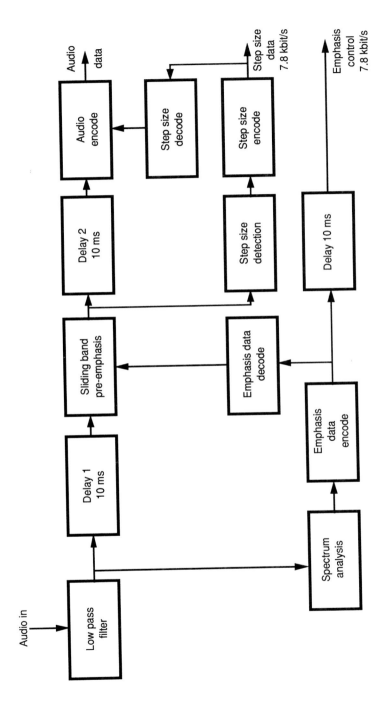

Figure 6.5 Block diagram of Dolby ADM encoder. (Courtesy of Dolby Laboratories)

every TV line. The additional sound capacity is used for the transmission of two digital stereo radio channels. Furthermore, Australian independent TV stations have recently adopted ADM for use in a professional distribution system handling a picture and up to four high-quality audio channels, with audio on a single subcarrier above the vision signal.

6.4 Recent audio data compression systems for transmission and broadcast links

6.4.1 Introduction

NICAM-728 and ADM are examples of a data compression system used for broadcast transmission, the aim being to reduce the bandwidth required for the digital audio signal. Such systems were originally designed some years ago, and since then a number of new audio data compression systems have appeared which have applications in broadcasting. Today, communications bandwidth is increasingly expensive, and it is purchased by the hertz. If broadcasters can reduce their requirement for bandwidth without reducing the quality of what is transmitted, then money can be saved, and a prime area of interest will be in satellite links for large television networks.

Bit rate or bandwidth reduction is a valuable means of saving money when purchasing space in a satellite band, broadcast band, or in any telecommunications environment such as ISDN (Integrated Services Digital Network). Alternatively, a data compression system allows the user to fit more audio channels into existing bandwidth which may be an important consideration for stereo sound broadcasting with television. Given the high sonic transparency of such systems, there is a strong and persuasive argument for their adoption. Two examples of approaches are described below, and it is acknowledged that this does not represent the full range of designs available at the time of writing. Currently there is debate within international standards organisations over the adoption of data compression systems for digital audio broadcast use, and there is also intense competition between the manufacturers of such systems, each of which naturally claims supremacy.

Both ADM and NICAM-728 are examples of successful efforts to reduce the bit-rate requirements of a digital audio channel to between 256 and 400 kbit s^{-1}. These systems are in use in broadcasting, particularly for stereo television sound transmission in parts of the world, but compared with recent data compression systems they use relatively simple techniques and thus result in a useful but only moderate reduction in the bit rate. The rapid rise of digital signal processing (DSP) hardware in integrated chip form at reasonable cost has led to the possibility for more complicated techniques to be developed. The developer has had a number of new doors opened owing to the increased number of calculations per second which are now possible, and which are needed in order to analyse and code an audio signal in an economical manner without involving long delays. Short delay times in coding and decoding are important for practical applications in broadcasting where delays may result in operational difficulties.

6.4.2 Principles of recent systems

The first aim of a high-quality audio data compression system is to ensure that there is no apparent loss of audio quality due to the data compression process, and a study of psycho-acoustic effects is important in ascertaining what side effects can be perceived and what cannot. In order to reduce the bit rate by substantial amounts there must be some exploitation of redundancies within the audio signal to be encoded, and such exploitation requires that the designer is able to anticipate the masking effects of certain signals on others, both in the time and frequency domains, and also to analyse the signal to determine the existence of repetitive or predictable components. Once the signal has been thus analysed it is possible to concentrate on accurately coding the components which are dominant or which have an appreciable effect on perceived sound quality, whilst relying on effects such as masking to hide the less important components. Essentially, the accuracy of coding is adjusted according to the nature of the audio signal, and optimised for the best audible result in each situation.

It is possible either to allow a data compression system to vary its output data rate, such that the system is free to adjust its coding accuracy according to the nature of input audio signals, or to fix the output data rate, which requires that the system always aims for the same output rate no matter what the prevailing signal situation, coding the signal to the best of its ability within the constraint of the target rate. The latter type is mandatory for applications in which one is dealing with a channel of fixed data rate, such as a transmission channel, but the former may be used in storage applications (such as in disk recording) where a fixed storage data rate may not always be of vital importance.

In order to exploit spectral redundancies in the audio signal one may analyse it either in the frequency domain or in the time domain. A technique known as adaptive transform coding, used by Dolby Laboratories, works by performing a discrete or fast Fourier transform on a group of samples, resulting in a set of values representing spectral components contained in the sample window (representing the Fourier analysis of a short portion of the audio waveform). From this the system ascertains which are the dominant components and will normally code these more accurately than the less dominant components. This, though, is not by any means the whole story, since certain less dominant components, especially at high frequencies, may still be important for representing transient information, and will have a marked effect on audio quality, so some assessment must be made, based on knowledge of subjective perception, to determine which components are important and which are not. Again, the principles of psycho-acoustic masking are taken into account.

In such a system, a 'side signal' is required, being a low bit-rate control pattern which signals to the decoder what coding scheme was involved at any particular time. This side channel must be heavily error protected, since its corruption could result in severe audible problems. Adaptive transform coding (ATC) of this type involves a codec delay time of around 55 ms at a sampling rate of 48 kHz. The ATC process used by Dolby in the DP501 and DP502 products codes two audio channels which originally were sampled at 48 kHz, 16 bits, at a data rate of 256 kbit s^{-1}, incorporating a low bit-rate (1200 baud) auxiliary data channel for user and control data. Audio bandwidth is limited to 15 kHz. The system incorporates error correction capable of correcting for random errors up to an error rate of 1 in 10^5.

The *apt-X 100* system, designed by Audio Processing Technology (a subsidiary of Solid State Logic), relies on a combination of backward-adaptive quantisation, linear prediction and sub-band ADPCM (adaptive differential pulse code modulation) to achieve its results. In many ways it is similar to the aforementioned technique in that it aims to exploit spectral redundancies in the audio signal, but it does this without the need for Fourier transforms and without the need for a side or control signal. Because of this it does not involve significant delays (~4 ms coder to decoder) and reacts more gently to conditions of high error rate.

In order to ascertain what dominant spectral components exist within the audio, the apt-X system looks at periodic aspects of the signal in the *time* domain, which obviates the need for a Fourier transform. Periodic emphasis in the signal shows up dominant frequency components. Linear prediction is a technique already well documented for speech coding, and research has shown that this technique also offers advantages for music signals since it is particularly efficient in cases of high spectral purity, such as might exist with pure tones or high-amplitude resonant sounds. Using this technique it is possible to attenuate such predictable signals (which normally show up unwanted modulation noise effects very prominently) before quantising, thus avoiding the need to resolve the frequency spectrum in order to code resonant components preferentially. More random signals, which are inherently unpredictable, do not gain any advantage from linear prediction, but these signals themselves have a masking effect on noise.

The 'sub-band ADPCM' part of the data compression process involves the splitting of the signal into four frequency bands, and adjusting the accuracy of quantisation according to the amount of signal energy in each band. This has certain parallels with the technique used in Dolby A noise reduction (an analogue system), in which the signal is split into bands before processing, such that dominant components in one band do not affect the processing in other bands, thus reducing the subjective effects of compansion). By using backward-adaptive quantisation it is possible to look at what has gone before in order to predict what coding accuracy is required in each band. This technique also obviates the need for a control signal to indicate the coding rules to a decoder, since the decoder is really a mirror image of the coder, also investigating past samples but performing the inverse action to the coder so as to restore the audio signal again (see Figure 6.6).

The performance of such a system under error conditions is likely to be a prime criterion of interest to anybody who wishes to use it in a transmission environment, and it has been proven to work well in simulated burst- and random-error tests. Random error rates of 1 in 10^4 have been judged to be audibly undetectable; at 1 in 10^3 the effect of the errors may just be noticed; but even at an error rate of 1 in 10 it is still possible to hear an audio signal, although distorted and noisy. The important factor is that the degradation appears to be very gradual as error rate increases.

The apt-X 100 audio data compression system may operate at any sampling rate up to 48 kHz, this rate being selected by a user-supplied word clock. The resulting output is a TTL data stream having a bit rate which depends on the initial sampling rate used. For example, with a 32 kHz sampling rate the output data rate is 128 kbit s^{-1} per audio channel, but with a sampling rate of 48 kHz the data rate is 192 kbit s^{-1}. A wide range of sampling rates can be used, locked to a master word clock, so it is possible to use the system in applications which require only 7.5 kHz audio bandwidth by sampling at 16 kHz, giving a data rate of only 64 kbit s^{-1}. In order to allow for the carrying of additional data, the facility has been provided for inserting auxiliary data into the compressed bit stream by overwriting the LSB of each 16 bit ADPCM code word which is output from the unit. One 16 bit output word is generated by the apt-X 100 system for every four 16 bit input words at the input, and the overwriting procedure necessary for the addition of aux data would necessarily reduce the overall audio fidelity slightly. The maximum rate of aux data is 8 kbit s^{-1} per audio channel.

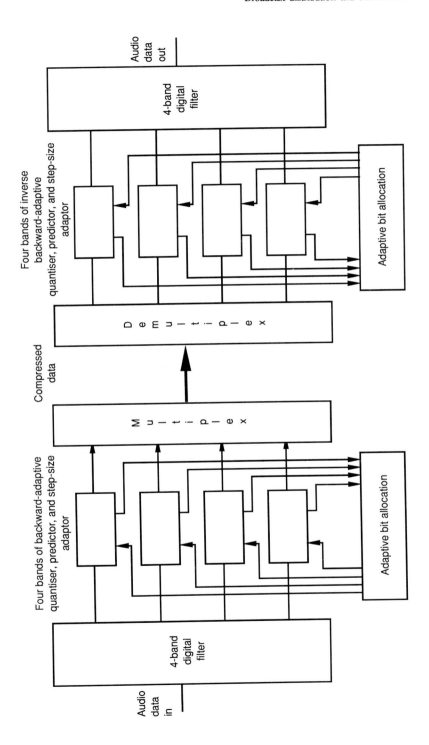

Figure 6.6 Block diagram of apt-X 100 audio data compression system. (Courtesy of Audio Processing Technology)

6.5 Digital audio for direct broadcast satellites (DBS)

Direct broadcast satellites are used increasingly for the transmission of television programmes throughout the world, and the C-MAC (Multiplexed Analogue Components) standard adopted by the EBU (European Broadcasting Union) allows for a number of digital audio options to suit different applications. In conjunction with a normal MAC picture, a data capacity of around 3 Mbit s^{-1} is available for audio purposes. Some countries will wish to use this capacity for transmitting a number of languages with each television programme, whilst others may prefer to use the capacity for additional digital radio channels, not necessarily associated with a picture. The EBU has specified that linear coding should be used wherever there is sufficient data capacity available, although companding processes such as NICAM may be used to increase the audio channel capacity if required.

For linearly coded PCM, up to six 15 kHz sound channels are possible, coded to 14 bit accuracy. This results from a data rate of 480 kbit s^{-1} per channel with simple error correction (parity only on the 11 MSBs). Alternatively, a smaller number of channels can be used with greater error protection, requiring a data rate of 608 kbit s^{-1} per channel (using a Hamming error correction code). Eight audio channels can be incorporated within the available capacity by the use of NICAM coding (see section 6.2), which reduces the data rate required per channel to 352 kbit s^{-1} (slightly lower than that used for NICAM-728 because the auxiliary data and control bits are not included).

6.6 Thames TV — a case study of digital audio in a TV centre

The recent successful installation at Thames Television's Euston site in the UK is a good example of digital audio signal distribution being used in a practical broadcast environment. It is also a good example of the principles of synchronous digital audio, video and timecode operation, as discussed in Chapter 14. The system was designed to take advantage of the digital stereo sound distribution and transmission systems now in use in the UK with terrestrial television (see section 6.2). In this installation AES/EBU digital interconnections (see section 10.2.4) are used for all signal routing, and Panasonic M-II VTRs (see section 4.17.2) are used for video recording, having two digital audio tracks which are available on AES/ EBU interfaces. Special switchers and mixers have been designed to route and level-control signals in the digital domain. Digital audio sources may be identified by the insertion of source data into the channel status bytes. Very soon, it is intended that signals will be able to remain in the digital domain all the way from source to domestic receiver.

The sampling rate used throughout the system is 48 kHz, although the sampling rate of the transmission and distribution system is 32 kHz. A sample-rate transcoder is being designed to interface between the studio centre and the sound-in-syncs network (see sections 10.3 and 6.1). Conveniently there is a simple relationship between the block rate of a 48 kHz AES/EBU signal (one block contains 192 samples, and carries a complete channel status word) and that of a PAL video signal. The AES/EBU block lasts 4 ms, whilst the PAL video frame lasts 40 ms, and thus there are ten AES/EBU blocks per video frame. As described in section 14.1, an in-house digital audio reference signal generator is locked to the 10 MHz rubidium reference which also locks the video sync reference. Video syncs lock the timecode

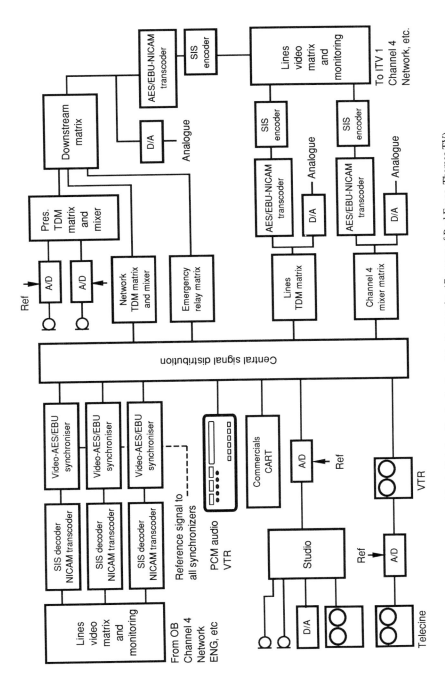

Figure 6.7 Block diagram of Thames Television's digital audio distribution at the Euston site. (Courtesy of Paul Evans, Thames TV)

generators, so that audio, video and timecode are all synchronous. Time-of-day timecode is inserted into the channel status bytes of the audio data, as bytes 18–21, and off-tape timecode is inserted into the bytes normally used for the AES/EBU sample address code (bytes 14–17).

The AES/EBU sync reference signal is distributed throughout the studio centre using much of the original cabling used for mono analogue audio, although with some modifications to suit the digital routing and to avoid signal corruption due to analogue-style patching and joining. Digital distribution amplifiers (DDAs) are used to distribute the signals, and these are capable of re-clocking the audio signals if required (see section 13.3). This reference signal carries a line-up tone at 18 dB below peak digital level (peak digital level is set at +18 dBu in the analogue domain). Operational peak level is set at 10 dB below the digital peak to allow for short high-level transients which might not be indicated on a conventional PPM. (Reference levels and line-up are discussed in section 8.2.3.)

A bank of A/D and D/A convertors is located in the central apparatus room, and these are used to interface with equipment which is still analogue, and to accept analogue signals from external sources. The eventual intention is that all signals will be digitally encoded as close to the source as possible, to maximise the benefits of digital audio routing. Gain-ranging 18 bit convertors are used which give the equivalent of 22 bit resolution, since the operational headroom required reduces the nominal signal-to-noise ratio of a 16 bit system to an unacceptable level. The AES/EBU interface carries the 20 MSBs of this signal, and the gain-ranging D/A convertors decode the 20 bit AES/EBU signal. Each stereo A/D convertor is equipped with a PROM (programmable read-only memory) which is used to identify the source in the status bits of the AES/EBU data.

The block schematic of the Thames digital audio distribution system is shown in Figure 6.7.

Chapter 7

Choosing a recording format

With such a wide range of digital recording options available, both tape and tapeless, the choice of system for a particular purpose may not be straightforward. The potential user will be faced with decisions over compatibility and interchange of recordings between systems, track capacity, synchronisation options (especially in video-related operations), as well as concerns over the robustness of the format in the face of drop-outs, flexibility in editing and available maximum recording time. One must not forget that many decisions will not be based on the recording *format*, but on its *implementation* in a specific product, since not all machines implement every facility of which a format is capable. With tapeless systems, since most currently make use of non-removable disks, the concept of a recording 'format' is somewhat meaningless, since recordings cannot be transferred between systems from different manufacturers. Once an optical disk interchange standard for sound files is agreed, this aspect of tapeless systems will become more important.

In this chapter a number of factors governing the choice of recording system will be set out, with reference to a range of possible end-user applications. The relative merits of disk- and tape-based systems are compared and contrasted. Since there are over 50 different tapeless systems on the market, with more appearing every month and with no standardisation, it is impossible to provide here a detailed comparison between such systems. For this the reader is referred to the latest edition of *The Tapeless Directory*, published by Sypha Consultants, the details of which are in the Bibliography at the end of this book.

7.1 Format or implementation?

It is possible to become confused over which aspects of a recording system are those of the recording format, and which are specific attributes of the product. It is not possible, though, to detach the consideration of machine facilities from the recording format, since, for example, a machine cannot offer splice editing if the format was not designed to allow it. An example is shown in Figure 7.1, where (a) shows some possible attributes of a *format*, whilst (b) shows the possible features of a tape machine. Although, for example, the format may allow for three sampling rates (32 kHz, 44.1 kHz and 48 kHz), the machine may only implement the last two. Similarly, although the format may have space for 20 bits per sample, the machine may only have implemented 16, since the format was allowing for future development. The format affects the potential for interchange of tapes between systems (see section 7.4).

Attributes of...

Recording format	Recording product
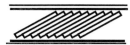	

Sampling rates (all possible)
Number of bits per sample (max.)
Tape speed
Drum speed
Angle of tracks
Number of aux tracks
Error handling mechanism
Tape type
Width of tape
Edit and punch-in/-out handling
Number of tracks
Track pattern
Channel code
Width of tracks
Housing of tape
Type of digital audio (e.g. linear PCM)

Sampling rate (selection)
Number of bits per sample
Editing options
Max. playing time
Number of aux tracks implemented
Timecode generator
Internal synchroniser
Other sync options
Error indication
Number of audio channels
Digital inputs and outputs
Punch-in and -out
Type of convertors
Varispeed range
Wind speed
Location options
Power supply options

Figure 7.1 Attributes of a recording format compared with attributes of a specific product or implementation of that format

Many 'formats' are manufacturer specific, rather than internationally agreed and ratified by standards organisations, and some have established themselves *de facto* through widespread use. A count of well-known digital tape formats (not all of which are in wide use) shows that there are at least 14 different ways of recording digital audio on tape. Formats which have been adopted by more than one manufacturer are DASH, PD, R-DAT, EIAJ, Video-8 (not really a professional standard), whereas the remainder (Mitsubishi X-80, Sony PCM-1610/1630, Decca, JVC, Akai A-DAM, Yamaha eight-track, 3M and Nagra-D) are used only in products from one manufacturer. S-DAT (stationary-head DAT) has yet to become properly established. From this it will be seen that there has been little success in standardising digital audio recording. The tables given in this chapter draw examples from the most widely used of recording formats and systems.

7.2 Cassette or open reel?

Digital tape machines use either tape on open reels or tape in cassettes. There are advantages and disadvantages to both approaches, and these are shown below:

Cassette
• Convenient to handle and store
• Tape is protected

- Does not easily allow splice editing
- Tape may be removed from machine without 'spooling-off'
- Allows thinner tape

Open reel
- More bulky than cassette
- Tape is not protected
- Allows splice editing
- Tape may be manually cued
- Theoretically allows any length of tape or reel size
- Possible psychological advantage in visible moving reels

Typically, cassette-based systems make use of rotary heads (see section 4.3), although there are exceptions such as S-DAT and the Yamaha eight-track format, whilst open-reel systems use stationary heads (although the Nagra-D format is an exception). Digital tape recordings are very easily damaged, since the tape is thin and the recorded wavelengths are high, and open reels make it easier to touch the tape or contaminate it. If splice editing is not a requirement then one has a strong argument for adopting a cassette-based recording format, although other aspects of an open-reel format should still be considered (see below). At the present time, the only large-scale multitrack digital tape machines available use open reels, so there is not a cassette option if a machine is required with 24 tracks or more, although Akai's A-DAM system offers 12 tracks on a rotary-head Video-8 cassette and Yamaha's DMR-8 integrated mixer and recorder offers eight tracks on a stationary-head custom cassette. Both of these machines may be synchronised to other machines of the same type, allowing greater track capacities to be obtained.

There is no overriding reason why the maximum playing time should be widely different between open reel and cassette, since although the cassette may be smaller than the open reel, its linear tape speed is also likely to be a lot lower, thus reducing tape consumption. The maximum playing time depends much more on the individual format (see section 7.5). An investigation of the costs of open-reel and cassette tape also does not show up any consistent bias towards one being more expensive than the other, although the cassette formats include those designed originally for consumer use (EIAJ and R-DAT) and thus tapes for these tend to be cheaper per hour than the professional formats.

7.3 How many channels?

7.3.1 Tape and disk compared

A distinction must be made between disk- and tape-based systems, since, as described in section 3.11, there is no clear definition of the term 'track' in a tapeless system. In such a system, there may be a certain number of channel outputs, and there may be a different number of inputs, allowing perhaps more channels to be replayed simultaneously than may be recorded simultaneously. In an application such as video dubbing this may be acceptable, since the inputs will be used for separately loading-up stereo effects, pre-recorded sync dialogue, sync effects and so forth. In a studio music recording system there may well be a need for a large number of inputs, for recording many microphone or line signals at once.

Potential users of disk-based systems should check on the number of output channels in a system compared with the number of input channels to see if their needs will be suited. They should also check to see whether all of the inputs may actually be *recorded* simultaneously. In a disk-based system there is no 'hard' relationship between internal tracks and channel outputs, since in most cases the relationship may be determined by the user. In a tape recorder it is the norm to encounter the same number of inputs as outputs, since inputs and outputs are wedded firmly to tracks on the tape, making it easier to state without any ambiguity what the track capacity of a tape machine is.

7.3.2 Expansion potential

One must also consider the expansion capability of any system. Tapeless systems are often very easy to expand, in terms of either storage time or track capacity, although this depends on the architecture of the design. In many cases disk systems are built on a modular basis, allowing the expansion of track capacity and playing time as the user's needs grow, by the addition of extra disk storage and additional channel outputs. The operating software may be designed to allow the addition of track capacity with no major changes to the user interface. This is not the case with all disk systems, though, as many are designed purely for stereo operation and have not allowed for expansion.

Digital tape recorders tend not to be built with expandable track capacity in mind, and one must normally decide on the maximum track capacity required and then stick to it. This differs slightly from the analogue situation in which one could purchase a 16 track tape recorder pre-wired for 24 tracks, and at a later date add a 24 track head block and the additional eight channels of audio electronics. There are other ways of expanding track capacity with tape recording, and these usually involve the synchronisation of more than one transport. It is worth noting that the DASH format allows for compatibility between 24 track recordings and 48 track recordings (see section 7.4.4).

7.3.3 Track capacity of tape recording formats

Table 7.1 shows the track capacities allowed for in a selection of current tape recording formats. Some formats are actually a family of formats which allow for a range of track capacities (e.g.: DASH and PD), whereas others are dedicated to a

Table 7.1 Track capacities

Format	Track capacity (min. – max.)	Current implementations
DASH	2 – 48	2, 24, 48
ProDigi	2 – 64	2, 16, 32
X-80	Stereo	Stereo
EIAJ	Stereo	Stereo
1630	Stereo	Stereo
JVC	Stereo	Stereo
Nagra-D	2 – 4	Not yet available
R-DAT	Stereo – 4	Stereo
Yamaha DMR-8	8	8
Akai A-DAM	12	12

Table 7.2 R-DAT modes

			Record/replay			
	Mandatory	Option 1	Option 2	Option 3	Pre-recorded	replay
Number of channels	2	2	2	4	2	2
Sampling rate	48	32	32	32	44.1	44.1
Bits per sample	16	16	12 non-lin.	12 non-lin.	16	16
Tape speed (mm/s)	8.15	8.15	4.075	8.15	8.15	12.225
Drum speed (rpm)	2000	2000	1000	2000	2000	2000
Playing time (min)	120	120	240	120	120	80

fixed track capacity (e.g.: EIAJ, PCM-1630). R-DAT is an example of a format which allows for a number of different modes, depending on such factors as tape speed, drum speed and sampling rate (see Table 7.2). It should be noted that only the 44.1 kHz and 48 kHz, 16 bit modes are in common usage. All DAT machines *must* record at 48 kHz and replay at 48 kHz and 44.1 kHz. Some machines are switchable between 44.1 and 48 kHz recording modes.

In Table 7.1 a distinction is made between 'stereo' formats and true two-channel formats, since many two-channel formats require that both tracks are recorded simultaneously and may not be treated independently (see section 4.1). All multi-track formats allow for the independent operation of each channel.

7.3.4 Trade-offs between track capacity and other factors

As discussed in sections 3.1 and 3.2, in any digital system there will be a trade-off between the number of channels to be recorded and the storage space required. Because of this, something has to give if track capacity is increased. In a disk system, provided that sampling rate and quantisation remain the same, it is the amount of storage time available from a given amount of disk storage, whereas in a tape system it may be the width of the tape, the length of the tape (either resulting in an increase in tape consumption), or the storage density. (See section 4.3 for a discussion of the way in which stationary-head machines achieve the increased bandwidth required for higher track capacity.)

To take an example from the DASH format (see Table 7.3) it can be seen that two audio channels may be obtained from a quarter-inch tape with four tracks per channel running at 7.5 ips, whereas 24 channels are obtained from a half-inch tape with one track per channel running at 30 ips, so tape consumption has been increased for the 24-channel version. Looking back to Table 7.2 it will be seen that in order to obtain four tracks from R-DAT the sampling rate has been reduced to 32 kHz and the quantisation has been changed to 12 bit, non-linear, although the tape consumption has not been affected when compared with the mandatory two-track version.

Table 7.3 Some implemented DASH-format configurations

Audio channels	Tracks per channel	Tape speed	Tape width
2	4	19	Quarter-inch
2	4 (twin DASH)	38	Quarter-inch
24	1	76	Half-inch
48	1 (double density)	76	Half-inch

7.4 Interchange of recordings

Perhaps the biggest problem in digital recording is the interchange of programme material between systems. In professional analogue recording, owing to many years of world-wide usage, a standard interchange format has arisen, there being only minor differences between recordings. By and large, it is true that none of the digital formats are compatible with each other, in that a tape of one format may not be replayed in a machine of another. This is not to be confused with the transfer of recordings from one format to another by *copying* via one of the standard digital interfaces (see section 10.2), since in most cases this is possible, provided that suitable track capacity exists on the recording machine. Even within one format there may be problems with interchange, and the likely difficulties are discussed below. Only the more universal formats in wide use are discussed below, it being taken for granted that the various manufacturer-specific formats (see section 7.1) are only replayable on that manufacturer's machines.

Currently there is very little to say about the interchange of disk recordings, since many systems use non-removable hard disks and there is as yet no agreed interchange format for sound files on optical disks (see Fact File 5).

7.4.1 Analogue recording interchange

The analogue interchange format is quarter-inch two-track tape for two-track recordings and 2 inch tape for 24 track recordings, this covering the majority of material that is moved between studios and locations within broadcast organisations. There are three tape speeds widely used in analogue recording, 30 ips (76 cm s^{-1}), 15 ips (38 cm s^{-1}) and 7.5 ips (19 cm s^{-1}), and two equalisation standards (NAB and IEC/AES). Nearly all machines can be switched to operate in any of these modes. The only difference between two-track machines is the NAB and DIN track format, the NAB format having a wider guard-band for true two-track recording. Timecode is sometimes recorded in a centre-track which runs down the guard-band, but this will not affect replay on non-timecode machines unless they have DIN heads. Noise reduction is often used on analogue recordings, and for many years this was to the Dolby 'A' standard, although latterly the Dolby 'SR' standard has become popular. It is possible to buy noise reduction cards which are switchable between Dolby 'A' and 'SR'.

It is true that non-standard analogue formats exist, there being a number of semi-professional machines from Japanese manufacturers which operate using narrower tape or cassettes, but these do not represent the mainstream of professional recording. It is also the case that some studios work to 1 inch eight track and 2 inch 16 track standards, although headblocks and guides may be fitted to 24 track machines to allow them to replay. Because of the measure of commonality between analogue machines, a tape made in the USA may be replayed in Japan or the UK with no difficulty.

7.4.2 Digital recordings made on video machines

Considering first systems based on PCM video adaptors (see section 4.6), interchangeability will depend on the video format involved. The EIAJ format has both PAL and NTSC versions, and for recording purposes an NTSC adaptor must be used with an NTSC VTR, resulting in an NTSC-format recording, and a PAL adaptor with a PAL VTR. PAL versions of the Sony PCM-701 have been modified by third parties (e.g.: Audio & Design) to allow them to be switched between PAL and NTSC video outputs, so that recordings may be made on either format of VTR. This modification is not possible with NTSC-format PCM-701s.

NTSC systems are found mostly in the USA, Japan and South America, whereas PAL is found in Europe, Scandinavia and Australia. For replay purposes NTSC recordings must be replayed on NTSC VTRs and PAL recordings on PAL VTRs, but some Sony PCM adaptors (PCM-F1, 501, 601, 701) will lock to and replay *either* PAL *or* NTSC video signals. There are one or two multi-standard VTRs available, but these are not common. If an NTSC tape is replayed in a PAL VTR, or vice versa, the VTR will not be able to replay the recording, and the result will be a muted audio output from the PCM adaptor.

The Sony CD-mastering format (PCM-1610 and 1630 systems) produces U-matic tapes which are of the monochrome 60 Hz/525 line format. These tapes can only be played back on other machines of the same type, via a Sony PCM-1610, 1630, or any future successor of the same format. Recordings made on the JVC digital mastering system, which may use either VHS or U-matic tapes, are not compatible with the Sony system. Tapes from either of these systems cannot be replayed via EIAJ-format decoders.

7.4.3 R-DAT recordings

R-DAT is a universal world-wide format which is not dependent on a video standard, and thus R-DAT tapes made in one part of the world should be replayable in another. Looking back at Table 7.2, though, it will be seen that there are a number of options within the standard. The only mandatory format is for recording at 48 kHz, 16 bit, the others being for purposes such as pre-recorded tapes and different playing times. All machines are also expected to replay in the 44.1 kHz mode designed for pre-recorded tapes, but not all machines will *record* in this mode. The reason for this is a historical and political one, since it would have allowed the direct digital copying of CDs via a digital output in the SPDIF format (see Fact File 17) which many CD players have. By preventing domestic machines from recording at 44.1 kHz, digital copying was made impossible, although analogue copying was not a problem. Professional users who bought older domestic DAT machines found that it was a relatively easy matter to modify some machines to allow recording at 44.1 kHz, this being a vital factor in enabling the machine to be used for CD mastering.

Since SCMS copy protection has been introduced (see section 10.6), more consumer machines have appeared which allow recording at 44.1 kHz via the digital inputs, and this is likely to become the norm. Potential purchasers should check, though, whether a machine will record via the *analogue* inputs at 44.1 kHz.

7.4.4 DASH recordings

The DASH format is supported by a number of manufacturers, principal amongst them being Sony, Studer and TEAC. As previously explained, the DASH format is a family of recording formats which has spawned a number of tape machines: two track, 24 track and 48 track. There being so many possible versions of the DASH format it is not a particularly straightforward matter to say which recordings will replay on which machines, since this depends on the specific capabilities of the tape machine involved. The DASH format allows for sampling rates of either 44.056, 44.1 or 48 kHz, with varispeed to ±12.5%, and all machines are designed to follow the recorded sampling rate on replay by adjusting the speed of the tape, so there is no problem in replaying tapes recorded at one sampling rate on another machine.

Considering two-track DASH first of all, it should be realised that the DASH format was revised in the mid 1980s to allow for so-called 'twin DASH'. In twin DASH all of the audio data is recorded twice, using two sets of tape tracks, one set of which has the odd-even sample arrangement altered so that the samples are arranged 'even-odd' instead. This was in order to make the format more robust when splice edited, and in the face of other replay errors, but has the effect of requiring the tape speed to be doubled compared with single DASH. Consequently Sony and Studer between them produced a variety of two-track DASH machines in combinations of the slow (7.5 ips) and medium (15 ips) speed formats, in both single- and twin-DASH formats, although Studer never produced a 7.5 ips machine. Initially, Sony produced the PCM-3102, which ran at 7.5 ips using four tracks per channel (single DASH), but the splice-editing performance was not particularly good, and so Sony produced the PCM-3202 which ran at 15 ips using the twin-DASH method. Then it produced the more advanced PCM-3402 which was switchable between the two speeds and could replay tapes made in either twin- or single-DASH formats. Studer's D-820X machine operates only in the twin-DASH format at 15 ips, and cannot replay 7.5 ips recordings. It seems likely that single DASH will disappear for two-track recording, to be replaced entirely by twin DASH, the only advantage in single DASH at 7.5 ips being the increased playing time available.

Currently, multitrack DASH-format recordings (both 48 and 24 track) are all made at the high speed of 30 ips. DASH-format recordings made on any 24 track machine will replay on any other machine, provided that the machine's mechanical alignments are correct. Furthermore, 24 track tapes will replay on 48 track machines without modification of the machine in any way. This is because the additional 24 tracks in the 48 track format are located inbetween those of the 24 track format. 48 track tapes may also be played back on 24 track machines, but only half of the tracks will be heard! Interchangeability of tapes has been successfully demonstrated between DASH machines from all three manufacturers, and between 24 and 48 track machines. Currently, both Sony and Studer manufacture 48 track DASH machines (the PCM-3348 and the D820-48 respectively). DASH-format tapes will not replay on ProDigi-format machines (see below), or vice versa.

7.4.5 ProDigi-format and X-80-format recordings

The ProDigi (PD) format was devised by Mitsubishi after the DASH format had been established, and is not compatible with it. It superseded the original format used by Mitsubishi on its early X-80 two-track machine, and is not compatible with this either (the sampling rate in this format was 50.4 kHz), although a Mitsubishi machine is available which can be used to replay two-track tapes of both formats. The PD format is currently supported by Mitsubishi, Otari and Telefunken. Like DASH, PD represents a family of formats ranging from 2 to 64 channels (see Table 7.4), although there is not as much commonality between the two-track and multitrack formats as there is with DASH. Real machines exist with up to 32 channel capacity.

A number of options exist with two-track PD, since there are two possible speeds (7.5 ips and 15 ips), the slow speed being intended for the longer playing time

Table 7.4 Some implemented PD-format configurations

Audio channels	Tracks per n channels	Tape speed (cm/s)	Tape width
2	8 per 2	19	Quarter-inch
2	8 per 2	38	Quarter-inch
16	10 per 4	38	Half-inch
32	10 per 8	76	1 inch

required in archiving applications which do not require splice editing, and in broadcast applications where longer playing time is valuable. Although the nominal sampling rate for PD recordings is 48 kHz, it is possible to record or replay at 44.1 kHz, as in DASH, and at 32 kHz, with an appropriate reduction in tape speed. There is also a Mitsubishi machine available (the X-86 HS) which samples at 96 kHz, although this does not conform directly with the tabled PD-format specifications. Tapes made at 15 ips will not replay on 7.5 ips machines or vice-versa.

All 32 track PD machines operate at the same speed as 24 and 48 track DASH machines (30 ips), but use 1 inch tape rather than half-inch tape. Mitsubishi's 16 track PD machine uses half-inch tape at 15 ips. Tapes may be interchanged between all 32 track PD machines, but not between 16 track and 32 track machines, since the track pattern is not compatible as it is in DASH.

One mode of the PD format (Mode 3) allows for up to 20 bits of audio data to be recorded per sample (this has been implemented in Mitsubishi's X-86 machine, although the machine itself only has 16 bit convertors, requiring an outboard convertor to achieve the full resolution) whereas DASH only allows for 16 bits per sample. A 20 bit recording may be replayed on a machine with only 16 bit convertors, but the additional audio resolution will be lost. However, 20 bit tapes may be recorded and replayed via AES/EBU digital interfaces (see Fact File 16), retaining full 20 bit resolution, using external 20 bit D/A convertors at an appropriate point.

7.5 Recording duration

Table 7.5 shows a comparison between the maximum recording times available in different tape formats using currently available machines. Not all formats place any limit on maximum recording time, since open-reel recording time depends on the size of the tape reels, but there are practical limits due to the usual maximum diameter of reels being 14 inches. It should be recognised that not all machines conforming to a particular format will offer this maximum storage capacity. The examples in Table 7.5 are taken from the most widely-used systems, and thus not every option in each format is quoted, since there is often no machine available in such cases. The table is intended as a working guide. Disk systems have not been included in this summary, since there are now over 50 varieties of disk system, each with a vast range of storage options.

7.6 Robustness of recordings

A vital factor in the regular use of digital tape machines is the reliability of a recording and its robustness in the face of such factors as physical damage, handling

Table 7.5 Guide to recording times

Format	Reel size	Recording time (min)
DASH 24/48 track (e.g.: Studer D820)	14 inches	65
DASH two track/7.5 ips (e.g.: Sony PCM-3402)	12.5 inches	180
DASH two track/15 ips (e.g.: Sony PCM-3402)	12.5 inches	90
DASH two track/15 ips (e.g.: Studer D820X)	14 inches	~120
ProDigi 32 track (e.g.: Mitsubishi X-850)	14 inches	65
ProDigi two track/7.5 ips (e.g.: Mitsubishi X-86)	14 inches	240
ProDigi two track/15 ips (e.g.: Mitsubishi X-86)	14 inches	120
EIAJ	ß L-750	195
1630	U-matic	75
JVC	U-matic or VHS	120 (VHS)
Nagra-D two track	7 inches	360
Nagra-D four track	7 inches	180
R-DAT standard mode (48 kHz, 16 bit)	-	120
Yamaha DMR-8, eight track	Custom	20
Akai A-DAM	Video-8, 60 min	16.5

and storage. Unfortunately there is not very much conclusive independent information available concerning the performance of tape or disk formats in this respect. Furthermore, it is very difficult to make generalisations about the robustness of *formats*, since this depends considerably on the alignment of machines and the way in which tape is handled and stored, as well as the type of tape used. It is more appropriate to discuss the ways in which the possibility of errors can be *minimised* in various systems, and this is covered in Chapter 9.

Each format is designed with an error-correction mechanism intended to be appropriate for the types of errors to be found on real tapes. Replay of recordings will fail when the error correction system is overwhelmed by a lack of correct data from the tape, and this may result when the tape is spliced, when it is damaged, when it is handled, or when it has deteriorated in storage. It may also result from random errors due to dirty heads, worn tape, poor tape, interference, or misalignment of the machine.

Although some systems can be seen to have more comprehensive error correction systems than others, this is not necessarily a guide to the relative robustness of the system, since, for example, R-DAT has a very comprehensive error correction system with many different levels of detection and correction (much more advanced than that used in the Sony CD-mastering format, for example), but this is because the system *requires* much greater protection against errors owing to the nature of the recording process (smaller tape, finer tolerances, etc.).

It would be true to say, though, that the 14 bit mode of the EIAJ format is more robust than the 16 bit mode, because of the reduced error protection in the 16 bit mode (see section 4.7), and also that the low-speed versions of the two-track single-DASH and ProDigi formats will be more prone to errors resulting from handling and splicing, since single DASH has reduced error protection compared with twin DASH and 7.5 ips PD involves a higher data density on tape than 15 ips PD.

7.7 Sampling rates

Two sampling rates should be considered as most important in any digital recording system: the 44.1 kHz rate which is used for CD mastering, and the 48 kHz rate which has been standardised as the professional recording rate (although in fact this rate may end up only being used in broadcasting as it is the only rate which can be used on some digital video recorders). The 32 kHz rate is much less important in recording systems, and is hardly ever used in professional environments. The 32 kHz rate is important in broadcast transmission systems and sound-in-syncs links (see Chapter 6). Although digital broadcasting often uses the 32 kHz rate, the 48 kHz rate is typically used in broadcast studio centres, using sample rate conversion (see section 10.3) to match the output of a studio centre to a digital network. The 44.056 kHz rate, once adopted in NTSC PCM adaptors, is not likely to survive as a standard, but the reasons for its use are discussed in Chapter 14. (See Appendix 1 for a description of the sampling process.)

Rates above 48 kHz may result from the upward varispeeding of digital recordings, or from higher non-standard fixed rates. The value of higher fixed sampling rates is dubious, although hotly promoted by some, since it only results in marginal improvements in sound quality, if any, but will involve a major increase in storage requirement (see section 3.1). There are more effective ways of ensuring a flat, uncoloured audio band than raising the recorded sampling rate. Such methods involve a technique known as 'oversampling' which is described in Appendix 1, as well as the use of carefully designed convertors and good analogue and digital filters. Using a combination of these three, high sound quality may be achieved whilst keeping storage requirements within sensible bounds.

Table 7.6 shows the sampling rates used by a collection of widely used recording formats. The rates shown in parantheses are allowed for in the format but rarely implemented in real machines, whilst the rates marked with the '•' symbol are not part of the format but have been implemented in real machines. The rate of 44.1 kHz is important if the user wants to make CD masters, otherwise 48 kHz has been recommended as the norm for professional recording. Disk-based systems often allow the user-selection of sampling rate, some allowing perhaps three fixed rates whilst others allow any rate over a wide range. Storage capacity is directly traded-off against sampling rate in such cases.

It is important to realise that in the formats which allow for varispeed replay (e.g.: DASH, PD, R-DAT) the output sampling rate is likely to change with the tape speed. Thus the quoted sampling rate is only correct at the nominal tape speed. This may present problems when tapes are replayed via digital mixers which expect a fixed sampling rate digital input, in which a sample-rate convertor will be required. This also applies to some disk-based systems, although some of these have integral sample-rate convertors.

Table 7.6 Sampling rates

Format	Sampling rates (kHz)	Comment
DASH	(32), 44.1, (44.056), 48	Tape speed changes pro rata
ProDigi	44.1, 48, 96 (•)	96 kHz only on special X-86
X-80	50.4	
EIAJ	44.056, 44.1	44.056 NTSC / 44.1 PAL
1630	44.056, 44.1	44.056 when locked to NTSC video
JVC	44.056, 44.1	44.056 when locked to NTSC video
Nagra-D	(32), 44.1, 48	
R-DAT	(32), 44.1, 48	See Table 7.2
Yamaha DMR-8	44.1, 48	Tape speed changes pro rata
Akai A-DAM	44.1, 48	Tape speed changes pro rata

7.8 Recording resolution (quantising accuracy)

The number of bits per sample used in a recording has a direct relationship to sound quality, affecting the dynamic range of the system (see Appendix 1). As with sampling rate, there is some conjecture over how many bits are required in professional systems. The CD format has made 16 bits per sample the standard for CD mastering, although there are many operators who would like to have greater resolution than this on professional systems, in order to allow for greater freedom in level setting (see Chapter 8). Provided that recordings of greater than 16 bit resolution are correctly truncated to 16 bits before mastering on to CD then a greater resolution would be valuable (see section 10.4), otherwise the result may be a reduction rather than an increase in sound quality.

The AES/EBU interface (see section 10.2.4) allows for 20 bits of audio data per sample (or 24 if the auxiliary word is used), and it might be suggested that such resolution should be allowed-for in recording *formats* even if a machine's convertors do not convert to this accuracy. Higher-resolution external convertors may then be used if required, and interfaces to other equipment may be made without potential loss of audio resolution. Table 7.7 shows the number of bits per sample allowed in a number of common recording formats. It will be seen that Mode 3 of the two-track PD format, as used in Mitsubishi's X-86, is really the only currently available two-track format capable of handling 20 bits (although Nagra-D will change this when it is available), and that both DASH and ProDigi multitrack formats are only capable of handling 16 bits. More recent multitrack systems, such as Yamaha's DMR-8, are provided with space for greater resolution, and indeed the convertors available for this system offer 19 bit quantisation.

When most of the tape recording formats were designed, 16 bit quantisation was seen as the standard, and many either believed that resolution greater than this would either never be available, or they simply could not believe that greater resolution would be demanded. Now that digital audio is moving into a more mature phase there has arisen a considerable interest in higher recorded resolution, yet few formats are able to take advantage of the increasingly large selection of 18–20 bit convertors now available. The advantage of using higher-resolution convertors may still be apparent with 16 bit formats, since such convertors usually offer better 16 bit performance than many dedicated 16 bit devices, provided that they are optimally dithered for 16 bit operation (see Appendix 1).

A number of the tapeless systems offer higher resolution than 16 bits within the file format, with systems currently catering for between 16 and 24 bits per sample,

Table 7.7 Sample resolution

Format	Bits per sample	Comment
DASH	16	
ProDigi	16, 20	20 bits only on Mitsubishi X-86 two track
X-80	16	
EIAJ	14, 16	16 bits only in Sony-modified version
1630	16	
JVC	16	
Nagra-D	20 + 4	20 bits audio + 4 bits aux from AES/EBU IF
R-DAT	(12 non-lin.), 16	See Table 7.2
Yamaha DMR-8	20	
Akai A-DAM	16	

although again the on-board convertors do not always operate to the full potential of the file format. Greater resolution, as with high sampling rates, reduces the maximum recording time of a disk system for any given size of disk (see Table 3.1).

7.9 Confidence replay

Systems built for professional usage are normally expected to offer confidence replay facilities, that is the option for monitoring a recording 'off tape' whilst recording, in order to check for drop-outs and any other problems which might have affected the recording. Such a facility has always been available on professional analogue recorders.

It should be realised that such facilities are rarely a function of the format, being a design feature of the tape machine. Some formats make it easier to provide off-tape monitoring than others. In stationary-head systems the facility involves a replay head mounted 'downstream' of the record head, as in an analogue tape machine, whereas in rotary-head systems it requires an extra head or heads on the rotating drum, mounted so as to follow the record head(s). It should be noted that none of the formats specifically *precludes* the facility being offered.

Disk systems would also be capable of offering confidence replay, but the means of achieving it would be rather different. Since the recording device would be a standard computer-industry disk drive, it would not be possible simply to add another head to monitor a recording. Confidence replay would involve the reading of a file block immediately after writing it (called 'verification' in computer terms) to determine whether it had been written correctly. At the same time a monitor audio signal could be reproduced, although if this was not considered necessary the system could report on file errors by means of a warning message. Normally, in hard disk systems, if a block fails on verification the system attempts to write it again, either in the same place or in a different place. Disk controllers keep maps of 'bad blocks' in order that they are not written to in the future.

In digital recorders, as in analogue recorders, confidence replay is usually slightly delayed when compared with the audio input, corresponding to the distance between record and replay heads coupled with any digital processing delay.

7.10 Access time

Access time to a distant section of pre-recorded material is an important factor in editing environments where many takes are to be auditioned, perhaps recorded in widely separated parts of a tape or disk. Access time is largely a function of the mechanics of the machine as opposed to the format, but by specifying certain mechanical aspects of a tape format the various standards have prepared the ground for differences in performance between real systems. For example, R-DAT uses small cassettes and transports, all with very low inertia, allowing for very fast winding speeds, whereas the Sony 1630 system relies on standard U-matic transports which have limited winding speeds.

By and large, DAT systems offer the fastest access time of any of the currently-available tape formats (usually less than a minute from end-to-end of a cassette), with all other systems falling often an order of magnitude behind. There is not a great difference between the access times of other cassette and open-reel systems. The thin tape used in digital open-reel systems can sometimes suffer poor packing and leafing if wound too fast, and this can result in edge damage to the tape. For this reason the high winding speed on open-reel machines is often limited.

Disk-based recorders, as is the the nature of random access devices, have very fast access time to any part of the store, it being only a matter of moving a head across the rotating surface of the disk. This can be achieved in milliseconds, as opposed to seconds or minutes, although some disk drives are slower than others (see section 3.12). RAM, used as the main store in some systems, has even faster access time than disks, being of the order of nanoseconds (10^{-9} seconds). The great strength of random access systems is this extremely short access time.

The importance of fast access time to a potential user will depend on the amount of editing envisaged, since this is the application in which the most-regular comparison of remotely located material will be required.

7.11 Flexibility in editing

Table 7.8 shows the editing capabilities of different digital tape systems. Some formats allow both splice (tape-cut) and electronic editing, whilst others may only allow one or the other. Some formats allow no editing at all. In many cases the crossfade times available are a function of an external electronic editor, whilst in splice-editing situations the crossfade is usually fixed for all edits, being controlled by an internal crossfader. It may be taken that all of the tapeless systems allow for editing, although the facilities offered by such systems vary so enormously between products that it would be difficult to tabulate them. Editing is covered in greater detail in Chapters 5 and 11.

7.12 Timecode

This subject is covered in detail in section 14.2, but here is given a short résumé of the facilities offered in different digital recording systems. Table 7.9 shows whether or not a timecode track may be recorded alongside the audio tracks, and the notes show any comments which apply.

In the R-DAT system, an IEC standard method for recording timecode has been agreed, such that the timecode is recorded within the subcode area of the helical DAT track. Earlier DAT machines, such as Sony's PCM-2000, recorded timecode on the narrow analogue edge track which was subject to damage and was only just adequate for the purpose. Fostex implemented its own timecode format for DAT in advance of the IEC standardisation, and thus future Fostex machines are likely to implement both IEC timecode and the in-house version. The IEC DAT timecode standard involves the conversion of true SMPTE/EBU linear timecode (LTC) into the equivalent 'DAT running time', which is a code relating to the DAT frame rate of 33.33 frames per second; thus all IEC-standard DAT machines will incorporate a 'gearbox' to achieve this conversion. It has the advantage that any frame rate of timecode may be derived on replay, no matter what was used whilst recording. Static 'user bits' data may also be recorded in the IEC format. In the Fostex implementation, LTC from the input is written unmodified, including all user bit data, into an area of the DAT subcode, without passing via a gearbox of any kind. See Fact File 29 for further details of the IEC timecode format.

Table 7.8   Editing options

Format	Manual splice (S) Electronic (E)	Comment
DASH	S, E	Splice only reliable at 15 ips and above
ProDigi	S, E	Splice only reliable at 15 ips and above
X-80	S, E	
EIAJ	(E)	See section 4.7
1630	E	
JVC	E	
Nagra-D	S, E	
R-DAT	E	Only on professional machines
Yamaha DMR-8	E	
Akai A-DAM	E	

Table 7.9 Timecode track provision

Format	Timecode track?	Comment
DASH	Yes	
ProDigi	Yes	
X-80	Yes	
EIAJ	Yes	Audio channel of videotape
1630	Yes	Audio channel 2 of videotape
JVC	Yes	Audio channel 2 of videotape
Nagra-D	Yes	
R-DAT	Yes	Timecode in subcode except Sony PCM-2000 (IEC-standard 'pro' machines only)
Yamaha DMR-8	Yes	
Akai A-DAM	Yes	

Most of the disk-based systems allow for timecode values to be stored alongside audio whilst recording, although the timecode is not recorded on a separate 'track' but entered in the directory (see section 3.8) as start and end points, as well as sometimes in a look-up table of timecode values against block locations on disk, to help in synchronisation of replay. This subject is covered further in Chapter 15.

Timecode is important for electronic editing and in any work which involves synchronisation of machines, such as in operations involving video machines. If digital recordings are cut and spliced then any contiguous timecode track will be broken up, whereas electronic copy editing often requires an unbroken contiguous timecode track on both player and recorder machines. Some recorders have inbuilt timecode generators, whilst others require an external feed of timecode, so it is wise to check on this feature. Most formats allow for timecode of any standard to be recorded on the timecode track, but those which are based around a particular video standard should normally be used with the appropriate timecode for that standard, otherwise synchronisation problems may arise (see Chapter 14).

7.13 Auxiliary tracks and subcode data

In addition to the high-quality audio tracks available on digital recorders, many offer a small number of tracks for auxiliary information. In most cases two of these tracks may carry an analogue version of the programme recorded on the digital tracks (although in the case of multitrack machines with only two cue tracks this may be

Table 7.10 Number of longitudinal auxiliary tracks

Format	Number of aux tracks	Comment
DASH	2	
ProDigi	3	Two cue audio, one for user data
X-80	1	Other aux track required for timecode
EIAJ	1 or 0	Depends on analogue tracks on VTR
1630	1	Other aux track required for timecode
JVC	1 or 0	Depends on analogue tracks on VTR
Nagra-D	1	
R-DAT	(2)	Rarely implemented
Yamaha DMR-8	2	
Akai A-DAM	0	Single aux track required for timecode

a rough guide track). The analogue cue tracks can then be used for rough location purposes, and for monitoring at speeds outside the range of normal digital replay, using a separate analogue replay head. Often the bandwidth and dynamic range of the cue tracks is fairly poor, due to the narrowness of the tracks and the fact that the tape is not optimised for analogue recording.

On some systems the auxiliary tracks may also be used for storing auxiliary digital data such as subcode information for CD mastering (suitably encoded to fit within the bandwidth of the track) and low baud rate control information for editing and cueing purposes. Some companies have found it possible to use pulse width modulation techniques (PWM) to record the auxiliary tracks, and these may offer slightly higher audio quality than ordinary biased analogue recording over a range of speeds. Mitsubishi uses a companding process followed by PWM to record the cue tracks in multitrack PD machines. Table 7.10 shows the number of auxiliary tracks available in some common recording formats, although these may not always be made available to users (e.g.: the edge track in R-DAT is hardly ever used). In the video cassette formats, the number of aux tracks depends on the facilities of the VTR used for recording. In the table the number of aux tracks is quoted *after* allowing for a timecode track.

Auxiliary tracks will be most useful for cueing purposes in open-reel machines where the reels may be moved by hand, such as during splice editing, at which speeds the normal digital tracks cannot be used. They are less useful in cassette-based systems for cueing, since it is unlikely that the reels will be moved by hand at non-normal speeds, and in such cases they can be used for auxiliary data or for low-quality slating information such as the identification of takes during a recording session.

The R-DAT format allows for subcode data to be stored in the same helically scanned track as audio data, having separate data blocks for this purpose (see Fact File 8). As the use of this format develops, machines may develop facilities for using this capacity, the only current usage of subcode data being for the recording of timecode and track location/timing information.

7.14 Synchronisation options

Digital tape machines may be synchronised to a variety of timing references, including video sync pulses, composite video, word clock, timecode, and the AES/EBU digital interface. The subject of synchronisation is not discussed further here, and the reader should refer to Chapters 13–15.

7.15 Punch-in and punch-out

In multitrack machines it is very important to be able to punch in and punch out of record mode on individual tracks, in order to allow for the replacement of sections of a track. In digital machines, gapless punch-in is achieved in a similar way to electronic editing, except that the material to be punched in does not usually come from another tape machine. At a punch-in the machine crossfades between replayed material (from the advanced replay head, see section 4.5) and new material from the audio input, and at a punch-out it crossfades back again, ensuring a seamless join. Both of the major multitrack formats (DASH and PD) are designed to accommodate this facility, and two-track machines of these formats allow punching-in also. Again, punch-in and -out is very much a feature of the *implementation* of a format, and not the format itself. Consumer DAT machines and EIAJ-format systems are not made to allow punching-in in most cases.

Punching-in is also possible with nearly all disk-based systems, although many of these systems are designed more for video post-production and audio editing than for multitrack music recording (where punching-in is most used.)

7.16 Track bouncing

In multitrack recording it is often necessary to 'bounce' tracks, that is either to move a track on to another track, or to combine two or more tracks into one recording on another track (this is sometimes called 'ping-pong'). Some machines incorporate track-bouncing facilities on-board, but this only allows for one track to be copied on to another, rather than allowing for any level control or mixing. It is usually necessary to have at least one spare track on to which source tracks may be recorded, once mixed externally, but Yamaha has shown in its DMR-8 system that it is not even necessary to have *one* spare track, allowing all eight tracks on its tape to be bounced to any other track or tracks. It achieves this by means of the read–modify–write process (see section 4.5) which can take material off the tape from an advanced replay head and re-record it on the same track with modifications (which could involve mixing the signal with that from other tracks).

7.17 Delays between input and output

Digital tape machines, unlike analogue machines, will introduce a delay between the input and output of each channel. This is due to the encoding and decoding process which audio data is subject to before and after recording on to tape (see Fact Files 6 and 7). The delay may only be a matter of milliseconds, but may affect the synchronisation and sound quality of foldback and cue feeds to artists if signals which have passed through the machine are mixed with signals that have not, resulting in 'comb-filter'-type cancellations and additions of the signal at various frequencies. The magnitude of any delay through a digital recorder should be checked and considered carefully. In the future, the AES suggests that the delay between inputs and outputs is clearly marked on sockets in terms of the number of AES/EBU frames involved (see Fact File 16).

Chapter 8

Recording levels and metering

This chapter is concerned with the interpretation of metering and the setting of recording levels in digital disk and tape systems. In analogue recording it is known that distortion gets gradually worse as the recording level rises, and it is known that noise gets worse as the recording level falls, and thus one attempts to record at a level which stays above the noise and below the distortion. It also known that it is possible to record at quite high levels on analogue tape without distortion being particularly objectionable, since the onset of distortion and high-frequency saturation is gradual and not unpleasant. A digital recording system does not behave in quite the same way as an analogue system, and one must learn to use the medium to best advantage.

8.1 Recording levels

The dynamic range of a linear PCM system (that is one which does not use any form of data compression and where each quantising step represents an equal increment in signal level) is governed principally by the number of bits per sample, and is limited at high signal levels by the sudden onset of distortion which results from clipping when the convertors run out of headroom (corresponding to the maximum positive or negative binary number within the range of the digital system, see Appendix 1). This point is sometimes referred to as 'peak bits', 'digital saturation' or 'over level' (see Figure 8.1), and the reference level designation '0 dB FS' has been applied to this point (FS stands for Full Scale). Most digital recorders have an indicator for each channel to show when this situation has arisen, and this may only illuminate when the clipping lasts for a number of consecutive samples, since it is widely accepted that very short durations of digital overload are inaudible (a typical figure is four samples' duration, or around 90 μs at 48 kHz, and at high frequencies it may be possible for overloads to last longer than this without being audible). For signals just below this clipping point the distortion of a 16 bit linear PCM system is very low (it is at its lowest level with relation to the audio signal), and thus there is a sudden audible transition from a very clean signal to a very distorted signal as the overload point is exceeded.

There is a fixed maximum level of quantising noise (referred to the clipping point described above) in a non-oversampling linear PCM system (see Appendix 1), and, provided that the system is correctly dithered (see section 16.1.5), this noise will be of a broadband nature, not correlated with the signal. In a companded system, or one

124

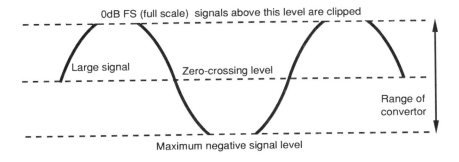

Figure 8.1 Audio signals exceeding peak recording level (0 dB FS) will be hard-clipped

relying on data compression (see section 6.4), it may be that noise and distortion will change with signal level, but systems intended for high-sound-quality applications are optimised such that the wanted signal masks the noise as much as possible. Modern oversampling A/D convertors exhibit noise and distortion levels which fall slightly as the signal level falls, such that in one example of a commercial 20 bit convertor (the UltraAnalog ADC 20048) the large-signal THD+N (Total Harmonic Distortion plus Noise) measurement is –98 dB FS, whilst the small-signal THD+N figure is –108 dB FS. Noise shaping (see Fact File 31) is used to shape the noise spectrum such that it is the least subjectively annoying, and thus the noise spectrum is not flat with frequency.

The trend, nonetheless, is for distortion and noise (as a proportion of the signal) to get smaller as signal level rises, until the clipping point is reached. Thus it might be suggested (at least on systems of 16 bits and lower) that one should control the recording level so that the highest-level signal comes as close to clipping (0 dB FS) as possible without actually exceeding it, although normally a number of decibels of headroom would be allowed for unexpected peaks. There is no gradual onset of distortion as recording level increases in a digital system. In this way the maximum dynamic range of a digital recording may be obtained within the constraints of a system's performance.

Now that resolution greater than 16 bits is available on some systems it will become possible to leave a useful headroom margin for operational convenience, without incurring the penalty of unacceptable noise. The EBU and AES are working on the standardisation of relationships between electrical input and output levels and 0 dB FS, since there is the distinct possibility that users of 20 bit systems will record well below 0 dB FS once they have 120 dB of dynamic range to play with, whilst 16 bit users will have to record nearer the top in order to achieve maximum dynamic range. The problem would thus arise that systems adjusted so that 0 dB FS always replayed at a fixed electrical level (say +24 dBu) would typically replay 16 bit recordings louder than 20 bit recordings. Proposals exist for there to be three electrical output level standards for 0 dB FS on 16, 18 and 20 bit systems, namely +12, +18 and +24 dBu respectively. Other problems arise when different resolutions of recordings are copied between systems in the digital domain, and these are discussed in section 10.4.

8.2 Interpretation of meters

In order to arrive at the optimum recording level described above, it is necessary to know how meters should be interpreted on digital equipment, and how recording levels relate to accepted analogue reference levels.

8.2.1 PPMs and VUs

The meters on analogue mixers, which many may use for digital recording in the studio, were designed for analogue broadcasting and recording equipment. The response of the PPM (Peak Programme Meter) was carefully optimised for the best correlation between visual and audible monitoring of the signal, being based on psycho-acoustic tests which determined the duration of peak signals which caused audible distortion in cases of peak overload, and thus may have a more lasting value in the digital age than slower mechanical meters. The PPM, as developed by the BBC, has an integration time which results in it being less sensitive the shorter the signal peaks, such that, for example, 10 ms peaks show 2.5 dB lower than continuous signals and 5 ms peaks show 4 dB lower. The rise time of PPMs is faster than the fall time, so that the meter does not swing uncontrollably and present a confusing visual analogue of the signal.

British or EBU PPMs read on a scale from 1 to 7, with PPM 4 usually corresponding to the system reference level, there being 4 dB between each gradation except between 1 and 2 where there is 6 dB. DIN-standard PPMs have a scale which is measured in decibels, rather than in arbitrary numbers, and have a wider dynamic range (55 dB). VU meters and EBU PPMs both display a dynamic range of about 26 dB. Electronic bargraph versions of VUs and PPMs simply mimic the ballistic responses of these two meters, although sometimes the dynamic range is made larger.

The VU (Volume Unit) meter has little practical value for digital recording, since it has a slow response time (300 ms) and does not respond adequately to peaks which cause audible distortion. Level differences between a VU and a PPM on the same programme material may be anything from 8 to about 20 dB, depending on the nature of the peaks in the material. It must be admitted, though, that the VU is a popular meter in music recording studios.

8.2.2 Metering and reference levels in analogue recording

Many analogue metering systems have a reference level marker at some point towards the upper end of the scale, with a number of decibels of 'headroom' above this point (see section 8.4). This area of the meter is often coloured red to show that users should regard signals above this as 'dangerous', although precisely how far 'into the red' one may record on an analogue system depends on how much distortion one is prepared to tolerate (see section 8.1). The 0 dB point on VU meters (and the PPM 4 mark on PPMs) normally corresponds to a system's electrical reference level, which may typically be 0, +4 or +6 dBu (0 dBu = 0.775 volts). This in turn can be set so as to correspond to a given magnetic flux level on analogue tape in nanowebers per metre (nWb m^{-1}). This is shown diagrammatically in Figure 8.2.

One typically peaks recordings at around PPM 6 in broadcasting, which is 8 dB above PPM 4, so as to avoid overmodulating the transmitter, and this can be made to correspond to a suitable peak magnetic recording level on analogue tape. For

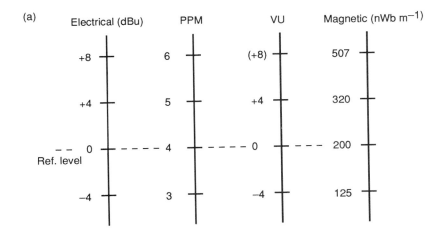

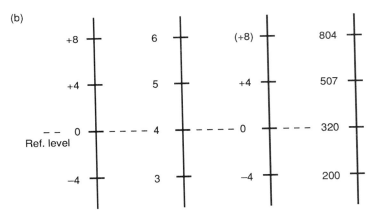

Figure 8.2 A number of relationships are possible in analogue recording between electrical, metered and magnetic levels. At (a) is shown a situation in which reference level at 0 dBu corresponds to 200 nWb m⁻¹, and thus the nominal peak recording level at PPM 6 corresponds to 507 nWb m⁻¹. At (b) the magnetic level corresponding to reference level has been raised to 320 nWb m⁻¹, and thus peak recording level is at 804 nWb m⁻¹

example, if PPM 4 ≡ 0 dBu ≡ 320 nWb m⁻¹ (reference level), then PPM 6 ≡ +8 dBu ≡ 804 nWb m⁻¹, which corresponds quite closely to the 3% MOL (Maximum Output Level) point on a good analogue quarter-inch tape.

8.2.3 Metering and reference levels in digital recording

There is no such thing as a magnetic reference level in digital recording (at least not as far as the user is concerned), and thus a relationship must be established between the electrical level in a system and the peak recording level in the digital system (0 dB FS). In many professional digital recorders the electrical level required to give 0 dB FS is in excess of +20 dBu (the Sony PCM-3348, for example, requires

+24 dBu), and this is well above the highest level indicated on a conventional VU or PPM used in a mixer, aligned so that PPM 4 or 0 VU equals, say, +4 dBu. Furthermore, some digital processors (the Sony PCM-1610 is an example) show 0 dB well below the top of their internal meters, in an attempt to imitate analogue conditions, making the top of the meters read some +20 dB. All of these things only add to the misunderstanding of level setting in digital recording.

If a digital recorder were to be driven from an analogue mixer, using the mixer's internal meters as a level reference, a number of things might happen. Firstly, there would be a danger of under-recording, since peaking at the normal point (say 8 dB above reference level) would result in a recording peaking well below the maximum level of the digital system, the effect of which would be perhaps a 14 bit recording from a 16 bit system. Secondly, if VU meters were used on the mixer the engineer would have hardly any idea of what the peak level on the digital recorder was. Thirdly, the effects of any pre-emphasis used in the digital recorder would not be seen (see section 8.3). Fourthly, if levels were to be increased at the mixer such that the digital recorder were modulated optimally (perhaps by as much as +10 dB) the needles on the mixer's meters would be bending against the end-stops.

A number of partial solutions exist to the above problems. It is possible in many cases to modify the input stages to a digital recorder or PCM adaptor in order to increase the input sensitivity, making peak level occur at a lower electrical output from the mixer. Secondly, it may be possible to use the meters on the digital recorder or PCM adaptor as the main meters when recording, and if this is not possible then a remote digital meter (such as one of those shown in Figure 8.3) may be used, of which a number exist, both multi-channel and two-channel. The meters associated with digital recorders often have a much better dynamic range than a mixer's meters (perhaps 60 dB) and have an optimised peak response, with lights for digital overload. They also often work in the digital domain (that is the segments are directly controlled by the states of the bits in the digital audio signal), and are thus a true representation of the digital signal level. Thirdly, it is becoming recognised by digital equipment manufacturers that they may have to put the 0 dB mark at the top of their meters, since other labellings have tended to result in confusion and low-level recordings, and that they might have to re-think the high input levels required for maximum modulation. It is worth considering, though, the possibility that as professional digital equipment begins to offer 18 and 20 bit resolution it may be that we will be able to return to the concept of a reference level with headroom (see section 8.4, below).

Semi-professional and consumer digital equipment requires electrical input levels which are much lower than those of professional equipment in order to

Figure 8.3 Remote digital metering is available for monitoring the precise levels of digital audio signals over a wide dynamic range, such as this example from Totalsystems, the DBM-1. (Courtesy of Totalsystems)

achieve peak recording level, and thus it is much easier to modulate these correctly with standard level outputs from a professional mixer, since 0 dB FS corresponds to around 2 volts in many such cases (consumer R-DAT, PCM-701, PCM-F1, etc.). It is also easier to overmodulate such systems because of the increased input sensitivity. In Sony consumer digital equipment the nominal input level is 0 dBu (0.775 volts), and this corresponds to −14 dB on the recorder's internal meter (a small mark is usually made here). A number of third-party modifications exist for such equipment, which provide balanced professional level inputs, with variable input gain to match the system to whatever output level is available from a mixer. It is important to consider the effects of pre-emphasis (see below) when setting the relative level between equipment, since this may cause signals to clip at high frequencies when they would not at low frequencies.

Some early consumer digital equipment (and indeed some of the cheaper designs today) used meters which measured the analogue signal, but had overload lights which worked on the digital signal (the Sony PCM-F1 is an example). Thus it was possible for the 'over' lights to show without the signal apparently reaching peak level, particularly when the peak concerned was of short duration. It should be noted that 'over' lights indicate overload during *recording*, but may not do so at the same point on replay, since an overload on recording will be clipped to peak recording level (the system cannot represent anything more). Some systems show overload exactly *at* peak level (which is not strictly an overload), and these systems would show the status on replay as well. Even more intelligently, some systems show overload when more than, say, four samples are at peak level, which is very likely to represent a recorded overload condition.

Further standardisation is required in the design of digital metering systems and in the relationships between analogue and digital levels. Once signals remain in the digital domain for a greater proportion of the time, the relationship between analogue and digital levels will become less important, since, provided that the most-significant bit (MSB) of digital samples is considered as the reference, no matter what the resolution of the system, digital meters will always show the correct digital level and 0 dB FS will become the internal reference. Digital mixers currently used in CD mastering have adopted the concept of a peak-reading bargraph with 0 dB at the top of the scale, and these are interfaced digitally to the recording system, thus eliminating the problems noted above.

In some PCM adaptors, the meters are fed from a point in the replay chain, prior to de-emphasis (see below), and thus they may not measure what is being *recorded* in a case where the replay chain is being used independently from the record chain (see section 4.6).

8.3 Effects of pre-emphasis

A number of digital recording formats specify high-frequency pre-emphasis in the recording chain, with subsequent de-emphasis on replay. Pre-emphasis was designed to reduce the subjective annoyance of quantising noise in 14 bit systems, and is considered less appropriate in 16 bit (or greater) systems. In most cases it is switchable, and usually follows the 50/15 μs time-constant curve, which was shown back in Figure 4.9.

The practical result of using pre-emphasis, as far as the setting of recording levels is concerned, is that signals with a large high-frequency content will result in a higher-than-expected indication on the recorder's meters, since metering normally comes after pre-emphasis has been added, showing the level of the signal actually being recorded on to tape. This can be checked by comparing the indication on the recorder's meters for a tone sent at reference level at 1 kHz with a tone sent at the same level at 10 kHz. For this reason, if using pre-emphasis, it is wise to set the nominal recording level slightly lower than that used without pre-emphasis (around 6dB lower is suggested).

If pre-emphasis is added during recording, a flag will be set in the digital recording to indicate this fact on replay, whereupon de-emphasis will happen automatically. The pre-emphasis switch on most systems, therefore, simply controls the mode of the recording chain. If a pre-emphasised recording is copied over a digital interface such as SDIF-2, SPDIF or AES/EBU (see section 10.2), the correct flag should be set in the digital interface data format, to signal a pre-emphasised signal to the receiving device. The receiver should then automatically de-emphasise it. Unfortunately this flag is not always set, and a number of processors are available for dealing with such signals, enabling the user to de-emphasise a signal manually when the flag is not set (see section 10.5).

8.4 Does headroom exist in digital systems?

The correct theoretical answer to the above question is 'no', but this does not allow for the *operational* concept of headroom. Traditionally, analogue systems have been used with a nominal reference level at which the system is aligned, and to which all signal levels are referred (usually 0 dB on VU meters, and PPM 4 on PPMs). At this level the distortion of an analogue tape recorder is within acceptable bounds, and the signal is well above the noise. Above this is the so-called 'headroom', where the recording gradually moves into greater and greater tape distortion and high-frequency saturation. The magnetic recording process may allow some 10–12 dB of headroom above reference level before the distortion becomes too severe, whilst a mixer and the tape recorder's electronics may allow over 20 dB of headroom before electrical clipping.

Operationally, the concept of headroom is an important one, since it makes possible the setting of a nominal recording level with a margin for occasional peaks. It is an approach that the recording engineer is familiar with, and it allows a margin for error and creative flexibility. It is perhaps difficult to adjust in a digital system to the concept of a reference level which is also the peak recording level (0 dB FS, as discussed above). Many people are now claiming the need for operational headroom in digital recorders, and with the advent of 18 and 20 bit convertors there will be ample dynamic range to enable slight 'under-recording', so as to allow for unexpected peaks, whilst still obtaining at least a 16 bit recording. Provided again that the recording is correctly post-produced optimally to reduce its resolution to 16 bits for Compact Disc (or whatever the resolution of the eventual medium) it may be that it will still be possible to retain the concept of headroom in digital recording.

A fully-modulated 16 bit recording has an adequate dynamic range for most conceivable purposes in professional recording, and to achieve this full 16 bits it is necessary to record as close to peak level as possible. The problem in the past has been that 16 bit convertors have not all operated to full 16 bit accuracy, perhaps offering the equivalent of only 14 or 15 bits in practice. This has led people to criticise 16 bit recording for inadequate sound quality, when in fact they have not been considering true 16 bit recording. One of the major benefits of oversampling convertors with greater accuracy (18 and 20 bit) has been that they can be used with 16 bit recording systems, offering truly accurate 16 bit recording. If used with recording systems capable of 18 or 20 bits on tape, then the additional headroom might be used for operational convenience, and could allow greater flexibility in level setting. The important point, though, is still that any recording made at such high resolution should be correctly handled in post-production, since simple truncation of unwanted LSBs is not the answer when reducing the resolution of an 18 bit recording to, say, 16 bits for CD or 14 bits for broadcasting. Digital post-production equipment is becoming available with suitable dithering algorithms and gain correction processes which maintain the optimum resolution of the signal during such operations.

Chapter 9

Understanding error rates and drop-outs

In an analogue recorder a number of factors may contribute towards deteriorating sound quality as time passes. Additionally, the various contributions from noise and distortion in the recording and replay processes will influence the integrity of replayed audio. Heads may wear, become magnetised or become dirty. Tape may also wear, become damaged, suffer print-through, become de-magnetised and suffer drop-outs. Tape machine transports may become misaligned, or tapes from an outside source may have been recorded on poorly aligned-machines.

One has become familiar with the effects of such phenomena in analogue recording, knowing that the result of dirty heads is a lack of high frequencies, the result of magnetised heads is low-level modulation noise and unevenness in the sound quality (a type of 'bubbling' or 'burbling' on steady continuous sounds), and the result of a drop-out is a momentary loss of signal, although perhaps not a total loss (it may just be a reduction in amplitude or a slightly 'broken-up' period of replay). When working with a digital recorder it is necessary to know how to interpret the effects of similar problems, since these may not manifest themselves in the same way as in an analogue system.

9.1 What are digital errors?

A digital recording system relies for its success on the premise that the difference between a binary one and a binary zero will be discernible in the replay process. Figure 9.1 shows the factors which may mitigate against this, and it will be seen that timing errors affect the system's decision because they may result in confusion over *when* an event occurred, and amplitude errors can affect the decision because they may result in confusion over whether the datum was a one or a zero. Noise and distortion in the recording or replay chain can affect both timing and amplitude of the signal.

Errors occur in replayed data when the timing or amplitude of a signal is so badly affected that a particular bit is reproduced in the incorrect sense (that is a one is detected as a zero or vice versa). Error detection mechanisms are incorporated within the audio data to check for the presence of errors (see Fact File 13), and these are used to signal the presence and location of an error to the error *correction* circuits which follow.

Typically, the types of phenomena described above which affect replayed sound quality in an analogue system (drop-outs, dirty heads, etc.), result in replay errors

<table>
<tr><td>FACT FILE
13</td><td># Error protection</td></tr>
</table>

There are two stages to the error correction process used in audio systems. Firstly the error must be *detected*, and then it must be *corrected*. If it cannot be corrected then it must be concealed. In order for the error to be detected it is necessary to build in certain protection mechanisms.

Types of error

Two principal types of error exist: the burst error and the random error. Burst errors result in the loss of many successive samples and may be due to major momentary signal loss, such as might occur at a tape drop-out or at an instant of impulsive interference such as an electrical spike induced in a cable or piece of dirt on the surface of a CD. Burst-error-correction capability is usually quoted as the number of consecutive samples which may be corrected perfectly. Random errors result in the loss of single samples in randomly located positions, and are more likely to be the result of noise or poor signal quality. Random error rates are normally quoted as an average rate, for example: 1 in 10^6. Error correction systems must be able to cope with the occurrence of both burst and random errors in close proximity.

Interleaving

Audio data is normally interleaved before recording, which means that the order of samples is shuffled (as shown conceptually in the diagram).

Samples which had been adjacent in real time are now separated from each other on the tape. The benefit of this is that a burst error which destroys consecutive samples on tape will result in a collection of single-sample errors in between good samples when the data is de-interleaved, allowing for the error to be concealed. A common process, associated with interleaving, is the separation of odd and even samples by a delay. The greater the interleave delay, the longer the burst error that can be handled. A common example of this is found in the DASH format,

Effect of interleaving

Original sample order

| 1 | 2 | 3 | 4 | 5 | 6 | 7 | 8 | 9 | 10 | 11 | 12 | 13 |

Interleaved sample order

| 3 | 7 | 13 | 9 | 4 | 10 | 1 | 5 | 11 | 8 | 2 | 6 | 12 |

Burst error destroys three samples

| 3 | 7 | 13 | 9 | 4 | | | | 11 | 8 | 2 | 6 | 12 |

Consequent random errors in de-interleaved data

| | 2 | 3 | 4 | | 6 | 7 | 8 | 9 | | 11 | 12 | 13 |

and involves delaying odd samples so that they are separated from even samples by 2448 samples, as well as reordering groups of odd and even samples within themselves.

Error checking

Cyclic redundancy check (CRC) codes, calculated from the original data and recorded along with that data, are used in many systems to detect the presence and position of errors on replay. Complex mathematical procedures are also used to form codewords from audio data which allow for both burst and random errors to be corrected perfectly up to a given limit.

Redundancy

Redundancy, in simple terms, involves the recording of data in more than one form or place. A simple example of the use of redundancy is found in the twin-DASH format, in which all audio data is recorded twice. On a second pair of tracks the odd–even sequence of data is reversed to become even–odd. This results in double protection against errors, and allows for perfect correction at a splice, since two burst errors will be produced by the splice, one in each set of tracks. Because of the reversed odd–even order in the second set of tracks, uncorrupted odd data can be used from one set of tracks, and uncorrupted even data from the other set, obviating the need for interpolation (see Fact File 14).

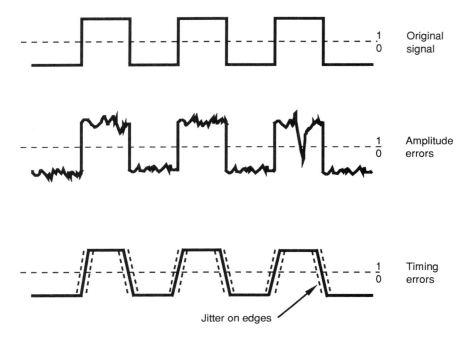

Figure 9.1 An original data signal may be corrupted by both timing and amplitude errors

in a digital system. Whether or not these errors then go on to manifest themselves as changes in sound quality depends on how good the error-correction system is at coping with them. In a well-designed system, performing as it was intended, replay errors are fully corrected in normal operation, and it is only occasionally that errors occur which are beyond the correction capacity of the system.

In tapeless systems the situation with errors is rather different, since the disk drives and controllers which are used as stores handle their own error correction. These drives have come from the computer industry, in which any error in data could be fatal, and thus the effective error rate tends to be extremely low. Disks are mapped by the disk controller to avoid writing data in any so-called 'bad blocks', and thus data tends only to be stored in error-free locations. There can be no such thing as 'interpolation' or 'hold' in a computer system used for, say, text processing, since an ASCII character is either correct or it is not. It is not normally possible to interpolate between the letters of a word to guess the missing letter!

9.2 Indication of errors

Most professional recording systems indicate error status to some extent, and it is important to know how to interpret these indicators. Common labelling for error-correction indicators shows lights in order of seriousness of the error. For example, the Sony DMU-30 digital meter unit (which may be attached remotely to the PCM-1630, see Figure 9.2) displays in the order CRC, Parity, Average, Hold, Mute (see Fact File 14). In many cases the lights are coloured green, orange and red, again to indicate the seriousness of the error. 'Green' errors such as 'CRC' and 'Parity' are

Figure 9.2 The Sony DMU-30 remote digital meter for the PCM-1630 has comprehensive error status indication. (Courtesy of Sony)

normally fully correctable and will not affect the output, whereas 'orange' errors such as 'Average' or 'Interpolate' may have a marginal effect on the sound quality, usually resulting in a short-term halving in audio bandwidth. 'Red' errors, such as 'Hold' or 'Mute', indicate that the system cannot attempt to correct or even hide the error and thus it resorts to holding the last known sample value, or, finally, muting the output. Often these error status lights have an artificial 'permanence' which keeps them alight for a second or so, even if the error only lasts a millisecond. A short 'hold' on the light does make errors easier to see, but too long-a hold may hide the true state of affairs and make it difficult to tell the difference between indicator hold and error conditions which are prolonged.

Most professional or 'professionalised' DAT machines have been equipped with only two lights to indicate error status, a red one and a green one. The red light usually indicates an error which is likely to affect the audio output (a serious one, in other words), whilst the green light indicates an error which will be fully corrected. The front panel of Sony's PCM-1630 only shows 'Mute' and 'CRC' states, although the intervening states may be seen by removing the front panel. This

FACT FILE 14 — Error handling

True correction

Up to a certain random error rate or burst error duration an error correction system will be able to reconstitute erroneous samples perfectly. Such corrected samples are indistinguishable from the originals, and sound quality will not be affected. Such errors are often signalled by green lights showing 'CRC' failure or 'Parity' failure.

Interpolation

When the error rate exceeds the limits for perfect correction, an error correction system may move to a process involving interpolation between good samples to arrive at a value for a missing sample (as shown in the diagram).

The interpolated value is the mathematical average of the foregoing and succeeding samples, which may or may not be correct. This process is also known as concealment or averaging, and the audible effect is not unpleasant, although will result in a temporary reduction in audio bandwidth. Interpolation is usually signalled by an orange indicator to show that the error condition is fairly serious. In most cases the duration of such concealment is very short, but prolonged bouts of concealment should be viewed warily, since sound quality will be affected. This will usually point to a problem such as dirty heads or a misaligned transport, and action should be taken (see text).

Hold

In extreme cases, where even interpolation is impossible (when there are not two good samples either side of the bad one), a system may 'hold'. In other words it will

Interpolation

Original sample amplitudes

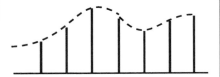

Sample missing due to error

Mathematically-interpolated value inserted

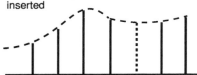

repeat the last correct sample value. The audible effect of this will not be marked in isolated cases, but is still a severe condition. Most systems will not hold for more than a few samples before muting. Hold is normally indicated by a red light.

Mute

When an error correction system is completely overwhelmed it will usually effect a mute on the audio output of the system. The duration of this mute may be varied by the user in some systems. The alternative to muting is to hear the output, regardless of the error. Depending on the severity of the error, it may sound like a small 'spit', click, or even a more severe break-up of the sound. In some cases this may be preferable to muting.

is true of many systems which do not always show the full error status on the main display, preferring not to worry users unless they decide to invite worry by removing the cover over the error status lights.

Some systems have optional error analysers, such as the Sony DTA-2000 shown in Figure 9.3, for displaying or printing the number, type and location of errors on

Figure 9.3 The Sony DTA-2000 can be used for logging errors of each type, and may be connected to a printer for hard copy. (Courtesy of Sony.)

a recording. These can be useful in quality-controlled environments when it is vital that tapes are either error-free or only contain correctable errors. Such a printed analysis also provides an insurance policy in the event of a tape being damaged by someone, or not replaying correctly in another location, since it is then possible to state (in time-honoured tradition) that the tape itself was 'alright when it left you'.

9.3 Effects and interpretation of errors

Only true *correction* will result in an unaffected audio output, since true correction restores erroneous samples to their original state perfectly, in which case there is no difference between a corrected sample and the equivalent original sample. Some professional systems have been designed so as either to correct perfectly or to mute the output and show a warning. In this way a master recording being checked could not pass if it contained any uncorrectable errors. This is a good approach in cases where perfection is important, but there may be instances in which being able to replay a tape is more important than the precise fidelity with which it is replayed. Some systems may be switched between these two states in order to allow the replay of erroneous tapes without muting (this mode is called 'PB Muting Off' on Sony EIAJ-format PCM adaptors such as the PCM-701).

In most consumer systems (e.g.: CD players), error correction status is not shown, since presumably it would result in too many complaints about faulty hardware or software! In such systems interpolation and holding is often allowed, since it is assumed that replay of some sort is preferable to a muted output. For this reason, errors in consumer digital systems are often audible on the system output as spits and clicks, or even broken-up audio in bad cases.

The regularity and seriousness of errors is an important indicator of the state of replay, the state of the tape and the state of the replay machine. Prolonged periods of interpolation-type errors should be regarded with concern, since the audio bandwidth will be halved during a prolonged bout of interpolation. If such errors continue on every tape that is replayed, it may indicate that heads are dirty or worn. If the errors only accompany particular recordings then the fault clearly lies with the tape, and may indicate a worn or faulty tape. Errors which accompany particular tapes may also be the result of differences in mechanical alignment between the record machine and the replay machine. Prolonged periods of 'green', correctable errors (CRC, Parity) will not affect the quality of the audio output but still should give cause for concern, since a correctly working system should only show the occasional flash of 'green' error during normal operation.

9.4 Minimising error rates

Error rates can be minimised in a number of ways, some depending on the tape machine and some depending on the tape. It has also been shown that the environment in which the machine and tape are housed can affect error conditions.

Any physical handling of a digital tape will cause fingerprints to be left on the surface, and although these might be considered unimportant they are in fact a good sticking point for dirt and represent a considerable contamination at the wavelengths involved. Fingerprints can result in replay errors of varying seriousness, and should be avoided. It is sometimes possible to clean a tape (especially the open-reel varieties) by carefully wiping the recording surface with a slightly moist cloth around the area of the fingerprint, and this has been shown to reduce the resulting errors in many cases. This technique also helps around difficult splice edits, where the tape has been handled and glue from the splicing tape may have caused dirt to stick, resulting in a poor join. Splice edits on both DASH and PD machines may sometimes be made to play in cases where previously they did not in this way.

Machine alignment is paramount to good performance, just as it is in analogue systems, and many people forget this aspect of studio life once they start using digital equipment. Mechanical alignments may need to be performed regularly, using manufacturers test jigs and test tapes, in order to keep the error rates low on digital recorders. It is not so necessary to align the system electronics regularly, since such adjustments as bias and EQ (required in analogue recording) are not required in the same way in digital systems. The mechanical tolerances required for good performance in a digital system are much finer than those required in analogue recording.

Head and guide cleaning is an important aspect of regular maintenance, as it is in analogue recording, although greater care is usually required than with analogue machines. Each manufacturer may recommend particular cleaning materials, and it is wise to use these. Isopropyl alcohol is not good for cleaning digital heads and guides, since it is slightly greasy, but ethyl alcohol or freon sprays are usually good. Any cleaning cloths or wipes should be free from stray fluff or anything else which might contaminate the mechanism. It is not wise to use much pressure when cleaning the heads, or to scrub them at all, since they are more delicate than analogue heads. For DAT recorders, the use of head-cleaning tapes has been recommended by leading manufacturers and distributors as a means of combatting head-clogging. One clogged replay head out of the pair in a DAT scanner will result in replay with many interpolation-type concealments, although replay may still be possible.

It is possible that tapes made on other machines may not replay so well as recordings made on the replay machine itself, and this again is normally the fault of poor mechanical alignment of one or both of the machines. Just as one adjusts the azimuth of the replay head to optimise the replay of tapes from other machines, using tones at the start of the tape, so it may be necessary to adjust the alignment of a digital machine to accommodate a poorly aligned recording, although it must be admitted that no standard procedure has been adopted for this purpose and that there is still some way to go in defining the alignments that most affect replay. In systems which use VTRs as the recorder (EIAJ format, JVC format and PCM-1610/1630 format), tracking adjustments are often required to minimise replay errors, since the tracking affects how accurately the replay head scans the recorded track. The only solution in the case of incompatible tapes may be to replay the recording on the machine on which it was recorded and make a digital copy on to a properly-aligned machine.

The Sony PCM-1630 system in conjunction with its DMR-4000 recorder offers 'read-after-read' facilities (see section 4.5) which involve the reading of each helically scanned track twice, offering additional protection against replay errors by automatically deciding which data to use in the event of errors from one of the heads. The R-DAT system is due to spawn an in-car replay machine (the so-called 'Car-DAT') which is built to withstand the greater tracking and alignment errors which would be likely in the hostile conditions of mobile use. Such a machine, with its multiple replay heads, might form the ideal basis for a studio system to replay badly aligned or damaged tapes.

Humidity and temperature may also affect the rate of replay errors, although many recorders have built-in 'dew' indicators to show when the humidity or condensation level is too high for them to operate (they usually prevent themselves from being turned on in such situations). Some users have found that digital tape recording equipment appears to perform better in a cold environment, although the precise reason for this has not been discovered. It may be that static electricity and high humidity are not so prevalent in these conditions.

Although tape type does not directly affect sound quality, as it does in analogue systems, the principal measure of a digital tape's performance is its error rate. This is discussed further below.

9.5 Coping with drop-outs and other major errors

A severe error condition may result in a muted audio output, or very broken-up sound, and there are a number of things which can be tried to get the tape to play.

Firstly, if the major error is due to tape damage or contamination it may be possible to smooth out and clean the tape, although this should be attempted with great care and is only really feasible with open-reel tapes. A soft, slightly-moist cloth may be used to wipe the recording surface, and the tape may be smoothed out on a clean, flat surface. The flatter the tape can be made the better. Secondly, the replay muting on the tape machine or PCM adaptor can be turned off, if this is possible, so that the audio output can reproduce the sound complete with errors, which may be preferable to no sound at all. Thirdly, playing over the damaged spot a number of times, once the tape has been smoothed out, may help to smooth it even further because the tape will be squeezed between the capstan and pinch roller of the tape machine in most cases. Winding or playing the edited section will also cause the damaged section to be packed with other layers on the supply or take-up reels which will smooth it further. If the tape can be made to play, make a digital copy immediately (see section 10.2).

If the major error is due to a tape drop-out then it is unlikely that anything can be done, since tape drop-outs are due to a lack of oxide on the surface, arising from wear or poor manufacture. Again, turning off replay muting may help to get over a moderate problem, but this depends on how severe the drop-out is. Sometimes, replaying the tape on a different make of machine (of the same format) may allow it to be played, owing to minor differences in alignment or superior error correction.

Head cleaning and machine alignment may also help to ensure that errors from other sources do not compound the problems faced by the error correction mechanism, since if the error correction is already working at full strength to deal with errors which have nothing to do with the drop-out it will not have the capacity to handle further errors.

If the major error is due to a poor tape splice, it may be possible to remake the splice by carefully unsticking it and using new splicing tape. This, though, is rarely successful because of the thinness and delicacy of the magnetic tape and the splicing tape, and also because of the handling of the tape required to pick apart the edit.

9.6 Tape performance

In systems which use a VTR as the recorder, videotape will be used as the recording medium, although it is recommended that one of the videotapes specially developed for digital audio use is employed. In dedicated digital recorders, special digital audio tape is used, which is thinner than analogue recording tape and has different magnetic properties. The thinness helps to maintain good contact with the heads, which is vital with such short wavelengths involved.

In general it is advisable to use the shortest length of tape that suits the purpose, since longer tapes may be thinner and more prone to damage and wear. For example, although 75 minute tapes are available for U-matic recorders in digital audio applications (for the purpose of mastering long CDs) Sony recommends that they are only used when absolutely necessary, since they are not as robust as shorter cassettes. It also suggests that the higher-quality VTRs, such as the DMR-4000, are used for longer tapes, since improved performance results. 3 hour consumer VHS and Beta tapes are also extremely thin, and 2 hour tapes should preferably be used for EIAJ-format digital audio.

Many manufacturers of digital audio tape for professional usage quote an average CRC error rate per reel, or per hour. Many also claim to check their tapes for drop-outs before they leave the factory, using sophisticated laser scanning methods. Users have found that some brands of DAT tape appear to perform better than others, and it would be wise to consider sticking to one of the brands that is reliable once it has been discovered. Because DAT tapes are so small, professional users have found it useful to employ the larger boxes provided by some manufacturers, which hold two DAT tapes and afford greater protection.

Open-reel digital audio tapes come in three widths — quarter inch, half inch and 1 inch — and are suitable for use on either DASH or PD machines. These tapes are specially back-treated to avoid static build-up and to allow good packing during spooling. The latter aspect is of prime importance to digital recordings, since 'leafing' which may occur during winding can expose the tape to serious edge damage and thus errors. It is advisable, therefore, to use the limited fast spooling speed of some machines when preparing a tape for transportation or storage, since this usually results in better packing.

Chapter 10

Copying and interfacing

Having looked at some of the important factors influencing the quality and care of digital recordings, the subject of copying and digital interfacing between devices will now be discussed.

10.1 Copying in the analogue domain

Digital recordings may be copied from one machine to another either via one of the standard digital interfaces (see below) or via the analogue inputs and outputs. In the case of the latter, replayed audio is converted back to the analogue domain by the replay machine's D/A convertors, routed to the recording machine via a conventional audio cable, and then re-converted to the digital domain in the recording machine's A/D convertors (see Figure 10.1). The audio is subject to any gain changes which might be introduced by level differences between outputs and inputs, or by the record gain control of the recorder and the replay gain control of the player. Analogue domain copying is necessary if any analogue processing of the signal is required in between player and recorder, such as gain correction, equalisation, or the addition of effects such as reverberation. More and more of these operations, though, are now possible in the digital domain.

Copying in this way is perfectly feasible, although it will involve a slight increase in quantisation noise of about 3 dB per generation of copying. If a recording has been copied in this way it is no longer quite correct to say that a recording has remained in the digital domain throughout its production and post-production (a fact indicated by the 'DDD' symbol on CDs), although very few people would notice the

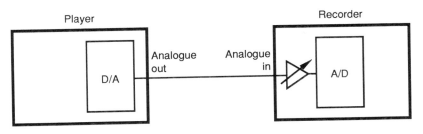

Figure 10.1 Connections for analogue domain copying. The record gain control will affect the level of the copy

difference introduced by a single generation of copying in the analogue domain, provided that levels were carefully matched between recorder and player. Multiple generations of copying via the analogue domain should be avoided.

An analogue domain copy cannot be said to be a 'perfect copy' or a 'clone' of the original master, since the data values will not be exactly the same (due to slight differences in recording level, differences between convertors, etc.), and for this it is necessary to make a true digital copy.

10.2 Copying and interfacing in the digital domain

In order to make a perfect 'clone' of a digital recording it is necessary to copy the binary audio data directly from the player to the recorder, without passing through conversion stages. Professional systems, and some consumer systems, have digital interfaces conforming to one of the standard protocols (see below), and allow for a number of channels of digital audio data to be transferred between devices, with no loss of sound quality. Any number of generations of digital copies may be made without affecting the sound quality of the latest generation, provided that errors have been fully corrected.

The digital outputs of a tape recorder are taken from a point after the error correction block (see Figure 10.2), which results in the copy being error corrected. Thus the copy does not suffer from any errors which existed in the master, provided that those errors were within the ability of the player's error correction system to correct (see Chapter 9). This is why it has been suggested that damaged recordings are copied digitally as soon as possible, provided that they can be made to replay, since a fresh error corrected master will result.

Digital interfaces may also be used for the interconnection of recording systems and other digital audio devices such as mixers and effects units, and this will become more prevalent as more digital signal processing equipment becomes available. It will eventually become common only to use analogue interfaces at the very beginning and end of the signal chain, with all intermediate interconnection performed digitally.

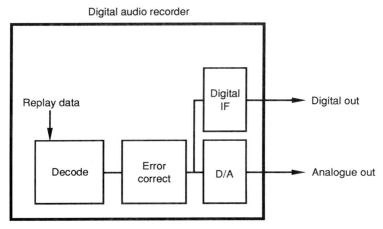

Figure 10.2 The digital output of a device normally comes after error correction has been performed on replayed data

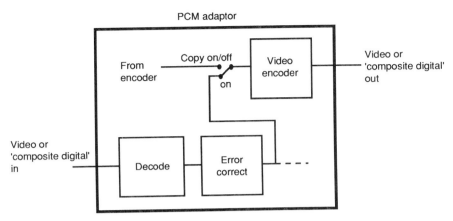

Figure 10.3 When copy mode is used on a PCM adaptor, video from a player is decoded and error corrected before being re-encoded and sent out to a recorder via the video or 'composite digital' output

10.2.1 Digital dubbing with PCM adaptors

The digital inputs and outputs of a tape recorder *must* be distinguished from the video or 'composite digital' interfaces of a PCM adaptor or VTR used for digital audio. The video or 'composite digital' outputs carry a digital audio signal encoded into a pseudo-video waveform for recording on to a VTR (see sections 4.6 and 4.7), and are not the same as the digital outputs of a system. Although it is possible to make copies by simply connecting the video output of a player VTR into the video input of a recorder VTR (like copying an ordinary video tape), the copy will not be error-corrected, and is likely to have more errors on it than the original. The correct procedure in this case is to copy the recording by using the relevant PCM adaptor in the 'dub' or 'copy' mode (see Figure 10.3) in which the video signal from the player is first decoded and error-corrected before being sent back out to the recorder. Video or 'composite digital' outputs must not be connected to ordinary digital inputs in any circumstances, even if they use the same BNC-type connectors.

On the Sony PCM-1610 and 1630, the input selector has three positions: 'analogue', 'digital' and 'dubbing'; it is the 'dubbing' position which refers to the above mode.

10.2.2 Digital interfacing

There are a number of types of digital interface which may be used for copying digital recordings. These are described in detail in Fact Files 16 to 23, contained in this chapter. They all carry digital audio with at least 16 bit resolution, and will operate at the standard sampling rates of 44.1 and 48 kHz, as well as at 32 kHz if necessary, with a degree of latitude for varispeed. Most of the interface standards are one- or two-channel only, but one of them, known currently as MADI, is a multi-channel interface (see Fact File 22). A number of interface standards are manufacturer specific, in that they are not the subject of AES recommendations or IEC standards, and this refers to such as the various Sony interfaces (see Fact File 19), the Mitsubishi interfaces (see Fact File 20) and the Yamaha interface (see Fact

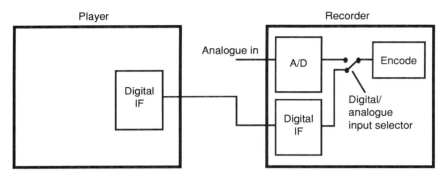

Figure 10.4 Devices which accept a digital input normally have a switch to select whether the input to the encoder will be fed from the A/D convertor or from the digital input

File 21). Manufacturer-specific interfaces may also be found on equipment from another manufacturer if it has been considered necessary for the purposes of signal interchange, especially on devices manufactured prior to the standardisation and proliferation of the AES/EBU interface. The interfaces vary as to how many physical interconnections are required, since some require one link per channel plus a synchronisation signal, whilst others carry all the audio information plus synchronisation information over one cable. The reader should also refer to the chapters on synchronisation of digital audio signals (Chapters 13–15) for further information, since this aspect of digital audio recording is becoming more important as devices are interfaced digitally on a regular basis.

Making a copy using any of the interface standards involves the connection of the appropriate cables between player and recorder, and the switching of the recorder's input to 'digital' as opposed to 'analogue', since this sets it to accept a signal from the digital input as opposed to the A/D convertor (see Figure 10.4). It is necessary for both machines to be operating at the same sampling rate and may require the recorder to be switched to 'external sync' mode, so that it can lock its sampling rate to that of the player. The recorder should be capable of at least the same quantising resolution (number of bits per sample) as the player, or greater, otherwise audio resolution will be lost. If there is a difference between the systems it may be advisable to use a processor in between the machines which optimally dithers the signal for the new resolution (see section 10.5) and may be able to offer sample rate conversion as well (see section 10.3). It will also be necessary to consider the digital level relationships between the two systems (see section 10.4).

10.2.3 Simple two-channel copies

The procedure for making a copy from one video machine to another via a PCM adaptor has already been shown in Figure 10.3. This applies to all such systems (PCM-F1, 701, PCM-1610/1630, JVC system, etc.) when using one PCM adaptor with two VTRs. For a two-channel copy between one digital system and another (say between two PCM adaptors, or two digital tape machines, or between a disk-based system and a tape machine) it is necessary to use a digital interface such as AES/EBU or SDIF-2. The two possibilities are shown in Figure 10.5, and it will be seen that in the case of the AES/EBU link only a single balanced line, terminated in XLR connectors, connects the two devices, whereas in the SDIF-2 link three

(a)

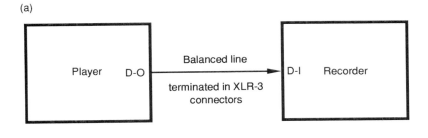

(b)

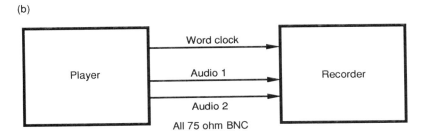

Figure 10.5 (a) AES/EBU and (b) SDIF-2 interfacing compared. AES/EBU requires a single XLR cable for the clock and two channels of audio. SDIF-2 requires three BNC cables

75 ohm BNC leads are required, one for word clock (WCLK) and one for each audio channel. This difference results from the fact that the AES/EBU signal is 'self-clocking', having a clock component inherent in the modulated data (see Fact File 16), whereas the SDIF-2 requires a separate clock. It has been demonstrated in practice, though, that some devices appear to interface better without the WCLK signal in SDIF-2 interfacing, requiring only the two audio signals, and this is a matter for experimentation in each case. WCLK should be linked between devices wherever possible, and in the case of a synchronised system (see Chapter 13) it is vital that each device is locked to a common word clock or other sync reference.

Signals are normally transferred over the interface with whatever flags are needed to indicate the status of the player tape. For example, a replayed tape may be pre-emphasised and copy protected, and thus flags will be set in the interface which signal this fact to the recorder, using data embedded within the audio data. In occasional cases such flags may not have been set, or may have been set incorrectly, in which case some manual intervention will be required (see section 10.5). A machine receiving copy-protected data will normally refuse to record such data, and indicates the copy-protection status on its front panel. This is normally only common in consumer equipment, where digital copying may be considered inappropriate (see section 10.6). In some systems the record-gain controls of a recorder will be inactive in the case of a digital copy, since they normally operate on analogue signals, but there are increasingly examples of systems which have digital record gain controls allowing level correction in the digital domain. Such a digital gain control should be bypassed or set to unity (0 dB) if a perfect digital 'clone' copy is required.

FACT FILE 15 Interface troubleshooting

If a digital interface appears not to be working (that is no signal is present on the receiving device (recorder) when connected digitally to a transmitting device (player)), it could be due to one or more of the following conditions. (Refer to the main text for further details.)

1. Sampling rates of transmitter and receiver are different. Set the two to be the same, preferably locked to a common reference (see Fact File 28).

2. Receiver is not locked to transmitter sample clock. Ensure that receiver is in external sync mode and that a synchronising signal (common to the transmitter) is present at the receiver's sync input. Alternatively, use an AES/EBU interconnect, which should be self-synchronising.

3. Receiver is not switched to accept a digital input.

4. Received data is in the wrong format. Both transmitter and receiver must operate to the same format.

5. There may be a consumer–professional conflict in channel status (see text). Use a format convertor (see section 10.5) to set the necessary flags.

6. Cables or connectors may be damaged.

7. Cable may be too long or of poor quality.

8. Copy protect or SCMS flag may be set by transmitter. For professional purposes, use a format convertor to set the necessary flags.

9. Incompatible channel status, user or validity data (see Fact File 18 and text).

10. Receiver is not in record mode. Some recorders must be at least in record–pause before they will give an audible and metered output derived from a digital input.

11. Digital signal may be of poor quality. Check eye-height on scope against specification, and check for possible interference sources. Alternatively make use of an interface error analyser (see Fact File 18).

Fact File 15 contains some ideas which may be tried if a digital interconnection does not appear to be working. When the interconnection is working correctly, the recorder should indicate the same signal on its meters as the player, the recorder's 'WCLK lock' or 'ext sync' light (or equivalent) should be illuminated (indicating that the recorder is correctly locked to the incoming signal) and sound should be audible from the recorder's outputs when monitoring its inputs.

10.2.4 Use of AES/EBU interface and SPDIF (IEC 958)

The AES/EBU two-channel interface (also known as the IEC two-channel interface for professional usage) is becoming more widely available on digital audio equipment, as it is a universal interface not specific to one manufacturer. The IEC two-channel interface also has a consumer version, sometimes called SPDIF (Sony–Philips Digital Interface), or 'CD/DAT', which has some striking similarities to the professional version, although there are also important differences. The technical characteristics of these two interfaces are described in Fact Files 16 and 17.

FACT FILE 16 AES/EBU interface

The AES/EBU format allows for two channels of digital audio (A and B) to be transferred serially over one balanced interface, using RS422 drivers and receivers. It has been standardised by the IEC as IEC 958 (1989). The interface allows two channels of audio to be transferred over distances up to 100 m, but longer distances may be achieved using combinations of appropriate cabling, equalisation and termination. Standard XLR-3 connectors are used, often labelled DI (for digital in) and DO (for digital out).

Subframe format

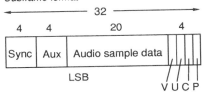

Each audio sample is contained within a 'subframe' and each sub-frame begins with one of three synchronising patterns to identify the sample as either A or B channel, or to mark the start of a new channel status block.

These patterns violate the rules of bi-phase mark coding and thus are easily identified by a decoder. Additional data is carried within the subframe in the form of 4 bits of auxiliary data (which may either be used for additional audio resolution or for other purposes such as low-quality speech), a validity bit (V), a user bit (U), a channel status bit (C) and a parity bit (P), making 32 bits per subframe and 64 bits per frame.

Sync patterns

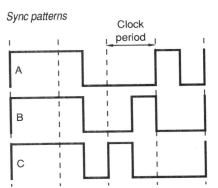

One frame (containing two audio samples) is transmitted in the time period of one audio sample, and thus the data rate varies with the sampling rate. Channel status bits are aggregated at the receiver to form a 24 byte word every 192 frames, and each bit of this word has a specific function relating to interface operation. Examples of bit usage in this word are the signalling of sampling rate and pre-emphasis, as well as the carrying of a sample address 'timecode' and labelling of source and destination. Bit 1 of the first byte signifies whether the interface is operating according to the professional (set to 1) or consumer (set to 0) specification.

Bi-phase mark coding, the same channel code as used for SMPTE/EBU timecode, is used. The interface has to accommodate a wide range of cable types, and a nominal 110 ohms characteristic impedance is recommended. Currently up to four receivers with a nominal input impedance of 250 ohms may be connected to a single transmitter, but a modification to the standard is expected to recommend the use of a single receiver per transmitter, having a nominal input impedance of 110 ohms.

Revisions and further clarifications are anticipated from the AES during 1991.

Hardware interface

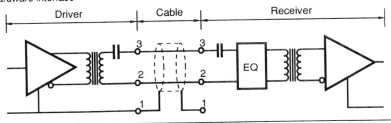

FACT FILE 17 Sony/Philips digital interface (SPDIF)

The SPDIF is very similar to the professional AES/EBU interface. When the IEC standardised the two-channel digital audio interface, two requirements existed: one for 'consumer use', and one for 'broadcasting or similar purposes'. A single IEC standard has resulted with only subtle differences between consumer and professional implementation (IEC 958). The electrical interface for the consumer version is shown below.

The data format of subframes is the same as that used in the professional interface, already described in Fact File 16, but the channel status implementation is different after the first 6 bits of the first byte. The second byte of channel status in the consumer interface has been set aside for the indication of 'category codes', these being set to define the type of consumer usage. Currently defined categories are (00000000) for the general category, (10000000) for Compact Disc, (01000000) for a PCM adaptor (such as a Sony PCM-601) and (11000000) for a DAT machine. Once the category has been defined, the receiver is intended to interpret certain bits of the channel status word in different ways, depending on the category. For example, in CD usage, the four control bits from the CD's 'Q' channel subcode are inserted into the first four control bits of the channel status block (bits 1–4).

The consumer format interface can be found on many items of semi-professional or consumer digital audio equipment, such as CD players and DAT machines. It usually terminates in an RCA phono connector, although some hi-fi equipment makes use of optical fibre interconnects carrying the same data. Format convertors are available for converting consumer format signals to the professional format, and vice versa (see main text).

For further details on AES/EBU and SPDIF, see:
1. AES 3-1985, Serial transmission format for linearly represented digital audio data.
2. IEC 958 (1989) Digital audio interface.
3. ANSI S4.40-1985.
4. *Proceedings of the AES/EBU Interface Conference*, AES British Section publication.
5. Watkinson, J. (1989) *The Art of Digital Audio*, Focal Press.

Hardware interface

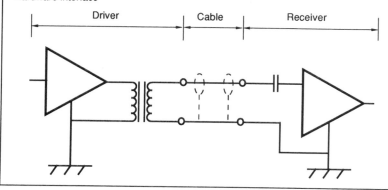

AES/EBU links are useful because they can be run over distances up to 100 metres without equalisation, and over this with equalisation. The interface can also carry 20 bits of audio data in normal operation, and was designed to be carried over ordinary screened, twisted-pair microphone cable, and to use ordinary XLR audio connectors. Microphone leads may in practice be suitable for AES/EBU interconnections, but see Fact File 18 on minimising interface errors. There is only

Minimising interface errors

Cabling and connections

Although the specification allows for the use of microphone cable, the characteristics of microphone cable vary widely. AES/EBU signals are very-high-frequency data signals requiring a bandwidth considerably greater than the clock rate of 3.072 MHz (48 kHz sampling rate). They cannot be treated just like audio signals. AES/EBU data signals may suffer when subjected to changes in cable and interface impedance, and such changes may arise if two dissimilar cables are connected together, if the signal is split between multiple receivers, or if the cabling used within any receiver or equipment bay does not match the impedance of the signal cable. The corruption of the data which results may affect sound quality, since errors may arise, although this is only likely in extreme cases. The design of the receiver also plays a major part in the effective operation of the interface. Any audio distribution amplifiers (DAs) in the signal chain must be replaced with DAs suitable for handling the bandwidth required.

It has been suggested that the use of 75 ohm coaxial cable with unbalanced 75 ohm interfaces at either end may provide a better transmission line than the standard balanced interface, and a modification to the standard may appear to allow for this possibility. Nonetheless, the better transmission line would be replaced by the problems suffered by an unbalanced interface. Microphone cables may well be found to work successfully over long distances, but this is often only reliable when a single device transmits to a single receiver over a single cable, and depends on the quality of the receiver.

Data incompatibilities

Not only may there be electrical difficulties with interfacing, but also there may be data incompatibilities. These arise principally out of the vague interpretation of how validity, channel status and parity bits should be interpreted by receivers. The validity bit is asserted to indicate an invalid sample (one which has been found to be erroneous by a previous device) and some receivers ignore this bit whilst others may mute or interpolate. Parity errors will only be signalled when an odd number of bits are in error, and even numbers of errors may be passed without attention. The standard does not incorporate any sophisticated error checking or correction mechanisms and thus errors on the interface will affect sound quality. Furthermore, channel status implementation is not fully standardised, and certain receivers may expect bits to be set in a particular fashion, which may or may not match that presented to them.

Clock recovery

The AES/EBU receiver may extract a clock signal from the incoming bi-phase mark data, and it is common for this clock to be noisy after it has passed over a lengthy interconnect. Receivers vary as to the quality of their clock-recovery circuits, it being most important to reconstruct a stable, jitter-free clock signal if such a derived clock is to be used to reference other parts of a system. Two examples of dedicated AES/EBU transceiver chips, one from the BBC (called AESIC) and one from Motorola (CP-340), promise low-jitter clock recovery in the face of poor input signals.

Testing the interface

New test equipment is appearing, specifically designed for the purpose of testing digitally interfaced equipment. Audio Precision's 'System One Dual Domain DSP' is an example of a set which can perform selected tests on AES interfaces, to check for errors, measure performance, and to set certain data conditions to check the implementation of the standard on different receivers. Some receivers and receiver chips have provision for the indication of a 'near failure' status, which monitors the state of received data. An oscilloscope may be used to view the 'eye pattern' of the received data, to check the minimum difference between high and low voltages of each bit cell (which should be 200 mV), although the scope must be triggered from the transmitter clock output to view the eye pattern correctly.

one socket for the AES/EBU output of a two-channel device, because both audio channels and sync information are carried over the same cable. SPDIF links are intended for use with consumer and semi-professional equipment, and as such these interfaces tend to be found on DAT machines and CD players. Terminated in a single phono connector and being unbalanced, these interconnects are usable over shorter distances than the professional interface. It is not necessary to use a separate word clock connection with either of these interfaces, since it will normally be ignored in any case by the receiving device. The receiving device extracts its synchronising signal from the data itself, which is self-clocking, and should be able to lock its sampling rate to that of the incoming data (although see Chapter 13 on synchronisation).

It can be seen in the fact files concerned that the professional interface is a fully balanced circuit, whereas the consumer interface is an unbalanced circuit. The professional interface normally involves a transformer at both ends (although it is only the EBU which insists on this), whereas the consumer interface has a transformer only at one end. Concerning the possibility for consumer-to-professional interconnection, one should note that the consumer version operates at peak-to-peak voltages of around 0.5 V, whereas the professional version operates at a higher voltage conforming to the RS422 standard. Nonetheless, the professional receiver must accommodate a minimum eye height of 200 mV, and thus most professional receivers will accept signals from consumer interfaces, provided that cable and termination losses are not too severe.

The real problems, though, are not in getting electrical interconnection to work, but in overcoming incompatibilities in the data format. In very rare cases it may be feasible to make a straight connection from consumer to professional or vice versa, but normally some notice must be taken of the additional data in the subframe, such as channel status. Consumer and professional usages of the channel status block are different, with the first bit of the channel status block in the professional format being set to a '1', whereas the consumer format it is set to a '0' followed by five control bits. Devices intending to accept both consumer and professional data should be able to recognise this bit and alter their interpretation of channel status accordingly. In practice, devices vary as to how comprehensively they have implemented either mode, and may ignore many of the bits in the channel status block. It should also be borne in mind that most professional devices will simply refuse to decode data with the consumer flag set.

A number of bits have been left intentionally undefined in order that their usage could be defined later. Furthermore, uses for previously undefined bits have been defined since the original specification, and some equipment may not recognise these. Problems arise when a receiver is expecting certain bits of the channel status word to be set in a particular pattern, locking out any data which does not conform to this exact pattern. Conversely, other systems may be very loose in their AES/EBU implementation, and will accept virtually anything, provided that it looks like AES/EBU data. There is a danger in the latter approach that audio data will be transferred with something set wrongly (pre-emphasis for example), whereas a more rigorous implementation would ensure that transfer only took place if every bit was set in the correct manner. For trouble-free conversion between consumer and professional formats it is preferable to use one of the proprietary digital format convertors such as those described in section 10.5.

10.2.5 Copying to and from multitrack machines

It is possible to copy multitrack recordings between DASH and ProDigi machines in either direction, provided that the correct interface or interface convertor is used. For copying between two-channel DASH and ProDigi equipment it may be quite straightforward to use the AES/EBU interface if this is fitted to both devices, but in multi-channel equipment it is rare to find large numbers of such interfaces

---

FACT FILE

19

Sony digital interface (SDIF)

SDIF stands for Sony Digital Interface. The most common Sony interface is SDIF-2, and is intended for the transfer of one channel of digital audio information per cable, at a resolution of up to 20 bits (although most devices only make use of 16). The interface, as used on most two-channel equipment, is unbalanced and uses 75 ohm coaxial cable terminating in 75 ohm BNC-type connectors, one for each audio channel. TTL-compatible electrical levels (0–5 V) are used. The audio channel connectors are accompanied by a word clock signal on a separate connector, which is a square wave at the sampling frequency used to synchronise the receiver's sample clock. Sony's PCM-3324 and 3348 multitrack machines use SDIF also, but with a differential electrical interface conforming to RS422 standards and using D-type multiway connectors. A single BNC connector carries word clock as before.

In each audio sample period, the equivalent of 32 bits of data is transmitted over each interface, although only the first 29 bits of the word are considered valid, since the last three bit-cell periods are divided into

two cells of one-and-a-half times the normal duration, in order to act as a synchronising pattern. As shown in the diagram, 20 bits of audio data are transmitted with the MSB first (although typically only 16 bits are used), followed by nine control or user bits. The resulting data rate is 1.53 Mbit s^{-1} at 48 kHz sampling rate and 1.21 Mbit s^{-1} at 44.1 kHz.

A 256 word block is used (a word being the 32 bits described above), the first of which carries control information in bits 21 to 28, the subsequent words carrying user information in these bits. In this first word, bits 26 and 27 signal whether pre-emphasis is used or not (00 for no emphasis, and 01 for emphasis to the 50/15 μs standard), bit 28 signifies copy protection status (1 is copy protected), and bit 29 is used to signify the start of a 256 word block, being set to a one at this point.

The SDIF-2 interface is used mainly for the transfer of audio data from Sony professional digital audio equipment, particularly the PCM-1610 and 1630, but also from semi-professional equipment which has been modified to give digital inputs and outputs (such as the PCM-701 and various DAT machines). It is also apparent on a number of disk-based workstations for the loading and unloading of audio data.

Data format

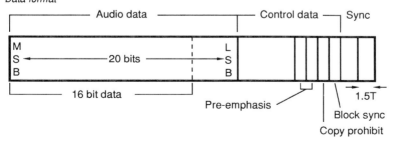

FACT FILE
20

Mitsubishi interface

Mitsubishi's ProDigi format machines use a digital interface similar to SDIF, but not compatible with it. Separate electrical interconnections are used for each audio channel. Interfaces labelled 'Dub A' and 'Dub B' are 16 channel interfaces found on multitrack machines, handling respectively tracks 1–16 and 17–32. These interfaces terminate in 50 way D-type connectors and utilise differential balanced drivers and receivers. One sample period is divided into 32 bit cells, only the first 16 of which are used for sample data (MSB first), the rest being set to zero. There is no sync pattern within the audio data (such as there is between bits 30–32 in the SDIF-2 format). The audio data is accompanied by a separate bit clock (1.536 MHz square wave at 48 kHz sampling rate) and a word clock signal which goes low only for the first bit cell of each 32 bit audio data word (unlike SDIF which uses a sampling-rate square wave). Status information is passed over two separate channels, which take the same format as an audio channel but carry information about the record status of each of the 32 channels of the ProDigi tape machine. One status channel handles tracks 1–16, and the other handles tracks 17–32 of a multitrack machine. The pin assignments for these connectors are shown below.

Interfaces labelled 'Dub C' are two-channel interfaces. These terminate in 25 way D-type connectors and utilise unbalanced drivers and receivers. One sample period is divided into 24 bit cells, only the first 16 or 20 of which are normally used, depending on the resolution of the recording in question. Again audio data is accompanied by a separate bit clock (1.152 MHz square wave at 48 kHz sampling rate) and a word clock signal taking the same form as the multitrack version. No record status information is carried over this interface, but an additional 'master clock' is offered at 2.304 MHz. The pin assignments are shown below.

Dub 'A'

Pin	Function
1, 18	Ch. 1 (+/–)
2, 19	Ch. 2 (+/–)
3, 20	Ch. 3 (+/–)
4, 21	Ch. 4 (+/–)
5, 22	Ch. 5 (+/–)
6, 23	Ch. 6 (+/–)
7, 24	Ch. 7 (+/–)
8, 25	Ch. 8 (+/–)
9, 26	Ch. 9 (+/–)
10, 27	Ch. 10 (+/–)
11, 28	Ch. 11 (+/–)
12, 29	Ch. 12 (+/–)
13, 30	Ch. 13 (+/–)
14, 31	Ch. 14 (+/–)
15, 32	Ch. 15 (+/–)
16, 33	Ch. 16 (+/–)
34, 35	Bit clock (+/–)
36, 37	WCLK (+/–)
38, 39	Rec A (+/–)
40, 41	Rec B (+/–)
17, 50	GND

Dub 'B'

Pin	Function
1, 18	Ch. 17 (+/–)
2, 19	Ch. 18 (+/–)
3, 20	Ch. 19 (+/–)
4, 21	Ch. 20 (+/–)
5, 22	Ch. 21 (+/–)
6, 23	Ch. 22 (+/–)
7, 24	Ch. 23 (+/–)
8, 25	Ch. 24 (+/–)
9, 26	Ch. 25 (+/–)
10, 27	Ch. 26 (+/–)
11, 28	Ch. 27 (+/–)
12, 29	Ch. 28 (+/–)
13, 30	Ch. 29 (+/–)
14, 31	Ch. 30 (+/–)
15, 32	Ch. 31 (+/–)
16, 33	Ch. 32 (+/–)
17, 50	GND

Dub 'C'

Pin	Function
1, 14	Left (+/–)
2, 15	Right (+/–)
5, 18	Bit clock (+/–)
6, 19	WCLK (+/–)
7, 20	Master clock (+/–)
12, 25	GND

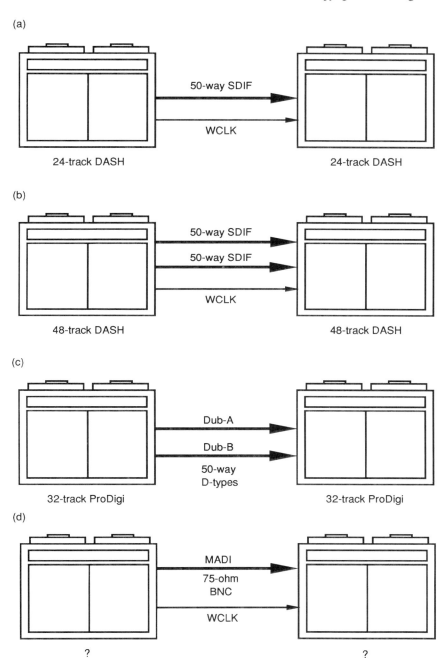

Figure 10.6 Methods of interfacing multitrack recorders. (a) 24-track DASH machines connected using a single 50-way SDIF cable and WCLK. (b) 48-track DASH recorders connected using two 50-way SDIF cables and WCLK. (c) 32-track PD machines connected using 50-way Dub-A and Dub-B cables. (d) Multitrack machines of any format equipped with MADI interfaces for transfer of up to 56 channels

(Mitsubishi makes an optional stand-alone 32 channel AES/EBU interface unit, the DIF-32). Sony fits a variation of the SDIF format to its PCM-3324 and PCM-3348 machines, the only difference between this and the SDIF-2 used in the PCM-1610 and PCM-1630 being that it is balanced rather than unbalanced, but ProDigi machines are not fitted with SDIF interfaces (since SDIF stands for Sony Digital Interface, and PD machines are not made by Sony!) and thus some other means of interconnection must be found. Hilton Sound in the UK designed an interface convertor which it called 'PDASH', and which took in signals of one data format and converted them to the other. This enabled the copying of tapes between formats, although clearly a 32 track PD tape could not be copied entirely to a 24 track DASH machine.

To copy between two Mitsubishi ProDigi machines it is common to use the Mitsubishi (Melco) interface format (see Fact File 20), which can also be used to

---

FACT FILE 21 — Yamaha interface

Yamaha digital audio equipment is often equipped with a 'Cascade' connector to allow for a number of devices to be operated in cascade, such that the two-channel mix outputs of a mixer, for example, may be fed into a further mixer to be combined with another mixed group of channels.

Connector

This interface terminates in an eight-pin DIN-type connector (as shown in the diagram)

and carries two channels of 24 bit audio data over an RS422-standard differential line. The two channels of data are multiplexed over a single serial link, with a 32 bit word of left-channel data followed by a 32 bit word of right-channel data (the 24 bits of audio are sent LSB first, followed by eight zeros). Word clock alternates between low state for the left channel and high state for the right channel (as shown below). Coils of 20 µH are connected between pins 6 and 7 and ground to enable suppression of radio frequency interference. The OUT socket is only enabled when its pin 8 is connected to ground.

Pin	Function
1	WCLK +
2	GND
3	Audio data −
4	WCLK −
5	Audio data +
6	20 µH coil to GND
7	20 µH coil to GND
8	GND (in), ENABLE (out)

Data format

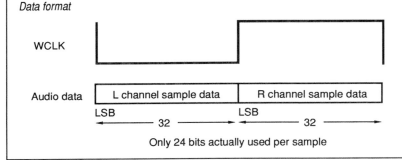

Only 24 bits actually used per sample

FACT FILE 22 — Multi-channel audio digital interface (MADI)

A number of manufacturers have combined forces to propose a multi-channel serial interface standard known as MADI (the Multi-channel Audio Digital Interface), which is based on the two-channel AES/EBU interface and is designed to be transparent to such data. It would have applications in large-scale digital routing systems, and for the interconnection of multitrack audio equipment. MADI naturally uses a higher data rate to carry the increased amount of information. The format has been submitted to the AES and EBU for consideration as a multi-channel standard. MADI allows for 56 channels of audio to be carried serially over one 75 ohm coaxial cable or optical fibre, such that one sample for each channel is transferred within one audio sample period.

MADI allows for subframes containing 20 or 24 bit audio data, together with the additional status bits of the AES/EBU data for each channel. The main difference in the MADI format is in the first 4 bits of each subframe (which in the two-channel interface break the bi-phase mark coding law to provide a sync pattern). Channel subframes thus formed are linked sequentially to form a 56 channel frame (as shown above).

Unlike the two-channel interface, the transmission data rate of MADI is fixed at 125 Mbit s^{-1}, irrespective of the sampling rate or number of channels, and the actual data transfer rate is 100 Mbit s^{-1} due to the use of a 4–5 bit encoding scheme. In this channel code each 32 bit subframe is broken up into 4 bit words which are then encoded to 5 bit words according to a look-up table, the reason being to maintain a low DC content to the code. A synchronisation symbol (11000 10001) is inserted at least once per frame, and in cases where the full bandwidth of the link is not being used, additional sync symbols are inserted to take up the capacity of the bus.

Communication is expected to be handled entirely by so-called TAXI (Transparent Asynchronous Xmitter/Receiver Interface) chips, which automatically take care of the insertion of sync symbols. Unlike the two-channel format, it is intended that the link will be asynchronous and accompanied by a separate synchronising clock (in the form of an AES/EBU signal, see Fact File 27), as it is not intended that the data be self-clocking. BNC 75 ohm connectors are to be used, and the maximum coaxial cable length is intended to be no more than 50 metres (although optical fibre would allow more). The modulation method used is to be NRZI in which a transition from high-to-low or low-to-high represents a binary 'one', and no transition represents a zero. Because of the asynchronous nature of the interface, buffers are required at both ends of the link so that data can be re-clocked from the buffer at the right rate. At the receiver, data is clocked out under control of the synchronising signal.

Further reading
AES10-19XX, Serial Multichannel Digital Audio Interface (MADI).

Data format

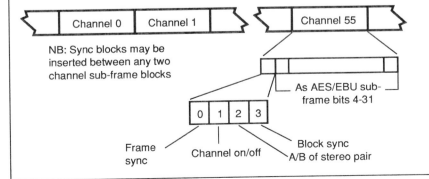

NB: Sync blocks may be inserted between any two channel sub-frame blocks

Channel 0 | Channel 1 | Channel 55

As AES/EBU sub-frame bits 4-31

0 | 1 | 2 | 3

Frame sync — Channel on/off — Block sync A/B of stereo pair

interconnect multitrack PD recorders to two-track PD recorders. To copy between two Sony DASH multitracks one can use the SDIF interface which is available on a 50 way D-type connector (two in the PCM-3348), carrying all the channels in a multicore cable. Alternatively, in the PCM-3324 (not the more recent PCM-3324A), the SDIF inputs and outputs for each channel are also available on BNC connectors. Studer's D820 DASH multitracks also have SDIF multi-channel D-type connectors, allowing them to be connected directly to the Sony PCM-3348 or PCM-3324, and all these machines have an AES/EBU input and output and an unbalanced SDIF-2 interface, assignable to any pair of channels, for copying to and from two-track systems. It should be remembered that copies of two-channel material to and from EIAJ-format or PCM-1610/1630 systems (and any others operating at the CD-mastering rate) may only be performed at 44.1 kHz, and thus this would force the multitrack machine also to operate at this rate.

The MADI interface format is a new multi-channel format based on the AES/EBU two-channel format (see Fact File 22), and may become more common on multi-channel digital audio equipment once it becomes accepted by either the AES or the IEC. It already has a number of supporters, having originally been formulated by co-operation between Sony, Neve, Solid State Logic and Mitsubishi in the UK. MADI will allow the copying of up to 56 channels of digital audio information, at

---

FACT FILE 23 — Optical interfaces

Optical fibres are capable of carrying large amounts of data at high speed, and as such are useful for carrying multi-channel digital audio, amongst other things. As indicated in the MADI fact file, TAXI chips can be used to transmit audio data over an optical fibre, but there are other developments which may allow for larger numbers of channels to be carried over a single fibre. The two primary advantages of optical fibres are their capacity and their ability to carry data over very long distances with minimal degradation and losses. A typical fibre may carry audio data over 2 or 3 kilometres satisfactorily, and thus may prove useful in large installations.

The BBC is working on a distribution system for 224 channels of digital audio, using optical fibres to accommodate the wide bandwidth required. In this system, four MADI-style multiplexes (see Fact File 22) will themselves be multiplexed over a single link operating at 500 Mbit s^{-1} (0.5 Gbit s^{-1}). The multiplex will be distributed to a number of locations within one studio centre using passive optical splitters, and rack-mounted terminators will be provided with individual AES/EBU-format inputs and outputs. Selection of signals is then a matter of demultiplexing the desired channel(s) from the 224 channel multiplex, rather than relying on the electrical switching of 'hard' channels.

Another system, presently at an early stage in its development, is Lone Wolf's 'MediaLink' protocol, designed to use optical fibres for the distribution of a wide range of different signal types over studio networks, covering distances of up to 2.5 km. Currently the company is using relatively low data-rate chips to transfer MIDI control data, but it is the intention to expand the system so that multi-channel audio data, timecode and video signals (to name but a few) may also be transferred over one network. Gateways to the network, to be known as 'Taps', will multiplex and demultiplex data into and from the proprietary multi-media protocol, each having its own address. Different configurations and routings of data may be set up to suit varying operational configurations. This system has its roots in computer LANs (Local Area Networks) such as Ethernet, and brings the concept of networking into the studio. If MediaLink proves workable and popular, it is possible that optical fibre interfaces conforming to this protocol may begin to appear on audio equipment.

the same resolution as the two-channel interface, over a single screened coaxial cable terminated in a BNC connector. A separate synchronising signal should accompany the MADI connection, in the form of either WCLK or an AES/EBU synchronising signal (see Fact File 27). In future, MADI data may also be transferred over optical fibres, since the transmitter and receiver chips were designed originally for this purpose.

Some examples of multitrack interfacing are shown in Figure 10.6.

10.3 Sample rate conversion

Since there are a number of possible sampling rates in use in digital audio it will be necessary from time-to-time to interconnect digitally devices whose sampling rates differ. In such cases a sample rate convertor is required, this being a device which takes in audio data at one rate and sends it out at another (see Fact File 24). This process either could be used between two tape machines which operate at different rates, for converting a 48 kHz recording to 44.1 kHz so that it could be used as a CD master, for example, or it could be used in between a tape machine and a digital mixer, in order that the tape machine could be varispeeded without affecting the input rate to the mixer. The 32 kHz rate is used widely in digital audio broadcasting (see Chapter 6), and thus the broadcaster will be interested in translating material at the professional rate of 48 kHz to the broadcast rate.

In fully-integrated digital systems, where most devices are interconnected digitally, it will become important for one common and fixed sampling rate to be used throughout, locked to a central sampling rate clock (see section 13.2). If any devices in the system do not conform to this rate they should be passed through a sample rate convertor in order to allow interchange of audio at the system rate, and a number of modern disk-based devices are now becoming available with internal sample rate convertors which ensure that, no matter what the internal operations of the system, the input and output sampling rates remain constant. This is important in any system which is varispeeded or synchronised to a timecode source, since without sample rate conversion the sampling rate of the digital outputs of the system would be likely to follow any speed variations of the replay.

It is now possible to perform high-quality sample rate conversion over a wide range of input and output rates which do not have to have a simple integer or fractional relationship. Older convertors were only capable of converting between a fixed input and output rate, and will be less useful.

10.4 Level relationships in digital copying

As discussed in Chapter 8, one may run into problems when considering where 'peak recording level' lies in relation to 0 dB FS (full scale or 'peak bits'). This may be a problem electrically when interfacing in the analogue domain, but it may also be a problem digitally when copying via interfaces such as the AES/EBU.

Now that 18 and 20 bit recordings are feasible, users will be freer to use the 100–120 dB of available dynamic range without needing to control the recording level in order to peak near full scale. Consequently higher-resolution recordings may peak perhaps 10–12 dB below 0 dB FS, whereas 16 bit recordings may peak very near to 0 dB FS. If a 20 bit recording peaking 12 dB below 0 dB FS is copied

FACT FILE 24
Sample rate conversion

Why is it needed?

The need for sample rate conversion arises out of the difference between the standard sample rates used in consumer and professional audio, and also in broadcast systems. The rate of 44.1 kHz is widely used in consumer equipment, and is the sample rate of Compact Disc, although older consumer DAT machines used the profes- sional rate of 48 kHz to prevent digital copies being made of CD s. Professional DAT machines can be switched to operate at the consumer rate of 44.1 kHz. PCM adaptors operate at 44.1 kHz, but when synchronised to NTSC video may operate at the slightly reduced rate of 44.056 kHz. Professional open-reel formats may be switched to operate at 44.1 or 48 kHz, whilst digital video recorders operate only at 48 kHz. Disk recording systems operate at one of a number of rates up to 100 kHz. Broadcast distribution and transmission typically takes place at 32 kHz.

Sample-rate conversion is further required when equipment is used at non-standard replay speeds, often resulting in a propor- tional change in sample rate. For example, +10% varispeed on a DASH machine results in a +10% change in sample rate. Many of today's digital mixers operate at a fixed rate, and will not accept audio at non-standard rates.

Types of conversion

The easiest way to convert from one rate to another is by passing through the analogue domain and re-sampling at the new rate, but this may introduce a small amount of extra noise. The most basic form of digital conversion involves the translation of samples at one fixed rate to a new fixed rate, related by a simple fractional ratio. This was the reason for the suggestion that 50.4 kHz should be the new professional sampling rate some years ago, since it was related to 44.1 in the ratio 8/7. Latterly, 48 kHz was chosen as the professional recording rate for

broadcast use because it has a simple fractional relationship to 32 kHz. Variable- ratio conversion is now also possible to other rates. Fractional-ratio conversion involves the mathematical interpolation of samples at the new rate based on the values of samples at the old rate. Digital filtering is used to calculate the amplitudes of the new samples such that they are mathematically correct based on the impulse response of original samples, after low-pass filtering with an upper limit of the Nyquist frequency of the original sampling rate. A clock rate common to both sample rates is used to control the interpolation process. Using this method, some output samples will coincide with input samples, but only a limited number of possibilities exist for the interval between input and output samples.

If the input and output sampling rates have a variable or non-simple relationship the above does not hold true, since output samples may be required at any interval in between input samples. This requires an interpolator with many more clock phases than for fractional-ratio conversion, the intention being to pick a clock phase which most closely corresponds to the desired output sample instant at which to calculate the necessary coefficient. There will clearly be an error, which may be made smaller by increasing the number of possible interpolator phases. The audible result of the timing error is equivalent to the effects of jitter on an audio signa. If the input sampling rate is continuously varied (as it might be in variable-speed searching or cueing), the position of interpolated samples with relation to original samples must vary also, and this requires real-time calculation of filter phase. Errors in such conversion should be designed so as to result in noise modulation below the noise floor of a 16 bit system, and preferably lower.

Commercial sample rate convertors exist, such as that included in Harmonia Mundi's bw-102 system for conversion between 44.1 and 48 kHz and vice versa, and DAR's DASS-100 for conversion between 32, 44.1 and 48 kHz ± 2%, with compensation for varispeed of ±10%. Other convertors also exist, such as an older model from Studer and a variable-ratio convertor from Sony.

digitally to a 16 bit device, using the convention of keeping the MSB (Most Significant Bit) at one resolution as the MSB at the other, the sixteen bit result will be seriously under-recorded. Clearly some form of digital level correction would be required between the devices in order to raise the level of the 20 bit example described above so that it peaked near the top of the 16 bit scale. A digital fader with optimal re-dithering at the output resolution may be used for this purpose, and some of the interface processors described below perform this function.

10.5 Use of interface format processors and convertors

As suggested in the preceding sections, a certain amount of intervention may be required between devices when interconnecting them digitally. This may be in order to modify status flags to suit a purpose, or to correct the status of certain flags to match the signal. It may also be necessary to perform operations on the audio signal, such as de-emphasis and gain correction, or to convert the signal from one interface format to another. One way of doing some of these things is to pass the signal through a full-blown digital mixer, but this may not be necessary in most cases, and a mixer may not allow the format conversion or flag modification. For this reason, a number of devices have been introduced which allow various degrees of modification to signals emanating from the standard digital interfaces, and some examples are described below by way of illustration.

The simplest operations of this type involve the conversion of AES/EBU signals to SPDIF consumer format or SDIF-2 format and vice versa, with possible modification of the copy prohibit status to allow copying of protected recordings. Audio & Design in the UK makes a range of 'Digital ProBoxes' for such purposes.

A more complex device is exemplified by the Audio Digital Technology FC-1, which has facilities for converting any of three input formats (SPDIF, AES/EBU and SDIF-2) to any of three output formats, with the possibility for de-emphasis in the digital domain to either CCITT J17 (used in broadcast) or 50/15 µs characteristics. It has two stereo signal paths which may be mixed together with the option of a mixer panel which can be used to perform level or channel balance correction and crossfades in the digital domain. It will also dither the digital signal optimally for one of three possible output resolutions (16, 18 or 20 bits), for conversion of signals between systems of different resolutions, ensuring the optimisation of sound quality when copying high-resolution signals to lower-resolution systems. A block diagram of this device is shown in Figure 10.7. As can be seen in the diagram, a number of other functions are also offered, such as DC-blocking (important for removing DC offsets introduced by badly aligned A/D convertors), digital high-pass filters, CTC (see section 4.7), channel phase and L/R reversal, and output status modification. There is also an oscillator for alignment purposes.

Another example of an advanced device in this vein is the Digital Audio Research 'DASS 100'. It takes the important step of offering sample rate conversion between any of the standard rates (32, 44.1 and 48 kHz, ±2%), as well as compensating for varispeed inputs of up to ±10% of these frequencies. There are optional interfaces to virtually every possible format (AES/EBU, SPDIF, SDIF-2, ProDigi, Yamaha DMP-7D and Sony 50 pin SDIF), and inputs may be mixed together with gain correction. Other features include the synchronisation of inputs to a reference (see Chapter 13), the variable delay of signals, the generation of a system sync signal

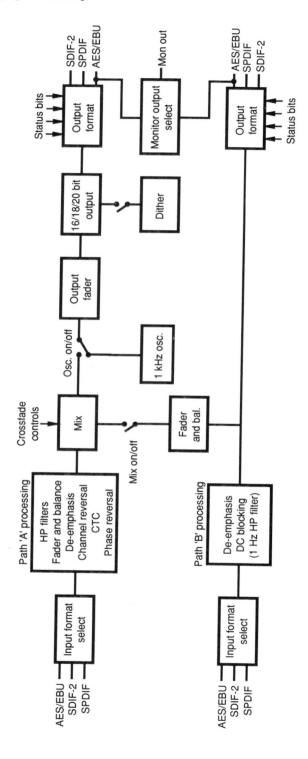

Figure 10.7 Block diagram of ADT FC-1. Such a device may be used for modifying digital audio signals conforming to various interface standards, as well as allowing them to be mixed. Any input format may be converted to any output format. (Courtesy of Audio Digital Technology)

from one of a number of sources, the pre- or de-emphasis of signals in the digital domain, and the generation of audio test waveforms in the digital domain.

10.6 Copying of DAT recordings and SCMS

A system known as SCMS, the Serial Copy Management System is designed to prevent the multiple serial digital copying of copyright material. It is now installed in all consumer (and some semi-pro) DAT machines, and introduces a flag into a first-generation DAT copy (only when made digitally) which prevents that DAT tape from being copied subsequently via the SPDIF. It does not prevent copying via the analogue outputs, which can be done as many times as one might like, neither is it likely to affect copies made using an AES/EBU interface if one is employed. There are some difficulties in working out whether or not a copy will be possible, especially when working with a combination of SCMS and older non-SCMS machines, and the following is a summary of the situation.

Included in the PCM audio area on a DAT recording is a block of identification bits (IDs). Two of these bits, named ID6, control copy protection. In pre-SCMS DAT machines ID6 could be either 00 (copying allowed) or 10 (copying prohibited), but in SCMS machines an additional code, 11, is used to mean 'one-time copying is allowed'. If an SCMS machine is asked to make a digital recording from its SPDIF input it first checks the category code of the source. If it is 'General', ID6 on the copy is set to 11, and one further copy is allowed (this would be likely when copying from early DAT machines). If it is other than 'General', the recorder must check for a copy-prohibition (CP) flag, and then check whether the category is one for which copying is allowed. SCMS allows for a first generation copy of a copyright CD, even if the digital output is set to CP, but sets the ID6 of the copy to 10. The same is true for pre-recorded DAT tapes whose ID6 is set to 11.

The means by which a copy is allowed between two DAT machines is complicated. A second DAT category code, 'DAT-P', has been introduced, which allows copying no matter what the status of the CP bit. If a DAT tape with an ID6 of 11 is to be copied, the category of the source's digital output is set to 'DAT-P' and the CP bit is asserted. Thus the copy is allowed but the receiver knows that it has made a copy of CP material and thus sets the ID6 of the copy to 10. Subsequently a player will only be able to set the category code on its output to 'DAT', and further copies would be prevented. In the rare case when a source tape has an ID6 of 00 an infinite number of digital copies are possible, since the CP bit is never asserted. Unfortunately, SCMS machines will set ID6 to 11 when recording from analogue inputs, thus only allowing one further copy, which can be rather annoying if the recording is perfectly legitimate. Bear in mind that pre-SCMS machines will not recognise the 'DAT-P' category code, and thus will not copy anything with a CP bit asserted on the SPDIF. Most will not recognise the difference between a recorded ID6 of 10 and an ID6 of 11, and thus will not allow you to copy tapes of either type.

This system will not be applied to truly professional recorders, since it would be unnecessarily restrictive, but might still be found in 'professionalised' consumer DAT machines. Professional users intending to purchase DAT machines would be wise to check whether or not SCMS has been implemented on the machine of their choice. SCMS would become obtrusive in professional operations such as editing, where digital copying might extend through more than one generation.

Chapter 11

Editing operations

There are many more ways of editing digital audio than there are of editing analogue audio, as has been shown technically in Chapter 5, but it is often difficult to decide which method is most suitable for a particular application. In the following chapter the relative merits of splice and copy editing are discussed, as are the relative merits of tape-based and tapeless systems. Operational advice is given on the use of digital editing equipment, and terminology and techniques specific to digital editing are described.

11.1 To splice or not to splice?

Firstly, to take a simple economic viewpoint, it might be suggested that splice editing of tape has clear advantages over any other form of editing, purely because it requires only one tape machine, a razor blade, a splicing block and some sticky tape. Splice editing also has the advantage of being fast, and it is a well-known technique; it is also quite flexible in that a change can be made in the middle of a programme by splicing a replacement section into an existing master without the need to re-copy. These are the reasons why splice editing has held its position as the primary technique in analogue circles. If it has so many advantages then why is it not widely used in digital recording?

Splice edits can be made to work successfully on digital formats designed for splicing (see section 5.7), although greater care is required than with analogue tape as discussed in section 11.9. (Splice editing was discussed in Chapter 7 with relation to specific formats, since there are many systems which do not allow splicing at all.) The use of timecode has become more widespread in digital recording, and splice editing has the effect of destroying a contiguous timecode track, which may subsequently confuse synchronisers, CD-mastering equipment and electronic editing systems. Furthermore, music editors have become used to the increased flexibility allowed by electronic editing systems, finding that the ability to preview edits and to experiment with different crossfades are valuable tools. In digital splice editing the crossfade time is fixed for every edit.

The creative tools provided in electronic editing systems have allowed edits to be made in music where they would previously have been considered impossible, making it possible to achieve a lot more in post-production could be done with analogue recording. This has allowed producers more leeway in creative decisions, and may even in some cases have made it possible to shorten recording sessions, although noone would want to admit to that. The possible increased costs of electronic digital editing seem to have been soaked up, at least in the music industry, in the greater profit margin which often exists in CD production when compared with LP production.

Digital splice edits, once made, may not easily be picked apart without destroying the tape, and thus the potential for modifications to edits is reduced when compared with analogue splices which can be picked apart quite a few times before there is any danger of a reduction in sound quality. There is the further problem with splice-editing formats that they are not accepted directly as CD masters, and must be copied to the Sony CD-mastering format (see section 4.8) before CD production. A CD master must also have a contiguous timecode track.

For the broadcaster splice editing of digital recordings ought to have many more benefits than for the music editor, since speed is often more important than creative flexibility where news and current affairs programmes are concerned. Indeed it was broadcasters who first pressed digital tape recorder manufacturers like Sony and Studer into designing digital formats which could be splice edited, since they said that electronic copy editing simply would not be viable in high-pressure news environments owing to the slow speed. Digital splice-editing machines have now been available for over 5 years, but there is little evidence that broadcasters have been falling over themselves to buy them. This may be attributable to the still-high cost of the machines (around four times that of the equivalent analogue machine), and the fact that broadcasters do not see increased sound quality alone as an overriding reason for switching to digital recording. Radio and TV studio centres often own many hundreds of analogue quarter-inch recorders, and the costs of exchanging them all for digital equipment would be prohibitive unless the operational advantages were seen to be great. There is the added disadvantage to digital formats that a lack of standardisation makes interchange of tapes difficult.

11.2 Tape or tapeless editing?

If splice editing is not proving popular for digital recordings, then the choice is really between the different electronic methods available, and here one must consider the major differences between tape-based and tapeless systems. Electronic editing of tape recordings to date has involved copying (see section 5.3), and this copying must normally be performed in real time; thus the minimum time required to edit a half-hour tape recording must be at least half an hour, even if only one edit is required. At least two tape machines and an edit controller are required, making it more expensive than splice editing. Furthermore, it is difficult to modify an edited master without time-consuming re-copying (see section 11.10).

There are ways of making this process easier, revolving around the use of EDL management and automatic assembly of a master tape, and these are discussed in section 11.6, but the fact cannot be avoided that copy editing is a laborious process. Interestingly, though, copy editing of just this type has been the norm in video post-production for many years, since modern video recordings cannot be spliced either.

Electronic copy editing has the advantages of allowing edit previews without committing the result to the master tape until the editor is satisfied that it will work (see section 11.8). Such systems also allow variable crossfades and variable pre-rolls, as well as memory rehearsal functions which speed up previews (see section 5.10); also the gain and channel balance of material may be adjusted in order to match sections together. These facilities add up to make electronic copy-editing of tapes more creatively flexible and reliable than splice editing, although perhaps not as fast in most applications. The copy-editing process results in a master tape which can immediately be taken away for the next stage of post-production or mastering without any further copying, and the tape will have a contiguous timecode track which makes it suitable for CD mastering or synchronisation with a videotape. It is becoming common for digital editing systems to accept video EDLs so that digital audio tapes can be conformed to an edited video picture (see section 14.10).

For the purposes of disposal editing (the removal of sections from a longer recording, such as might be used in speech editing to remove mistakes and coughs) the possibility exists for using a large RAM buffer to enable the skipping of unwanted sections without cutting the tape and without copying, as proposed in the Nagra-D format (see section 4.8). This may well be the answer to the broadcasters' dilemma in many radio current affairs situations where speed is of the essence.

Tapeless editing takes the creative flexibility aspect of electronic editing to even greater lengths, allowing instant comparison of recordings which were made at different times, and which would have required lengthy tape spooling in a tape-based system. As described in section 5.11, tapeless editors compile a finished master by controlling the playing order of prerecorded sound files, with crossfades of variable length introduced at joins. Such systems allow for endless modifications of the finished master until the operator is satisfied. Unlike copy editing, tapeless editing allows the insertion of new material into a finished master without the need to re-copy the master, simply because the master only exists in a tapeless system as a 'soft' playing order with edit commands. If a new take is to be inserted into the middle of an edited sequence, the replay schedule (see section 5.14) can be adjusted to take into account the length of the replacement section, shifting subsequent edit points either forwards or backwards in time as appropriate.

In many ways the tapeless editor has the speed and simplicity of splice editing with the creative flexibility of electronic copy editing, the only stumbling block being the need to load all the source material on to disks before it can be edited, and subsequently to copy the finished master off the disk on to a tape. Tapeless systems are also fairly expensive, although systems are beginning to appear which seriously challenge tape-based editors in terms of cost versus performance. As high-speed removable optical disks become more widely used (see section 3.12.7), hopefully with some degree of interchangeability between systems, there is a strong likelihood that recordings will be made directly on to disks which can then be edited without copying.

Tapeless editing is also proving very successful in video post-production, where it more closely resembles film sound editing than traditional multitrack tape post-production. Sound effects, music and dialogue may be moved around with relation to the picture, and large libraries of regularly used material may be stored on-line or on optical disks. This is discussed in greater detail in section 15.2.

Many tapeless editors also offer sophisticated DSP facilities for the processing of sounds in the digital domain during the editing session. These may include 'de-noising' of noisy recordings, equalisation, filtering, programmed gain changes and speed/pitch correction (see section 11.12).

11.3 Summary of relative merits of editing techniques

Splice editing is fast and relatively cheap, and does not require copying of original or edited material, but it is not always reliable: edits are hard to modify, crossfades are fixed and timecode tracks are broken up. Digital two-track recorders offering splice editing currently cost around four times the price of a professional two-track analogue recorder.

Electronic copy editing requires at least two tape machines, often with associated controller or synchroniser, and thus it is expensive compared with splice editing, but it offers greater creative flexibility and is widely used in music editing. Edits may be previewed and crossfades may be varied to suit the edit. Copy editing must be performed in real time, and thus it tends to be slower than splice editing. Edited tapes may be used directly as CD masters, and will have a contiguous timecode track.

Jump or skip editing involves the use of a large RAM buffer, but avoids the need to cut the tape (except perhaps roughly) or to copy it. It has its principal value in the removal of unwanted sections from a single recording. Such an approach may be combined with the type of real-time creative flexibility found in tapeless systems, since audio may be manipulated before it is sent to the output. Edit commands may be stored on the tape and used to control the replay process.

Tapeless editors require that material to be edited is loaded on to disks in real time, although eventually original sound recordings may be made on to removable disks. Editing can be as fast as splice editing (ignoring the time required to load material) and as creatively flexible as copy editing. Costs of systems vary enormously depending on facilities. There is little standardisation between systems, making the interchange of material difficult. Currently it is necessary to copy edited material back to a tape for mastering on to CD. Many tapeless systems also offer sophisticated DSP facilities for audio processing during post-production. Tapeless editing closely resembles film sound editing, because of the possibility for slipping tracks and inserting sound effects, and this makes it popular in picture post-production.

11.4 Timecode in tape editing

Electronic editing systems use SMPTE/EBU timecode as a positional reference (see section 14.2), uniquely identifying points in a recording. Timecode is also used in synchronising tape machines during copy editing, with offsets being introduced between machines according to the relative timings of player and recorder for each edit. A number of factors must be considered with relation to the handling of timecode in order that the system functions correctly. Readers should refer also to the sections on synchronisation of digital audio (see Chapters 14 and 15).

11.4.1 Recorder timecode

Electronic editing systems normally require the recorder tape to have a contiguous timecode track, throughout the length of the programme. This may either be 'pre-striped' before an editing session, or it may be assembled during editing. Some systems will only work with a pre-striped master tape (the Fostex D-20 DAT editing system is an example), operating in the 'insert' mode which simply records digital audio whilst leaving auxiliary information and timecode information untouched. The Sony DAE-1100 or 3000 systems, for example, allow editing in either insert or assembly modes (see Fact File 11), and in the latter the timecode track is assembled contiguously during the assembly of the master tape by the so-called 'jam-syncing' of the timecode generator in the editor or tape machine to the replayed timecode before the edit such that the newly recorded timecode after the edit carries on without a break from the old timecode.

In Sony CD-mastering systems, timecode should always be recorded on analogue audio channel 2 of the U-matic tape, rather than on the dedicated timecode track found on high-band U-matics. Timecode on a master tape should also be recorded along with digital 'silence' for at least 30 seconds before the start of the programme and 30 seconds after the end.

It is important that the timecode generator used for striping both player and recorder tapes is locked to the same sync reference as the digital tape recorder, so that 'time' as measured in terms of audio samples is the same as 'time' measured by the passing of timecode. This subject is covered further in section 14.8.

11.4.2 Player timecode

It is not always necessary to have contiguous timecode on the source tapes, but it is desirable. If source tapes have breaks in the timecode then any editing system or synchroniser will become confused whilst trying to locate particular takes. This is because many systems do not read timecode whilst spooling, preferring to read video control-track pulses or tachometer information, and this simply increments the time counter either up or down from the last known timecode value, resulting in confusion when the machine goes back into play as it finds a different value recorded on the timecode track. Manual location may be used in such cases, and it is generally accepted that even if there are timecode breaks in the tape the time should increment upwards from the beginning of the tape, not going over the 24-hour boundary.

Electronic editing systems require a short period of tape with timecode on it prior to an edit point on both player and recorder for the purposes of parking and pre-rolling. In order for machines to be synchronised it is usually necessary to have at least 10 seconds of contiguous timecode prior to any edit point on both machines, and if more than this can be left then it will leave a greater margin for error. It is possible to set a short pre-roll for edits which do not have much timecode before them, but the location process in some editing systems often spools back to a point before the pre-roll in order to play up to the 'park' point (see Figure 11.1), in which

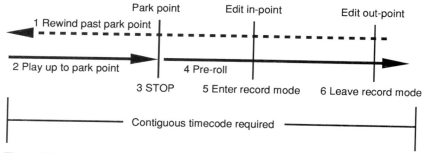

Figure 11.1 Contiguous timecode is required from before an edit in-point until after the edit out-point. The steps normally encountered in the execution of an automatic electronic edit are shown

case confusion could again arise.

Discontinuities in the timecode should not be allowed to occur during a particular recorded take, since this often results in error conditions on an editor. Nonetheless, some editors and synchronisers can be programmed to switch automatically from timecode synchronisation to digital word clock or video synchronisation once initial lock has been achieved, requiring only that timecode be contiguous during the pre-roll and first few seconds of locked play. After this, any jumps in timecode value will be ignored. Such an approach has other merits as well, because it avoids the possibility for speed variations in the master machine affecting the speed of the player. Timecode must be synchronous with word clock in order for such a method to be feasible (see section 14.1).

11.4.3 Type of timecode

Normally it is expected that the timecode on recorder and player machines will be of the same frame rate, since it is not usually possible to synchronise machines which have dissimilar timecode types. In the case of systems based on video formats (EIAJ, PCM-1610, JVC) the timecode type will normally be restricted to that used in the video format (e.g.: 30 fps for 525 line/60 Hz video systems such as the PCM-1610 or 1630), and the associated editor normally only accepts timecode of the right type. In the case of dedicated digital audio recorders, such as DASH, PD and DAT machines, the timecode format may be chosen from any of the available standards (24, 25, 29.97 and 30 fps), and may perhaps be selected to match a particular video format with which the edited tape may need to be synchronised.

Certain machines have built-in intelligent timecode generators, allowing for the replay of any timecode type no matter what was recorded on the tape, and this can be most useful in multi-standard environments. Sony's PCM-3402 DASH machine is an example of this approach. Also, IEC-standard DAT machines with timecode will allow the selection of the replay timecode frame rate.

11.5 Editing terminology and processes

Electronic digital audio editing has borrowed quite a lot of terminology from video editing, since the process is very similar. In music editing, the assembly of a digital audio master from source takes usually involves the systematic copying of material from the beginning of the programme through to the end, perfecting one edit at a time, after which it is committed to tape and recording continues until just after the next edit point.

The term 'out point' normally refers to the point on the master tape (recorder) at which old material is to cut into new material, whilst the term 'in point' normally refers to the point on a player tape at which the new material is to begin. At the edit point, therefore, the system fades out of old material from the recorder, and into new material from the player. Buttons may be provided, labelled 'mark in' and 'mark out', and should be used to mark the appropriate locations whilst tape is playing. Once the point has been marked roughly it may be trimmed using rock-and-roll replay by means of a wheel or equivalent (see sections 5.9 and 5.13), or by means of incremental 'nudging' in milliseconds.

In tapeless systems, these terms may still be used, but it is common to find tapeless systems which use terms borrowed from word processing, such as 'cut', 'copy' and

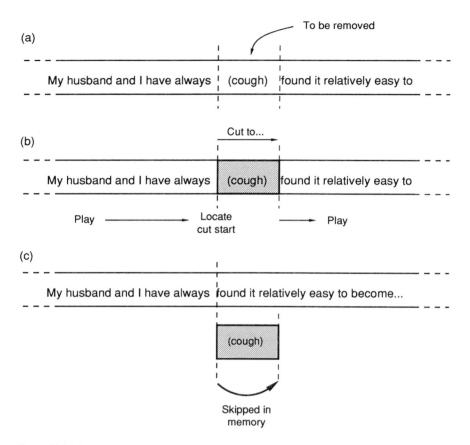

Figure 11.2 Disposal editing is fast and straightforward in tapeless systems, since an unwanted section can quickly be located and then skipped in memory. It would also be feasible to implement this function in tape-based systems, provided that the tape recorder's transport was responsive enough and the memory large enough to accommodate the jump

'paste'. In such systems, source material is 'pasted' into appropriate locations on a virtual 'tape', and the 'cut' and 'copy' functions can be used to remove portions and place them elsewhere. It is important to remember that the tapeless system does not physically dispose of sections which are removed from a recording, it simply does not play them. The original file remains intact. This type of approach is useful in so-called 'disposal editing', such as might be used with speech where sections of hesitation and mistakes are being removed from a long interview, for example. The principle of this type of editing is shown in the example in Figure 11.2, and has proved to be very fast in operation when using well designed editors.

11.6 Edit decision lists

An edit decision list (EDL) is a list of timecode locations and edit commands which dictates the edit-in and edit-out points on both player and recorder machines, often allowing for the handling of multiple players and source tapes. In a tapeless system the EDL is used to construct a replay schedule (see section 5.14) against which files are played out from the disk and joined in specific places. Digital tape editing systems have not typically stored the information for more than one edit at a time (both Sony's DAE-1100 and DAE-3000 only store one edit), although there are now examples of systems which keep data for every edit in a session, allowing the list to be modified and executed automatically.

In video editing systems the maintenance of an EDL for a complete session has been common for quite some time, and there are considerable advantages to this approach. Firstly, it allows for the re-doing of earlier edits based on the data originally stored, and secondly it allows for 'rippling through' of the effects of such changes to the times of subsequent edits if the new timings cause the subsequent edits to be wrongly located. Automatic execution of an EDL can often be performed provided that all tapes have contiguous unbroken timecode on them, because the editing system can go through each edit in the list in turn, locating the machines, synchronising them and performing each edit. This can be left to happen either overnight or during a lunch-break.

An interesting example of the above approach exists in the Fostex D-20 DAT editing system which allows for small portions of audio to be copied from source tapes to the master tape at the starts and ends of long edits so that the edits themselves can be finalised without copying all the intervening material. Once the edits have been programmed it is possible to leave the system to go through and compile the master tape automatically using the data stored in the EDL.

Currently there is no standardised format for audio EDLs, since there are few editing systems which use them. This is likely to become more important in the future if digital recordings are to be edited on a wider range of systems.

11.7 Closeness and accuracy of edits

Recording formats allow different minimum distances between splice edits, and this may also apply to tapeless systems although there are ways of getting round the problem, as described below.

In stationary-head formats, the minimum distance between edits is governed by the odd–even interleave delay (see Fact File 13) and in the case of DASH and PD formats this means that splice edits must be at least a few centimetres apart (e.g.: 21 mm in the high-speed DASH format). For most purposes this is adequate, and was designed to allow for the replacement of single notes in music. The accuracy of edits is normally limited by the sector size in the recording format, which typically limits edit-point accuracy to between 1 and 4 ms.

When using external electronic crossfading it is possible to make edits accurate to the sample (22 μs at 48 kHz) if required (Sony's DAE-3000 operates to sample accuracy), but in many operational cases this may be considered as excessive resolution. There is debate over the operational importance of sample-accurate editing, one view being that accuracy greater than one millisecond is pointless, since one millisecond corresponds to approximately one-hundredth of an inch (0.38 mm) at a tape speed of 15 ips (38 cm s^{-1}), and noone could guarantee to edit to that sort of accuracy with a razor blade on analogue tape. Nonetheless, as technology has made it possible to edit more accurately, the operational demands on editors have increased and standards of editing have become more strict. Razor-blade edits which would have been passed as 'OK' fifteen years ago are now often regarded as too audible. Producers often leave much more work to the post-production stage than they might have in the days of analogue editing, since they know that an edit can be made virtually anywhere in a programme, due to the crossfade options and positional accuracy possible with modern digital editors. It is also possible that very accurate electronic editing could be used for the removal of tiny clicks or other interference. There is no minimum distance between edits in electronic rotary-head editing systems.

In tapeless systems, edit points can theoretically be specified to sample accuracy, but in practice it depends on the software of the system. The minimum distance between edits depends on the way in which the system calculates and executes crossfades, since many systems execute crossfades between files in real time. In a real-time-crossfading system, it is usually not possible to start a new edit while a preceding crossfade is still taking place on the same track. Furthermore, depending on the size of the memory buffers for each channel (see section 3.9), the system may require a finite recovery time after an edit to replenish the buffer. Each system will perform differently in this way, and thus no minimum distance between edits can be stated categorically. It is sometimes possible to record a separate sound file which contains only a particular crossfade (see section 5.12), in order to make possible two edits in very close proximity or to make possible a very long crossfade which would otherwise have exceeded the capabilities of the system. In such a case, the crossfade file is treated as just another file of source material, and the real-time crossfader can then begin to crossfade new material into the middle of the first crossfade without having to do two jobs at once.

11.8 Preview modes

The ability to preview an edit before it is committed is a valuable feature of digital electronic editing. In tape-based systems, electronic editing involves the recording of a new master, whereas in most tapeless systems editing involves only the scheduled replay of existing material, with crossfades introduced in real time at joins (see section 5.11). For this reason, the preview is only really relevant in tape-based systems because there is not a lot of difference between a preview and a true edit in a tapeless system, since the EDL may be changed at any time.

Previews can be slow in older systems such as Sony's DAE-1100, because the edit simulation is made from tape, requiring that both the player and recorder U-matic machines are wound back, parked, pre-rolled and synchronised before each preview. Any changes in the edit point which result in the short crossfade memory capacity being exceeded require that the recorder is played over the edit point again to reload the memory, and low-band U-matic machines are relatively slow to cue-up because the tape must be partially unlaced before spooling. Later editors such as the DAE-3000 (and the electronic editor built into later DASH-format machines) have allowed previews entirely from memory, without the need to cue the tape, and have a six second window either side of the edit point. The memory stores stereo audio at full resolution, so the sound quality is equivalent to that which would be replayed from tape.

Most editing systems allow three preview modes: one that plays *up to* the out-point, one that plays *from* the in-point, and one that performs a full preview with crossfade. The first two modes are useful in determining exactly where the cut takes place in both sections, since it is then easier to hear whether the beginning of a note has been cut off at an in-point, or whether an out-point has been set too late, leaving an overhang into the next section. The first preview type (playing up to the out-point) can be achieved in earlier editors which do not provide it specifically (e.g.: DAE-1100) by pulling down the fader which controls player gain and performing a full preview. The system will then crossfade to nothing at the edit point, resulting in the same effect.

11.9 Successful splice-editing techniques

Although splice editing of digital recordings is not performed widely, it is some-times useful in multitrack operation for assembling tracks without the need for two machines, and it may be used to a limited extent for stereo editing. The following are some guidelines to help in achieving splice edits which have a high chance of working.

Firstly, cleanliness and care is of paramount importance, and many manufacturers recommend the use of cotton 'splicing gloves' to avoid fingerprints and sweaty hands affecting the tape. It is true that such things will affect the error rate on replay (see Chapter 9). Secondly, the correct splicing tape should be used, since analogue splicing tape will not work properly as it is too thick, has too much glue and is too wide. Thirdly, the use of too much splicing tape is to be discouraged (a centimetre or so is usually adequate) since excessive lengths of splicing tape affect the head-to-tape wrap and contact. Fourthly, it is advisable to leave a tiny gap in the tape at the edit point, especially in PD-format recordings, since the signal loss which results is used in PD machines to flag an edit point to the machine's crossfader. It also avoids the unevenness which may result from a slight overlap or butt join. Fifthly, a vertical cut should be used, not an angled cut, since an angled cut only destroys a greater number of samples and does not affect the crossfade. Sixthly, if the edit does not play correctly the first time, it should be played-through a few times as this will smooth the tape. If this does not work, careful cleaning of the tape should be tried on the oxide side with a very slightly damp cloth.

11.10 Re-doing earlier edits and inserting new material

Digital splice edits, once made, are difficult to modify due to the damage that may be caused to the tape, amongst other things. Cleaning and smoothing the tape may help to make it possible to play over damaged locations, but this is not always successful (see section 9.4). The ability to play over damaged sections depends largely on the error correction abilities of the system. If it is vital to pick apart a splice then the utmost care must be taken not to damage the tape.

In electronic copy-editing systems, completed edits may only be re-done by reassembly of the master. It is not usually possible to insert a changed section into the middle of an electronically edited tape, since it is unlikely that the new section will be exactly the same length as the old section it is replacing (see Figure 11.3). Even if the 'in-point' can be matched, the point at which the inserted material crossfades back into old material is likely to be early or late, depending on whether the replacement section is shorter or longer than the original. It is also possible that the point at which the replacement section crossfades back into existing material no

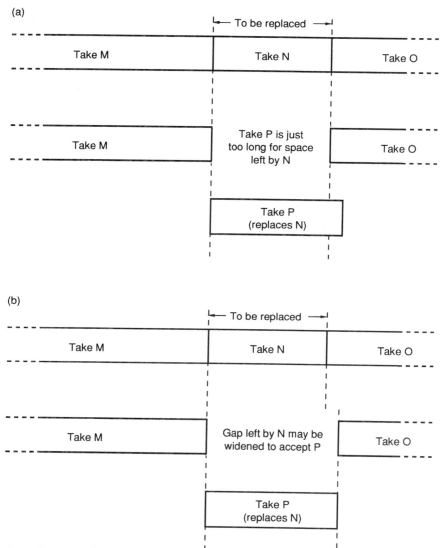

Figure 11.3 In tape-based copy editing it is difficult to insert a replacement take into a finished master, because the new take may not be exactly the same length as the one which it is replacing, as shown in (a). In tapeless editing, or with manual splicing, the gap left by the old take may be adjusted to fit the new take, as shown in (b)

longer works in the same place in the music as before, requiring the edit to be made in a different location.

It may be possible to avoid re-editing the whole programme by making a copy of the edited master, re-editing the section concerned, and then copying the originally edited material from there to the end, or, if the EDL has been stored (see section 11.6), re-doing the edits concerned and updating the EDL to take into account the changes to subsequent edit-out points on the recorder (the in-points on the player will normally remain the same if the edits are to occur at the same place in the music), and then automatically re-executing all the edits following the insertion. This is a laborious and time-consuming process.

In tapeless systems, material may be inserted and edits remade at any point in the programme at any time, since the subsequent edit points can be adjusted automatically (although of course the same artistic considerations apply as with copy editing). If material which has been edited has been off-loaded from the disk on to a master tape or backup it may be more difficult to re-do old edits, but this depends on the nature of the backup tape. Many systems allow for the contents of an editing job to be backed up in a form which can be restored complete with the original EDL. This allows the editing session to be resumed just as if it had never been finished. Simply reloading an edited master will not reload all the original sound files and edit information.

11.11 Working with crossfades

It is possible to engineer a variety of crossfade types at edit points, although older editing systems are limited to simple crossfades of one type. Greater flexibility in crossfade types and lengths has led to edits being possible in places where they would previously have been considered impossible, such as during sustained musical passages. Linear crossfades are often acceptable when short crossfade times are involved, but longer crossfades may exhibit an audible dip in level in the middle of the crossfade, depending on the nature of the material being joined, due to the additive and cancellation effects of incoming and outgoing programmes. In many cases, the cosine-law or log curves prove more successful over long crossfades, although it is possible that the log curve may even result in a slight *rise* in level at the mid-point. Many tapeless editors offer a choice of crossfade to the user, and each situation must be judged according to its requirements, the important point being that longer crossfades may be made without rises or dips in level by using the right curve. Additionally, it is often useful to shift the point at which the fade starts slightly in either the incoming or the outgoing take, in order to achieve the smoothest take-over. Fact File 25 shows some examples of crossfades from the Sonic Solutions editor, together with possible applications.

It is possible to introduce digital crossfades which would have been physically impossible with splicing, such as those in which the fade-down time is different from the fade-up. Such techniques might be used in music editing when, say, applause is to be faded down slowly at the end of one track, and to decay underneath the relatively fast entry of the next track.

The possible duration of crossfade in a tapeless system can theoretically be infinite, but in practice it is usually limited because of the need to accommodate the possibility for a wide range of operational situations, each of which will place demands on the transfer rate of the disk drive and the buffering processes (see section 3.10). During a crossfade the system needs to access both incoming *and* outgoing files, effectively doubling the demands on the disk drive and buffering. When a long crossfade is required on many channels at once it is not uncommon for tapeless systems to run out of buffer memory or exceed the performance of the disk drive, in which case one or more channel outputs will mute or break up. Good system software should be able to calculate when such a situation would arise and warn the user that he or she has requested an impossibility.

FACT FILE 25. An example of crossfade control

The diagram shows the crossfade modification page from Sonic Solutions' disk-based editor. It is possible to set the fade-in and fade-out to be the same, or to set their characteristics separately. 'Energy-balanced' crossfades are calculated in order that uncorrelated material may be joined with constant total power (no rise or fall in perceived volume), whilst 'gain-balanced' crossfades are for joining phase-coherent material with constant total voltage (again with no rise or fall in volume). The latter would be used when joining identical material (that is editing a take of a piece of music to itself.)

The cosine and linear curves are gain balanced, whilst the root-cosine and root-linear curves are energy balanced. The exponential curve introduces an identical but mirror-imaged exponential law into the two channels, and this is the simplest type of fade, as found in older editors. It is usually less effective operationally than the energy-balanced crossfade on normal musical material. The alpha-exponential setting allows the user to give the crossfade curve a customised shape, and to select energy- or gain-balanced operation.

It is possible to set a pre-play time for the source take and post-play for the destination which determines whether the source begins to fade up before the actual edit point, and whether the destination fades down after the edit point. For example if pre-play is set to 50% and crossfade duration is 1 second, the incoming signal will start to fade up half a second prior to the edit point and be at full level half a second after its edit point. If pre-play is 100%, the incoming signal will start to fade up 1 second before the edit point and be at full level at the edit point.

Sonic Solutions crossfade page

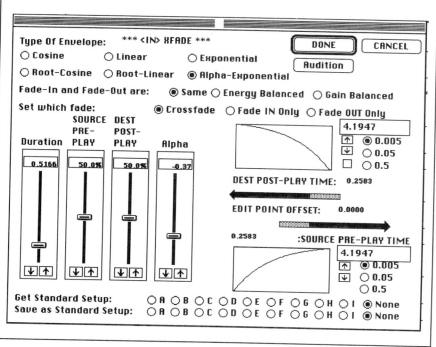

11.12 Additional audio processing during editing

It is desirable to be able to modify the gain characteristics of the sound during a programme. This may take the form of a level offset between one file and another, a channel balance adjustment, a gradual fade of some sort, or a cross-fade with an unusual gain contour, for example. These features are useful because they help in the artistic process of ensuring seamless joins, and they will also make possible programmed fade-ins and fade-outs. Simple digital signal processing is required for this purpose, and should be able to alter the magnitude of samples and perform basic additions. This is all that is required for cross-fade processing and gain control. The user interface can be designed in such a way that the user may programme points at which gain changes are to occur at particular points during replay, after which these will then take place automatically, executed against a timing reference such as timecode.

It is a short step from operations such as these to more complex DSP operations such as equalisation and mixing. In many tapeless systems the audio can be subjected to a variety of post-production processes, including level control, speed change, equalisation, time compression and effects. In tape-based electronic editing systems the master must be made up by copying source material, and any DSP will be introduced during the dub, but in a tapeless system it is possible to modify any characteristic of the programme at any time without re-copying the finished master, since this simply requires alterations to the replay schedule and any memorised DSP operations.

It is becoming common for tapeless editing to be fully integrated with digital mixing and effects, and this again is similar to the situation in video, where post-production may involve much more than just cutting pictures. Many video editing systems may be integrated with video mixers and effects units, in order that complex video processing may be performed at the same time as picture cutting.

11.13 Visual representation of edit information

Edit information may be presented to the operator in a variety of ways. Electronic tape editors are very much like video editors, simply having a keyboard and a display to show machine locations, status and EDL data. The aural judgement of edit points is not always backed up by any visual cues in such systems. In most tapeless systems, the user is presented either with a graphic representation of a piece of moving tape, with a virtual 'replay head' showing the current timecode location (see Figure 11.4), or an audio waveform display showing the waveform of the source material and that of the 'master' recording into which source material will be cut (as shown in the example in Figure 11.5).

Some editors find the waveform display a useful adjunct to their aural judgement, and it is possible to become used to identifying certain sounds visually as well as audibly. Such displays may be zoomed in and out to show various degrees of time and amplitude resolution. The virtual 'tape' display is useful in that it is often possible to enter titles which appear on the tape to identify the program segments as they pass. It is also useful when operating in the cut-and-paste mode (see section 11.5), because the user can treat the recording rather like a text document on a word processor, highlighting certain sections and removing them, or placing them somewhere else in the program. This approach comes into its own in video post-production (see section 11.6).

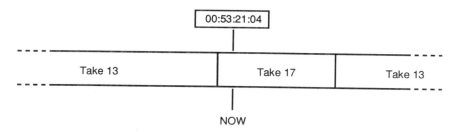

Figure 11.4 One way of illustrating the replay order to the user in tapeless systems is to display a graphic representation of moving tape, with a 'head' or 'now marker' to show the current time. Take numbers or cues may be displayed on the tape

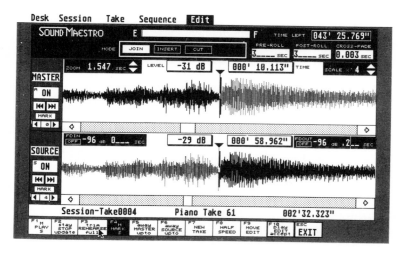

Figure 11.5 An audio waveform display may prove useful in locating edit points, as used in some tapeless editors. (Courtesy of Audio & Design)

Chapter 12

CD pre-mastering

Tapes to be presented for CD mastering should adhere to the guidelines shown in Fact File 26. It has become standardised *de facto* that the Sony CD-mastering format (PCM-1610 or 1630) is to be used as the final master for CD production, and although some pressing plants will accept other formats they will still copy the tape to the Sony format before cutting the glass master, and will sometimes charge extra for this.

Analogue tapes to be mastered for CD should be copied to the digital format along with a contiguous timecode track, and it is important that the version of the analogue master used for this copy is *not* the equalised (EQ) master which was produced for LP mastering, since this will badly affect the frequency response of the programme. Recording levels should be carefully adjusted to make optimum use of the dynamic range of the digital system (see section 8.1). Older analogue recordings may require additional work to make them suitable for high-quality CD reproduction (see section 12.3).

Any pre-emphasis set on the CD master tape (see section 8.3) will be copied on to the CD itself, along with a flag to indicate the pre-emphasis condition. CD players all have built-in de-emphasis circuits and a detector for the pre-emphasis flag, and thus are able to restore pre-emphasised signals to their original state.

Digital recordings having a resolution greater than 16 bits must be correctly truncated to 16 bits for CD mastering. In order for this to be done correctly, the recording must be copied and the signal dithered in the digital domain to suit the CDs resolution. This can be achieved by the use of a suitable digital mixer or interface processor (such as the one described in section 10.5).

12.1 Subcode editing and encoding

The subject of subcode editing of CD master tapes is complex (this is sometimes called 'PQ editing' since the P and Q subcode channels are those used principally, whereas the R–W channels have been either undefined or little-used to date). It involves the process of signalling the start and end points of tracks as well as index points and track numbers to the CD cutting equipment in order that the correct subcode information can be incorporated within the audio data and the table of contents (TOC) written at the start of the disc (this is an index to the contents of the disk). The subcode information then provides cueing and muting information to the CD player when the disk is replayed. The complexity lies in the different ways of

FACT FILE **26** | Guidelines for presenting CD masters

Tapes to be presented for CD mastering should normally be in the Sony format recorded by PCM-1610 or 1630 processors on U-matic tape, although some pressing plants may accept other formats and copy recordings to the Sony format themselves. The following are technical guidelines for the preparation of tapes to be presented for CD mastering:

1. Sampling rate should be 44.1 kHz (not 44.056 kHz).
2. Non-drop-frame SMPTE timecode (30 frames per second) should be recorded at 0 VU (100 nWb m^{-1}), ±3 dB, on analogue audio channel 2 of U-matic tape.
3. Timecode must be contiguous throughout programme and must not pass through midnight (00:00:00:00).
4. Timecode must be locked to video frame rate and sample frequency (see Chapter 14).
5. Timecode must be recorded along with digital silence for at least 30 seconds prior to the start of the first track and after the finish of the last track. More is preferable.
6. Tapes may be supplied with or without pre-emphasis.
7. Some tracks may be pre-emphasised and others not, but leave at least 2 seconds for pre-emphasis changes on the CD player between tracks.
8. Only use 75 minute tapes when absolutely necessary.
9. Supply a timing sheet as detailed in the text.
10. If supplying PQ code (see text) record this in a burst during first 30 seconds of tape on analogue audio channel 1 at 0 VU, ±3 dB.

providing the subcode information to the pressing plant, and in such things as the offsets necessary between actual start points and marked start points of tracks. If a tape is not PQ-coded by the recording studio it can often be done at the pressing plant or by a mastering facility, based on detailed timing sheets provided by the person who made the tape (see below), but this may incur extra cost.

The P bits of the CD subcode stream signify the start points of music in each track. P bits are set high for at least 2 seconds prior to the start of every track on a CD. The Q bits of the subcode contain a range of information about the track concerned, including track number (TNO), ISRC (see section 12.2), index number, track time, absolute time (mm:ss:ff), emphasis flag, and copy prohibit flag. This is shown diagrammatically with relation to an example programme in Figure 12.1.

The 'Red Book' standard for Compact Discs allows for a CD to begin with a track of any number from 1 to 99, although it should be noted that there are some CD players on the market which will refuse to play a CD which starts with anything other than track 1. Index points mark points within a track which the producer feels will be of interest, or will form suitable points for automatic location on replay. Not all CD players will locate index points. It is possible to set up to 99 tracks and up to 99 index points on one CD.

PQ data to be entered on the CD is normally recorded in a standard-format burst at the start of the CD master tape, recorded at 0 VU on analogue track 1 of the U-matic Sony-format recording which should correspond to a magnetic level of 100 nWb m^{-1}, or auxiliary track 1 of other formats (timecode is recorded on track 2). A stand-alone PQ editor is normally used for this purpose (e.g.: Philips/Studer LHH 3055 or Sony DAQ-1000), and most have an audio output which is used for recording the burst of encoded data on to the master tape (for which a standard is

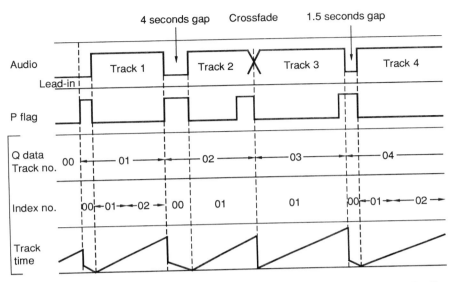

Figure 12.1 Status of Compact Disc P and Q subcodes shown with relation to an example of audio programme

defined), although one or two produce a floppy disk which may then be read by an identical PQ editor at the CD pressing plant (e.g.: Nippon). It is important to discover the format in which a pressing plant requires PQ information, and the tape should always be accompanied by a detailed track sheet in case any confusion arises. Some tapeless editors have PQ-editing software as part of the package, in which case the PQ data can be created in the same environment as the audio editing, and subsequently dumped to tape with the audio. One system even allows a write-once CD player to be attached to the editor for the production of a reference CD, complete with PQ data.

Figure 12.2 gives an example of a typical track sheet for a CD. It will be seen that two start points are given for each track: the actual start point and the 'begin-access' point (index 01). This is because the begin-access marker must be placed before the audio actually begins, in order that the CD player has time to unmute after it has located the track, and to allow for inaccuracy in location, as well as perhaps allowing the listener to return to his seat (although this might require slightly longer). The recommendation for the gap between these two points varies according to the source, but a widely used guideline is that the begin-access point should be set at a minimum of 15 timecode frames from the start of the track. This gives virtually every CD player on the market a little room for overshoot and unmuting time (in most players the unmute time is very short). Studer suggests that the first track should be allowed 0.6 seconds, and tracks 2–99 should be allowed 0.3 seconds. The begin-access points can be placed earlier than this if required, if sufficient silence exists between tracks. From the diagram in Figure 12.1 it will be seen that index marker 00 of the incoming track comes immediately after the end of the outgoing track (so 'end-access' = index 00 of the following track), and that time counts down from there (where the track number increments upwards) to the 'begin-access' point of the incoming track at index 01. Thus 'track 3, index 00' represents the end of

TNO	Title	Begin or end	Emph	Access	Actual	Duration
1	xxx	B	Off	00:01:45:00	00:01:45:15	
		E		00:05:00:00	00:04:59:00	00:03:15:00
2	xxx	B	On	00:05:03:00	00:05:06:00	
		E		(no end access)		00:05:27:00
				Crossfade between tracks		
3	xxx	B	On	00:10:30:00	00:10:30:15	
		E		(no end access) 00:13:01:00		00:02:32:15
				Only 1.5 secs between tracks		
4	xxx	B	On	00:13:02:00	00:13:02:15	
		E		00:20:04:00	00:20:03:00	00:07:02:00

etc...

Figure 12.2 Example of a track sheet to accompany a CD tape master

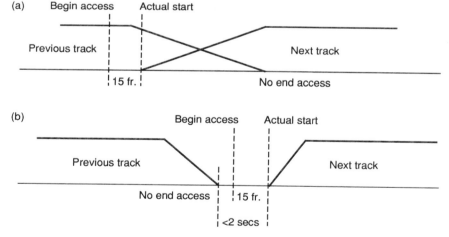

Figure 12.3 Use of begin- and end-access markers. (a) Situation in the case of a crossfade. (b) Situation in the case of a gap of less than two seconds between tracks. (Check with individual PQ editing software.)

track 2 not the beginning of track 3. It marks the start of the *real* pause between tracks (which may or may not be the same as the duration of the 'P' flag), and is the marker which denotes the point at which a player will skip to the next programmed track if in random-access mode.

The 'end-access' point for a track in the cue list (that is index 00 of the following track) must be located approximately 1 second after the actual end of each track in cases where a silent section of at least 2 seconds exists between tracks, and should be placed after all reverberation has died away. Where a crossfade is to be made between two tracks, or where less than 2 seconds gap exists between tracks, the begin-access marker of the incoming track should be placed the minimum 15 frames before the start of the fade-in, *and no end-access marker should be used for the fade-out or end of the outgoing track* (see Figure 12.3). The proviso should be made that, despite this, some PQ editors require the user to enter index point 00 in all cases even if it is the same as index point 01 (the begin-access marker), apparently for the sake of uniformity.

Where emphasis status changes between tracks, the begin access (index 01) of the incoming track should be set so as to lie at least two seconds after the end-access of the outgoing track (index 00 of the incoming track). In other words, it is not advisable to change emphasis with a gap of less than 2 seconds between tracks.

12.2 Additional information to accompany CD tape masters

The track sheet and notes which are sent along with a CD master should also contain indications of any noises, drop-outs or over-level occurrences on the tape, since this will make the mastering engineer aware that these either are intentional or have been chosen to be ignored.

It is possible on some PQ editors to enter information concerning the details of each track on the CD, some of which can be encoded within the subcode and some of which will simply be printed out alongside the track sheet if required. Within the subcode it is possible to include the ISRC (International Standard Recording Code) for each track, and this is useful in automated facilities such as radio stations for logging purposes.

Further subcode areas, denoted R to W, are available for purposes other than cueing, and these are gradually being defined more substantially. The intention is that these codes will be used for text and graphics information, to convey still pictures or words. In future these will be used for conveying such information as the lyrics of songs. For further information on the CD format the reader is referred to the book *The Compact Disc*, by Ken Pohlmann (see the Bibliography).

12.3 Editing old or noisy recordings

It is not intended to go into this subject in depth here, since it is a highly specialised area, but some pointers may be given towards the achievement of high-quality results from old or noisy recordings which need to be made into CDs.

A number of record companies have had success in the re-mastering of analogue tape recordings for CD. The dynamic range and frequency response of analogue recording is quite adequate for high-quality reproduction when optimised, and a CD made from an analogue recording will be an almost flawless copy of the master tape, offering great improvements over the original LP in many cases. Re-mastering may involve going right back to the source tapes if these are still available, and re-editing the recording digitally. If this is not possible then it may be possible to re-do some analogue edits digitally, having cleaned up the tape around the edit point and taken apart analogue edits. Given that it is possible to vary crossfade times and gains on an electronic editor (see above) it is often possible to make a better job of old edits when re-mastering.

In transferring analogue recordings to digital recorders care should be taken to align the analogue machine as well as possible with reference to the tones at the beginnings of reels, and to compensate for any differences in level or EQ between reels. Azimuth of the replay head of the analogue machine should be optimised for each reel, and heads should be kept clean and de-magnetised. Any noise reduction used should also be aligned correctly. Recording levels on a 16 bit digital system should be controlled so that the loudest sections on the analogue recording peak just below the peak recording level on the digital recorder (see section 8.1).

Various systems have been developed for removing the noise from hissy recordings, or taking the clicks out of recordings which originated on analogue disks. Most recent systems, such as Sonic Solutions' *NoNoise* option for its tapeless editor, operate using fast DSP to build up a 'template' for the noise to be removed, and can be successful in removing seemingly random hiss as well as clicks and interference.

When analogue recordings are mastered onto CD it is often obvious because of the sudden presence of background hiss at the starts of tracks. This results because analogue recordings will have been copied to a digital tape and then edited together digitally, often fading to digital silence in between tracks. Digital silence is particularly stark compared with analogue 'silence' because it is often some 20–30 dB quieter! Clearly the audibility of this depends on the replay level, but it is to be suggested that a steady low level of hiss is less objectionable than sudden onsets, and thus some 'ambient' hiss should be edited-in between tracks. At the start of the CD ambient noise should be faded up gradually, rather than cut in. This technique also applies to digital recordings in which a high degree of ambient noise exists from the location in which the recording was made, and it is wise to record a sample few minutes of noise when on location in order to be able to splice it into the edited recording between tracks, perhaps with a moderately long crossfade (see section 11.11).

Chapter 13

Signal synchronisation

There are two strands to the subject of synchronisation in digital audio. One is the synchronisation of digital recorders to other machines using timecode, and the other is the synchronisation of digital audio signals. The former is important in environments involving pictures of any kind, and also in editing operations (see Chapter 11), whilst the latter is important in any environment where digital signals from a variety of sources are to be combined, copied between machines or routed around a network. It is not possible to divorce the discussion of one from the other, since there is no point in having machines which are synchronised correctly using timecode if their digital outputs drift with relation to each other.

Digital audio signals differ fundamentally from analogue signals in that they are time discrete, and the preservation of the correct timing of these signals is vital to the correct reconstruction of the audio signal. Furthermore, if digital signals are to be combined in any way, or interconnected between devices, it becomes important that they are identically timed. The most important requirement in a digital audio system is the control of sample rate clocks, such that they are the same, it being less important that signals are synchronised to bit accuracy since this is usually achieved within equipment. In the following sections some strategies for signal synchronisation are discussed, which should be considered alongside requirements for timecode synchronisation (see Chapter 14).

13.1 Sync references

A number of reference signals may be used for locking the sampling-rate clock of a digital audio device. In a large system it is vital that all devices remain locked to a common sampling rate reference clock, and there are now AES draft recommendations for this purpose which are likely to become confirmed in the near future (see Fact File 27). As will be seen, they state that all machines shall be able to lock to a reference clock (provided as a standard AES/EBU interface signal whose sampling frequency is stable within the tolerance allowed), and that all machines should have a separate input for a synchronising signal (this takes the form of a single AES/EBU XLR socket).

Currently, digital audio recorders are provided with a wide range of sync inputs, and most systems may be operated in the external or internal sync modes. In the internal sync mode a system is locked to its own crystal oscillator, which should be accurate within ±10 parts per million (ppm) if it conforms to AES recommended

FACT FILE 27 · Criteria for signal synchronisation

The AES has published draft recommendations for signal synchronisation, a summary of which is given below.

Synchronous signals

Signals will be considered synchronous when they have identical sample rates. In order to achieve this, all devices within a system should be able either to lock to a reference signal in the form of a separate AES/EBU input, or to the clock rate implicit in the AES/EBU programme signal present at the device's digital audio input. Input signal frame edges must lie within ±25% of the reference signal's frame edge, and output signals within ±5% (see diagram), although tighter accuracy than this is preferable. It is normally unnecessary for signals to be synchronised to bit-accuracy (such that like-numbered bits from each input align perfectly) since such alignment is normally performed within a device if it is necessary for signal processing. If a number of frames' delay exists between the audio input and output of a device, this delay should be stated.

Conditions for synchronous signals

Reference signals

The AES/EBU-format reference signal may either contain programme or not. If it does not contain programme it may simply contain the sync preamble with the rest of the frame inactive. Two grades of reference are specified: Grade 1, having a long-term frequency accuracy of ±1 ppm (part per million), and Grade 2, having a long-term accuracy of ±10 ppm. The Grade 2 signal conforms to the standard AES sample-frequency recommendation for digital audio equipment, and is intended for use within a single studio which has no immediate technical reason for greater accuracy, whereas Grade 1 is a tighter specification and is intended for the synchronisation of complete studio centres (as well as single studios if required). Byte 4, bits 0 and 1 of the channel status data of the reference signal indicate the grade in use (00=default, 01=Grade 1, 10=Grade 2, 11=reserved). The reference signal may be distributed in a star configuration with a maximum of four spurs per circuit.

Further reading

AES11-19XX, Synchronisation of digital audio equipment in studio operations

Shelton, T. (1989) Synchronisation of digital audio. In *Proceedings of the AES/EBU Interface Conference*, AES British Section publication.

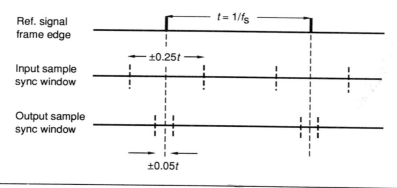

practice (AES5-1984). If in the external sync mode the system should lock to one of its sync inputs, which may either be selectable using a switch, or be selected automatically based on an order of priority depending on the mode of operation (for this the user should refer to the operations manual of the device concerned). Typical

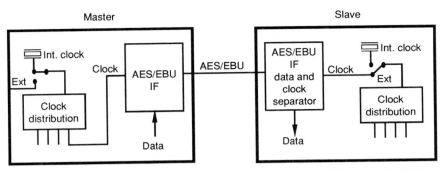

Figure 13.1 Genlock synchronisation. The slave locks to the master's clock by extracting it from the AES/EBU data stream

sync inputs are word clock (WCLK), which is a square-wave TTL-level signal (0–5 V) at the sampling rate usually available on a BNC-type connector; 'composite video', which is a video reference signal consisting of either normal picture information or just 'black and burst' (a video signal with a blacked-out picture); or AES/EBU, which is a reference signal conforming to the tolerances outlined in Fact File 27. In all cases one machine or source must be considered to be the 'master', supplying the sync reference to the whole system, and the others as 'slaves'.

It is also possible to lock a device to its own AES/EBU digital audio input (if one exists), and this technique is often known as 'genlock'. It can be used for small systems operating in a daisy-chain, or where an external reference is not available (see Figure 13.1). Alternatively, a separate WCLK may be daisy-chained between devices in cases where the AES/EBU interface is not available, such as when equipment is interfaced using SDIF-2. A 'sync' light is usually provided on the front panel of a device (or under a cover) to indicate good lock to an external or internal clock, and this may flash or go out if the system cannot lock to the clock concerned, because it has too much jitter, is at too low a level, or conflicts with another clock, or because it is not at a sampling rate which can be accepted by the system.

Video sync (composite sync) is often used when a system is operated within a video environment, and where a digital recorder is to be referenced to the same sync reference as the video machines in a system. This is useful when synchronising audio and video transports during recording and replay, using either a synchroniser or a video editor, when timecode is only used initially during the pre-roll, whereafter machines are released to their own video sync reference. It also allows for timecode to be recorded synchronously on the audio machine, since the timecode generator used to stripe the tape can be locked to video syncs also (see section 14.8). The relationship between video frame rates and audio sampling frequencies is shown in section 14.1.

13.2 Distribution of sync references

It is appropriate to consider digital audio as similar to video when approaching the subject of sync distribution, especially in large systems. Consequently, it is advisable to use a central high-quality sync signal generator (the equivalent of a video sync pulse generator, or SPG), the output of which is made available widely about the studio centre, using digital distribution amplifiers (DDAs) to supply different outlets in a 'star' configuration. In video operations this is often called 'house sync', and such a term may become used in digital audio as well. Each digital device in the system may then be connected to this house sync signal, and each should be set to operate in the external sync mode. In the future, as described above, it is most likely that house sync will take the form of an AES/EBU-format signal, and this should be adopted wherever possible for the sake of standardisation.

Using the technique of central sync-signal distribution (see Figure 13.2) it becomes possible to treat all devices as slaves to the sync generator. In this case there is no 'master' machine, since the sync generator acts as the 'master'. It is a concept which many analogue recording engineers may find unfamiliar, since analogue machines are typically 'free running', requiring no sync reference. It requires that all machines in the system operate at the same sampling rate, unless a sample-rate convertor and signal synchroniser are used (see section 13.4).

Alternatively, in a small studio, it may be uneconomical and impractical to use a separate SPG, and in such cases one device in the studio must be designated as the master. This device would then effectively act as the SPG, operating in the internal sync mode, with all other devices operating in the external sync mode and slaving to it (see Figure 13.3). If a digital mixer were to be used then it would be sensible to use it as the SPG, but alternatively it would be possible to use a tape recorder, disk system or other device with a stable clock. In such a configuration it would be necessary either to use AES/EBU interfaces for all interconnection (in which case it would be possible to operate in the 'genlock'-type mode described above, where all devices derive a clock from their digital audio inputs) or to distribute a separate word clock or AES sync signal from the master. In the genlock configuration, the danger exists of timing errors being compounded as errors introduced by one device

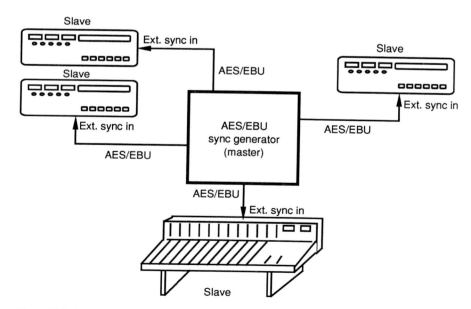

Figure 13.2 Central sync signal distribution. A high-accuracy master AES/EBU sync generator is used as a reference for all devices in the system. All devices operate in the external sync mode

(a)

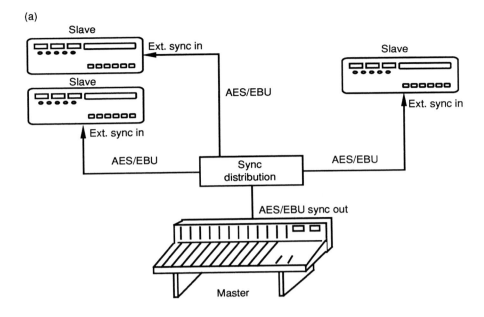

(b)

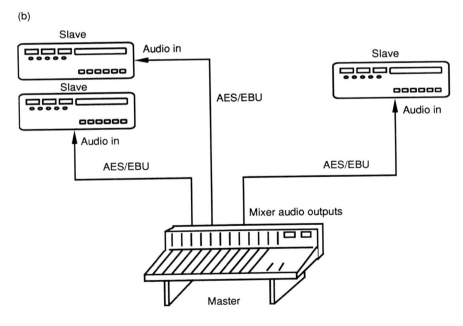

Figure 13.3 Where it is not economically viable to use a separate sync reference, one device must act as the master clock, as shown in (a). In this example the mixer operates in internal sync mode and sends a reference signal (either AES/EBU or WCLK) to all other devices (operating in ext. sync). Alternatively, as shown in (b), slaves may lock to the incoming AES/EBU audio signal, which contains a clock

are passed serially down the signal chain.

In situations where sources are widely spread apart, perhaps even being fed in from remote sites (as might be the case in broadcast operations) the distribution of a single sync reference to all devices becomes very difficult or impossible. In such cases it may be necessary to synchronise external 'wild' feeds to the house sync before they can be connected to in-house equipment, and for this purpose a sample rate synchroniser should be used (see section 13.4).

13.3 Control and effects of timing jitter in digital audio

In addition to the control of the nominal sampling rate of digital audio signals, it is necessary to consider the effects of short-term timing errors on signals which affect the positions of significant instants of the digital signal. This is known as 'jitter'. Jitter can arise through external interference, random noise and crosstalk between signals, and if not corrected may adversely affect the audio in a number of ways. Firstly, a larger number of errors may result during decoding due to the difficulty in determining the positions of bit edges, and secondly the audio quality of D/A conversion may be affected because of phase modulation of the analogue signal. Slower changes of timing may result in audible 'wow and flutter', a phenomenon well known in analogue audio but normally absent in digital audio recording.

From a systems point of view, devices should be able to lock to an incoming signal with a degree of jitter and clock modulation. In order to eliminate the subsequent effects of jitter on the audio signal it is important that each device 'de-jitterises' the incoming signal clock using a suitably filtered phase-locked loop at the sync-

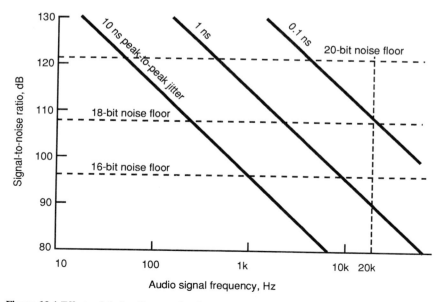

Figure 13.4 Effects of timing jitter on signal-to-noise ratio. For jitter-induced noise to be below the 18 bit noise floor, the clock must be stable to within 0.1 ns (100 ps). (After W.T. Shelton, with permission)

separation stage to re-clock the signal, and that synchronisers handling remote signals re-clock these before they are 'allowed in' to the rest of the system. If a 'genlock' arrangement is used for sync distribution (see above) it is vital that clocks are de-jitterised before they are passed on to further devices, since otherwise the jitter will simply accumulate. Clock de-jitterisers are becoming available with extremely high specifications to suit the requirements of modern high-resolution convertors, with the added advantage of a moderately wide lock-in range.

Buffering of audio signals, followed by re-clocking under internal crystal control (as described in Fact File 1), can be used to ensure that audio samples may subsequently be converted within the timing tolerances required for high-quality audio. Buffering, though, unavoidably introduces a delay, and this may not be acceptable in some operational situations; thus it may be preferable to re-time data by cleaning up the clock upon reception, using a suitable phase-locked loop. The AES has specified in its draft that sample clock modulation should be limited to less than ±1 ns, sample to sample, at all modulation frequencies above 40 Hz, in order to make 'wow and flutter' insignificant, and that jitter should be less than ±0.1 ns per sample clock period to keep noise modulation below acceptable limits in a 16 bit system. Jitter tolerance should be made even tighter, *pro rata*, in the case of systems operating to resolutions greater than 16 bits. Figure 13.4 shows this diagrammatically.

It should be remembered that consumer or semi-professional digital audio equipment may not operate to the same standards of timing accuracy as professional equipment, and thus audio signals from such devices should be treated with care. Such devices should not normally be used as sync references unless the clock accuracy can be verified, and tests have proven that the clock frequency error of such equipment regularly exceeds 50 parts per million. Furthermore, the stand-alone convertors used in expensive hi-fi systems do not always adequately re-clock the incoming signal before it is converted, and this may lead to severe modulation of the audio, resulting in noise or distortion. It is wise to consider passing the digital audio from consumer equipment through a synchroniser before contribution to a professional system.

13.4 Use and function of sample rate synchronisers

The sample rate synchroniser is not a well-established concept at the time of writing, although it is implicit in the AES recommendations for digital audio synchronisation. It will become most important in large-scale digital audio operations such as those likely to be used in broadcast networks and studio centres, although music studios and others should not ignore the concepts involved. A sample rate synchroniser is used to synchronise a non-synchronous digital audio signal to a reference signal (see above). In this context, the synchroniser is used only to lock signals of nominally the *same* sampling frequency, but whose sampling frequency may differ within the maximum tolerances allowed in the AES recommendation. The audible effect resulting from a signal which drifts with relation to the sync reference is usually the appearance of a glitch or click at the difference frequency between the signal and the reference, nominally at a level around 50 dB below the signal. This usually appears when attempting to mix two digital audio signals whose sampling rates differ by a small amount. Some systems may not operate at all if presented with asynchronous signals.

FACT FILE 28: Examples of sample-rate synchronisers

There are many methods for synchronising digital audio signals to a reference clock, and two possibilities are described below.

Buffer-store synchroniser

As shown in the first diagram, the buffer-store synchroniser, as described by Gilchrist, is a relatively simple device which makes use of a short-term memory buffer (holding perhaps 128 samples). The synchroniser calculates the difference between the input sample rate and the reference sample rate, re-timing the output from the buffer so as to conform to the reference rate. If the input is slower than the output the buffer will gradually empty, until such time when the synchroniser must intervene to allow the buffer to re-fill, during which time it must repeat samples at the output, whilst re-addressing the buffer to the mid-point. Conversely, if the input is faster than the output, the buffer will become full and eventually some samples must be discarded while the buffer is re-addressed to the mid-point. The jump in buffer address results in a signal discontinuity, but this is designed to occur within a silent portion of programme so as to avoid the audible effect which otherwise would result.

The delay of 128 samples is relatively short, and for the system to be viable the input signal would have to be within a small tolerance of the reference frequency, otherwise 'jumps' would occur too regularly.

Sample-rate conversion synchroniser

As shown in the second diagram, a synchroniser may also employ a short period of sample rate conversion (see Fact File 24) to correct for the accumulated error between input signal and reference signal. This technique has the advantage that it may be used within program material, rather than having to wait until a silent break, since the audible effect will be minimal.

Further reading
Gilchrist, N.H.C. (1980) Sampling-rate synchronisation of digital sound signals by variable delay. *EBU Technical Review*, No. 183, October.
Gilchrist, N.H.C. (1988) Sampling-frequency synchronisation with minimal delay. *Journal of the Audio Engineering Society*, **36.5**, May.

Buffer store

Sample-rate

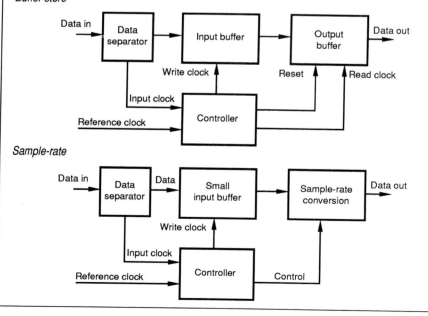

It may be necessary to correct for timing errors in signals synchronous to the master clock, but which have travelled long distances, since these may have been delayed slightly and thus be out of phase with the reference. This is more properly referred to as 'frame alignment'. Propagation delays are not great: for example, an AES/EBU signal must travel 3.7 km down a cable before it is delayed by one sample period. A 1 bit delay results when a signal has travelled through approximately 58 metres of cable (although this depends on the cable). For signals of different nominal sampling frequencies, a sample rate convertor (see section 10.3) should be used.

A synchroniser's job, when operating with serial data conforming to the AES/EBU standard, is to synchronise signals whose frame edges lie within ±25% of the reference signal's frame edges. This should result in signals at the output which are within ±5% of the reference signal (the definition of synchronous signals), although tighter lock is preferable in order that errors in later stages do not accumulate. The synchroniser is normally to be located in the operational area accepting remote or asynchronous signals, and may eventually be located on a chip within devices themselves. Depending on how far adrift the incoming signal is from the reference, a number of techniques may be used to bring it into lock, and some examples are shown in Fact File 28. The synchroniser could also perform the useful function of re-clocking noisy remote signals to remove short-term timing errors.

A commercial example of such a device exists in the Digital Audio Research DASS 100, described in section 10.5. This device switches between different types of sample sync depending on how far out of sync the input signal is. It also allows the generation of a stable sample rate clock signal from composite video, LTC (see section 14.2), or WCLK or from AES/EBU.

Chapter 14

Synchronising digital audio systems with video

Each digital audio recording format has its idiosyncracies when it comes to synchronisation with a picture, and there are particular problems when using digital systems which themselves are based around VTRs, since the frame rate may not be the same as that of the picture. There is also the question of how the sampling rate of a digital recorder relates to the video frame rate, and the question of how the synchronisation of disk-based systems may be achieved. Furthermore, the question of timecode synchronisation cannot be tackled without also considering the business of signal synchronisation, as discussed in the preceding sections.

Two things are important in this discussion, one being the synchronisation of a digital audio system to a house video reference signal, and the other being the synchronisation of digital audio recorders to VTRs using timecode. The concepts of synchronous recording and replay, including timecode recording, are also described, since these are not familiar concepts in analogue audio.

14.1 Audio and video reference clock relationships

In video systems all devices are locked to a reference source of sync pulses, provided by a sync pulse generator (SPG), just as digital audio devices should be in their own way (see above). In environments where digital audio and video are to be used together it is important that a relationship is established between the two reference clock signals, such that a fixed ratio of video sync pulses to audio samples exists. Once such a synchronous relationship is set up it becomes a relatively simple matter to stripe tapes with synchronous timecode and to synchronise transports using a combination of timecode and either video or digital audio syncs, since it would be taken for granted that a given number of timecode frames corresponded directly to a given number of samples, and that this relationship would not drift.

Table 14.1 shows the relationships that would need to exist between video frame rates and digital audio sampling frequencies, indicating the number of samples per television frame. It is possible that a common clock of high frequency could be used to reference both the video and audio SPGs, or that a stable source of video syncs could be used to drive an audio SPG. It would be possible in a simple stand-alone system to use a digital audio recorder capable of locking to video syncs as the digital audio reference for the rest of the system. Some example systems, with video and digital audio both locked to the same sync reference, are shown in Figure 14.1. Timecode generators normally lock to video syncs as opposed to digital audio syncs,

(a)

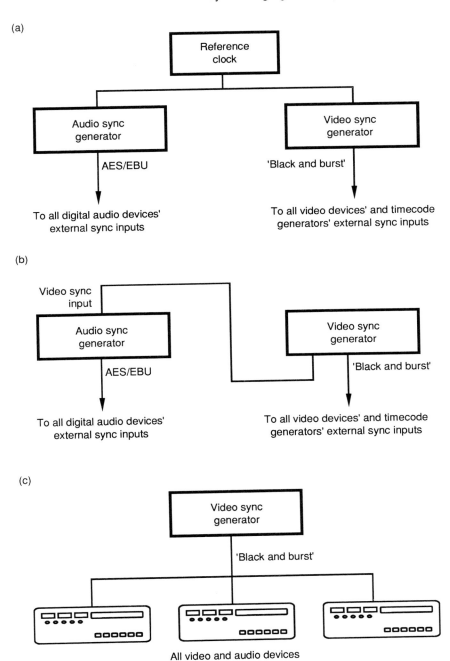

Figure 14.1 Methods of locking digital audio, video and timecode to the same reference. (a) Audio and video SPGs locked to a common reference. (b) Audio SPG locked to video SPG. (c) Audio and video devices all locked to video SPG

Table 14.1 Audio samples per frame for various picture frame rates

Sample rate (kHz)	24 fps (Film)	25 fps (PAL/SECAM)	30 fps (monochrome)	29.97 fps (NTSC)
32	4000/3	1280	3200/3	16 016/15
44.1	3675/2	1764	1470	147 147/100
48	2000	1920	1600	8008/5

although it is conceivable that this situation will change as synchronous timecode becomes more widely used in digital audio.

14.2 Timecode

The type of timecode normally referred to in operations involving audio and video recorders is the SMPTE/EBU time and control code, which is used for synchronisation and positional-location purposes. Some of the more detailed aspects of the code apply only to video recorders, and thus will not be covered here, but a description will be given of the factors which affect the use of timecode in audio systems.

Timecode comes in two basic forms, linear timecode or LTC, and vertical interval timecode or VITC. The former is modulated in such a way that it can be recorded on to an audio track of a tape machine, whereas the latter is recorded as part of a television picture on a video tape recorder, using two spare lines in the picture frame. Timecode can be made to conform to one of four standard frame rates, to be compatible with the television picture frame rates of the different countries in which it is used (the frame rate is the number of still frames per second which make up a moving television picture). It has been mistakenly dubbed SMPTE ('simply') by many people, but this refers only to one specific frame rate and can lead to confusion.

Each frame value is represented by an 80 bit binary word, which contains all the necessary information to describe the value of the frame in hours:minutes:seconds:frames (hh:mm:ss:ff) format. There is also space for user bits, which are set aside for the user to enter data of his or her choice. Additionally there are some signalling bits which refer mainly to video functions, and a sync word which is used to denote the end of a frame word and has a unique pattern which occurs nowhere else in any frame. The sync word pattern allows an LTC reader to determine whether the timecode is being played backwards or forwards, since either is allowed. Figure 14.2 shows the data format of the 80 bit timecode word.

The data is modulated before it is recorded, in order that it may be recorded as an audio signal, and a method known as bi-phase mark coding is used (the same channel code as used for AES/EBU digital interface signals, see section 10.2.4). This encodes binary information in a format which forces a transition from one state to another at the start of every clock period, there being 80 clock periods in a frame. If the datum in that clock period is a one then there will be an additional transition within that period; if the datum is a zero there will be no transition. The result is a waveform which looks a little like a square wave whose frequency changes continually between one rate and another (see Figure 14.3). The advantage of this kind of modulation method is that it can be phase inverted and yet still read correctly, since the data is represented by the transition from one state to another, whether that be low to high or high to low.

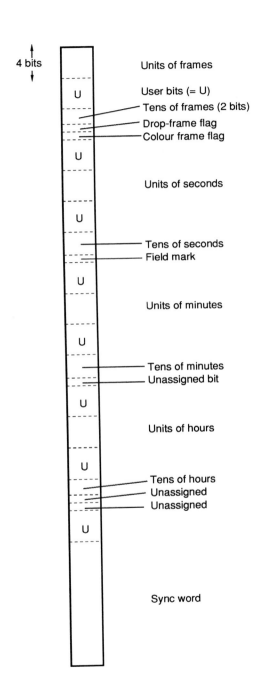

4 bits

Units of frames

User bits (= U)
Tens of frames (2 bits)
Drop-frame flag
Colour frame flag

Units of seconds

Tens of seconds
Field mark

Units of minutes

Tens of minutes
Unassigned bit

Units of hours

Tens of hours
Unassigned
Unassigned

Sync word

Figure 14.2 Contents of the SMPTE/EBU timecode frame

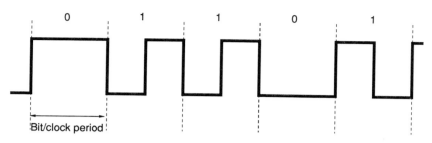

Figure 14.3 Bi-phase mark or FM channel code used for SMPTE/EBU timecode. A transition occurs at edges of bit cells, and also within the bit cell when a '1' is present in the data

The four standard frame rates used, together with their application, are as follows:

1. A frame rate of 24 frames per second (Film) is used for some film purposes, since the frame rate of film is usually 24 fps unless it is made specifically for television.

2. A frame rate of 25 fps (EBU) is used with PAL- and SECAM-standard TV pictures in Europe, Russia, Australia, parts of Asia, and other areas.

3. A frame rate of 29.97 fps (SMPTE drop-frame) is used with NTSC colour pictures in the USA, Japan, and other countries which operate at this frame rate. It is called 'drop-frame' because 30 frame code is used, but with two frames being dropped every minute, except for every tenth minute, in order to keep the average rate of the code the same as that of the picture. There will be short-term errors, but the long-term error is kept to a minimum.

4. A frame rate of 30 fps (SMPTE) is strictly only used with monochrome American-standard TV pictures, and thus is not widely used in modern video systems. It may be used in some digital audio systems which involve VTRs running at exactly 30 frames per second (e.g.: Sony PCM-1630).

There is also a standard for the transference of SMPTE/EBU timecode data over a MIDI interface (see section 1.4), known as MIDI timecode (MTC). This is used in situations where the majority of equipment is interconnected using MIDI, the original timecode being converted into the MIDI format using an SMPTE/MIDI convertor. Owing to the data rate of the MIDI interface, and the need for other MIDI information to be transferred over the same interface, timecode data is only completely transmitted once every other frame, requiring that receiving devices interpolate. It is beyond the scope of this book to cover MTC in further detail, and the reader is referred to the book *MIDI Systems and Control* by this author (see the Bibliography).

14.3 Timecode implementation in digital recording formats

The reader is referred to section 7.12 where a table of the timecode options in digital recording formats is given, along with a brief discussion. Fact File 29 contains

FACT FILE 29   IEC-format for DAT timecode

An IEC standard exists for the incorporation of timecode information within the subcode area of R-DAT recordings. This replaces the initial concept of recording timecode on an analogue edge track, as employed in Sony's early PCM-2000 recorder, and is also different from the timecode format initially employed by Fostex in the D-20 recorder. All manufacturers of professional DAT machines have agreed to implement the IEC-standard timecode format in cases where timecode is to be employed in DAT machines. The following is a brief description of the IEC timecode format and features.

As shown in the diagram, timecode is recorded in the subcode blocks at the ends of each helical scan. Timecode is only one of the data types which may be recorded here. The rotary head reads and writes timecode as well as audio, and timecode may be recorded either at the same time as audio or separately from it, since it is possible to turn the head current on for only the short segment corresponding to the subcode block. The 'frame rate' of DAT is 33.33 fps, and this does not relate easily to the SMPTE/EBU frame rates of 24, 25, 29.97 and 30 fps, so a translation process is required which converts from one to the other and back again.

IEC timecode works by recording running-time code at the DAT frame rate into a subcode area known as the 'Pro R-time' pack. This value is computed from the SMPTE/EBU frame value according to an appropriate 'gearbox' ratio. Clearly there will often be an error in conversion, since there is not a simple ratio between the two frame rates, and thus an 11-bit pointer is included in the Pro R-time pack which indicates the absolute phase relationship between the SMPTE/EBU frame edge and the DAT frame edge in terms of the number of samples' difference. Thus replayed timecode may be accurate to the sample. Replayed timecode may be converted to any of the standard SMPTE/EBU frame rates, no matter what was recorded, since this is a simple matter of changing the gearbox ratio on replay.

Timecode information encoded within the channel status bits of the AES/EBU interface (see Fact File 16) may also be recorded in the Pro R-time pack, as may user data from either the SMPTE/EBU frame or the AES/EBU channel status. User data is stored in a pack known as 'Pro Binary'.

DAT timecode recording

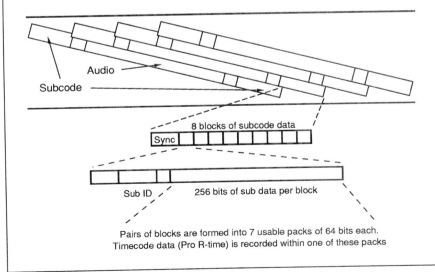

Pairs of blocks are formed into 7 usable packs of 64 bits each.
Timecode data (Pro R-time) is recorded within one of these packs

details of the proposed IEC standard for timecode in DAT machines. The implications of timecode in digital editing are discussed in section 11.4. Many digital audio recorders do not incorporate internal timecode generators, and require an external generator. The locking of this external generator to the same reference as the audio recorder is very important, as discussed below.

14.4 Video sync of EIAJ-format recordings

A distinction must be made between dedicated digital audio recorders (DATRs) and those which are based on helical-scan video recording (see sections 4.6–4.8). Dedicated DATRs may record timecode of any standard, and may be synchronised

(a)

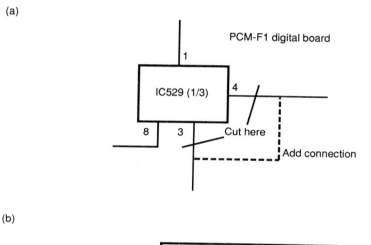

(b)

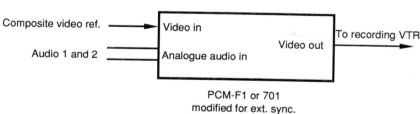

(c)

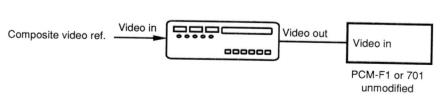

Figure 14.4 External sync options for EIAJ-format devices. (a) Sony PCM-F1 may be modified for external sync during recording as shown. (b) A modified F1 or 701 may be locked to a source of composite video for synchronous recording by connecting the video to its video input. (c) Synchronous replay may be possible by locking the replay VTR to a source of composite video

with video or film transports from any country in the world, but systems based on video recorders (e.g.: EIAJ format, JVC format and Sony PCM-1610/1630) present more difficulties because they are normally limited to one frame rate. The latter type of system is being gradually phased out, since VTRs were only used for early digital audio recording because they happened to have suitable characteristics and avoided the need to design a new transport, although it may still be necessary to attempt to use these along with VTRs carrying pictures.

EIAJ-format PCM adaptors come in both PAL and NTSC video standards, the sampling rate used in the NTSC format being 44.056 kHz, as opposed to the 44.1 kHz of the PAL format. It is possible to record timecode on the audio track of the VTR used with these systems, and such timecode should normally be of the same frame rate as that of the video standard, and should be locked to the same video sync source as the VTR and PCM adaptor. Not all EIAJ PCM adaptors can be locked to external sync in record mode, but a number exist (e.g.: Sony PCM-701, modified by Audio & Design) with modifications to allow this, as well as a switch to select PAL or NTSC record modes.

It is possible to modify the Sony PCM-F1 for external sync operation in record mode, in order that synchronous recordings may be made alongside video recordings, as shown in Figure 14.4(a). This allows the video encoder of the F1 to be locked to the device's video input, which should be fed with a source of composite video. The COPY switch should be set to OFF. Synchronous replay of EIAJ-format recordings can be established by connecting the VTR to a source of composite video (at its video IN or sync socket) and feeding the VTR output to the PCM adaptor, since these normally lock to the incoming video on replay. This assumes that the VTR can lock to its video input. Some examples are shown in Figure 14.4.

14.5 Video sync of Sony PCM-1610 and 1630 recordings

Sony's PCM-1610 and 1630 systems can operate at a sampling rate of 44.056 kHz as well as the CD-mastering rate of 44.1 kHz, in order to allow for sync with NTSC pictures. If the PCM-1610 or 1630 is locked to NTSC video syncs, its sampling rate is 44.056 kHz, and it should be noted that it is therefore difficult to make a recording which both synchronises correctly with an NTSC video recording and is also suitable as a CD master. In such a situation, the recording would have to be made at 44.056 kHz and sample rate converted to 44.1 kHz for CD production. If a 44.056 kHz recording is replayed at 44.1 kHz, there will be a pitch-shift of 0.1% upwards.

If it proves necessary to synchronise an NTSC or 30 fps digital audio recording to a PAL video picture then it may be possible to stripe the timecode track of the digital audio VTR with EBU (25 fps) timecode from a timecode generator locked to a source of NTSC or 30 fps video syncs converted to 25 fps via a suitable 'gearbox', of which a few commercial examples exist. The reference for the timecode generator could be the composite sync output of the free-running PCM-1630 if it became necessary to post-stripe a pre-recorded audio tape with EBU timecode. Audio Kinetics, for example, manufactures a gearbox which can be used to derive sync pulses at any output rate from pulses at any input rate, to drive the company's synchronisers (which also generate timecode). Using this method, the timecode track of the digital audio VTR will not then drift in the long term, even though it is operating at a different frame rate, and a timecode synchroniser may be

(a)

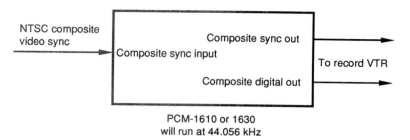

NTSC composite
video sync

Composite sync input

Composite sync out

Composite digital out

To record VTR

PCM-1610 or 1630
will run at 44.056 kHz

(b)

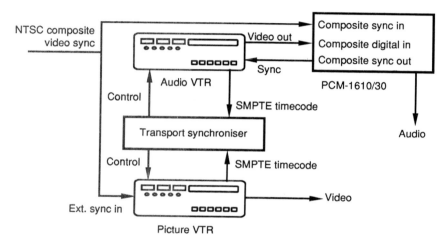

NTSC composite
video sync

Video out

Composite sync in

Composite digital in

Composite sync out

Audio VTR

Sync

PCM-1610/30

Control

SMPTE timecode

Audio

Transport synchroniser

Control

SMPTE timecode

Ext. sync in

Video

Picture VTR

(c)

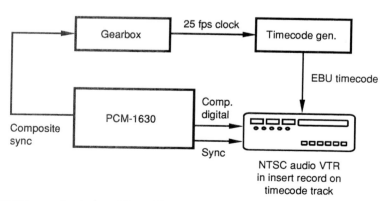

Gearbox

25 fps clock

Timecode gen.

EBU timecode

Composite
sync

PCM-1630

Comp.
digital

Sync

NTSC audio VTR
in insert record on
timecode track

Figure 14.5 Video synchronisation of Sony PCM-1610 or PCM-1630. (a) Locked to NTSC composite video for synchronous recording. (b) Locked to NTSC composite video for synchronised replay. (c) Post-striping a recording with EBU timecode, locked to PCM-1630 video reference.

(d)

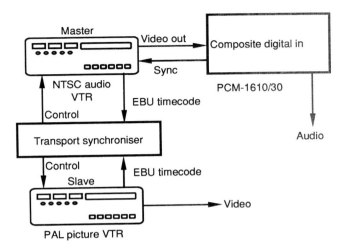

Figure 14.5 (d) PAL video replay locked to NTSC audio replay, using post-striped EBU timecode track on audio VTR (requires audio machine to be master)

(a)

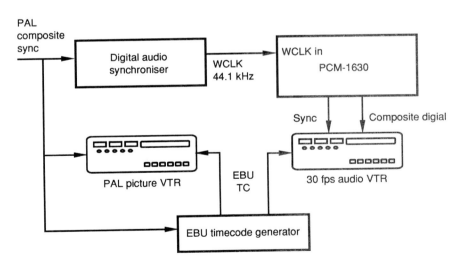

Figure 14.6 Use of DAR DASS-100 (or equivalent synchroniser) to derive 44.1 kHz WCLK from PAL video reference. (a) Recording situation

used to lock the video machine to the audio machine on replay, using the audio machine as master. Problems may arise if it is also necessary to lock the picture VTR to PAL composite sync, since this may be in conflict with the sync reference provided by the 1630 to the master machine. Some examples of synchronised operation are shown in Figure 14.5.

(b)

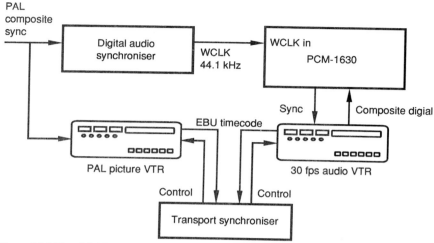

Figure 14.6 Use of DAR DASS-100 (or equivalent synchroniser) to derive 44.1 kHz WCLK from PAL video reference. (b) Replay situation

A solution to the above problem of mixed video standards may lie in the adoption of a suitable digital audio signal synchroniser and interface processor such as the DAR DASS-100, described in section 10.5, since this is a device which is capable of generating a digital audio reference signal such as word clock or AES/EBU, locked to video syncs of any standard. Using such a device, as shown in Figure 14.6, it would be possible to use the 1630 in a PAL environment, by referencing the PCM-1630's sampling rate to an external word clock, which itself had been derived from PAL video syncs. The same PAL video could lock a 25 fps EBU timecode generator which could stripe the timecode track of the NTSC audio VTR and the PAL picture VTR during recording. During replay, the transport synchroniser would lock the two VTRs using EBU timecode, and the 1630 and picture VTR would both be referenced to PAL syncs. This arrangement has the further benefit that it does not require the 1630 to be the master.

14.6 Video sync of JVC VP-900 recordings

The JVC VP-900 PCM adaptor operates similarly to the Sony PCM-1610, and also is switchable between 44.1 and 44.056 kHz. The timecode used is a unique JVC code recorded with the digital audio and called BP-code (bi-parity), which may be converted to SMPTE code using a separate timecode unit called the TC-900V. JVC developed a synchroniser for locking audio recordings made at 44.056 kHz using the NTSC video format to video recordings made in the PAL or SECAM formats, and this contained a digital audio buffer which adjusted the buffer delay to accommodate the difference between the internal system BP-code and the SMPTE/EBU timecode read from the video tape, thus maintaining sync between audio and video. A block diagram of synchronised operation using this device is shown in Figure 14.7.

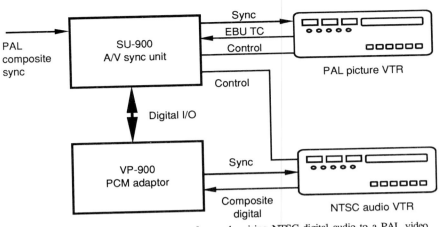

Figure 14.7 Block diagram of JVC system for synchronising NTSC digital audio to a PAL video recording

14.7 Video sync of other digital audio tape recorders

Dedicated digital audio recorders are not subject to the restrictions of PCM adaptors when concerned with video sync. Such dedicated recorders include DASH and PD open-reel formats, X-80 format, DAT, and the various in-house multitrack formats devised by Japanese companies (e.g.: Yamaha, Akai). Many of these recorders may be locked to a variety of sync sources including composite video, and may record timecode of any standard. IEC DAT machines and some open reel machines (e.g.: Sony PCM-3402) may be made to replay timecode of any standard, no matter what was recorded, owing to intelligent internal timecode reader/generators.

Machines which do not offer video sync as standard may have the option to install a video sync card which can lock to a range of video standards. The DABK-3000 board for the Sony PCM-3324 multitrack, for example, is able to lock to a wide range of sync pulses, including NTSC (monochrome and colour), PAL, and Film (24 fps), whilst the more recent PCM-3324A and PCM-3348 can lock to these references as standard features. Mitsubishi's X-850 and X-880 multitracks will lock to external video sync references as a standard feature. This also applies to Studer's D820X DASH machines. It is rare not to find a composite video sync input on modern digital audio equipment, since operation in conjunction with video systems is such a common occurrence these days.

It is most important to ensure that the correct relationship is set up between video frame rate and audio sampling rate, and most video synchronisation interfaces will have either DIP switches or a software set-up procedure for this purpose. The Fostex D-20 DAT machine, for example, has a number of switches on the rear panel for this purpose. Unless care is taken in selecting the correct video rate, the sampling rate which results may be wrong. Examples have occurred in the past of recordings being made on DASH-format machines locked to NTSC pictures at a sampling rate of 47.95 kHz as opposed to the 48 kHz intended, because the operator had left the video interface set to 30 fps instead of 29.97 for NTSC. The subsequent problems which may result from such mistakes can be very time consuming and expensive to rectify, since timecode, digital audio and video may drift with relation to each other.

14.8 Synchronous recording

Synchronous recording involves the recording of digital audio synchronously with an external reference, perhaps at the same time as timecode. It is not a concept which is common in analogue recording, although it is sometimes used when resolving an analogue audio machine to a pre-striped timecode track for recording synchronously with video. In synchronous recording, the timecode track should not drift with relation to the audio. In other words, a second in terms of timecode should be the same as a second in terms of audio samples. This requires that the timecode generator is locked to the same sync reference as the audio recorder. This could be achieved in a combined audio/video system using the technique of synchronous audio and video reference signals, as shown earlier in Figure 14.1. Alternatively, in a system not making use of a centrally distributed digital audio sync signal, the DATR and the timecode generator could both be locked to composite video, both operating in the external sync mode (see Figure 14.8).

Synchronous timecode and digital audio are important in editing systems and for video synchronisation, since many synchronisers and video editors initially lock transports using timecode for absolute positional location, thereafter releasing machines to their own external sync signal. If timecode was not synchronous there would be a loss of lock when switching from one sync reference to the other.

DATRs which have their own timecode generators ensure that the timecode recorded on to tape is synchronous with digital audio, even if the recording is made without reference to an external sync source.

14.9 Synchronous replay

Synchronous replay involves the replay of a digital recording synchronously with an external reference signal, such that the long-term speed stability of the replay machine is controlled by comparing the reference signal to the off-tape control track or digital audio word clock. If a recording is replayed without reference to external sync it will only be accurate in speed within the tolerance of its own internal sync reference, and this may result in drift in the long term with relation to other devices. In the short term this may not matter, but over an hour or more it may become noticeable with relation to a picture, in terms of loss of lip-sync.

Sync replay may involve the use of a timecode synchroniser, or video or audio

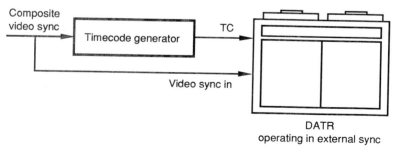

Figure 14.8 Video sync of dedicated digital audio tape recorder. Timecode generator and DATR are both locked to the same composite video reference

editor, to lock the two machines (whether audio and video or audio and audio) at the correct offset, but a sync reference signal should also be supplied to both machines. In the case of an audio–video pair, both could be supplied with composite video, or, alternatively, the video machine with composite video and the audio machine with an AES sync signal locked to the video reference. If two DATRs are to be operated in sync, such that they act as a locked pair (for 48 track recording using two 24 track machines, for example) it is vital that they are both locked to the same sample clock reference, and that the audio outputs are locked to sample accuracy. This is in order to achieve correct phase lock between the audio signals from the two machines. Often one machine of the pair will act as the master, and provide a sample clock signal to the other. Positional relationships are then maintained either using timecode or with reference to the control track on the tape.

If timecode is used to lock a DATR for more than the initial period of pre-roll, during which lock is established, it is possible that speed variations of the master timecode may be reflected in modulation of the digital audio signal on the slave, since a synchroniser will constantly attempt to adjust the slave speed to maintain a steady offset whilst the master wanders about, perhaps due to wow and flutter. For this reason, the technique of releasing slaves to external sync after initial timecode lock is preferable.

14.10 Conforming of digital audio recordings to video EDLs

Now that tape formats such as DAT are being used more in video work for the recording of both sync and non-sync material, it is necessary to consider how such recordings may be edited to conform with the edits made to the accompanying picture. The recording of separate sound has been used widely in film production, and is being used considerably in modern video production because of the high-quality sound available on DAT machines, which suits digital stereo television broadcasts well. DAT machines are also portable, being small and light, and studio machines are now appearing which allow the recording of timecode, as well as options for video sync. It will only be a short time before portable IEC timecode DAT machines with video sync are released. Video editing often involves many generations of copying (five to ten is not unusual), and, if this involves analogue copying of analogue VTR sound tracks, the final edited sound track often ends up in a sorry state. The use of separate sound editing allows for first-generation sound to be laid back to the edited video.

A number of the DAT machines on the market have such stable and accurate sampling rate and speed that they can be synchronised initially to a picture and then left to free-run over the length of a short programme without loss of lip-sync. Although this is fortuitous, it does not solve all the requirements of separate digital audio with video. What is required is a means of synchronising a DAT machine to timecode, locking it to video sync, and editing the separate audio tapes to match the picture. The Japanese company, Fostex, makers of the professional D-20 DAT machine, have produced a system which is a good example of this approach, and this will be outlined.

Audio recordings are made on a Fostex D-20 synchronously with the picture being recorded on a VTR, with the same timecode being recorded on each. The D-20 is locked to video sync during recording. The videotape is then edited in the normal way, and an EDL is produced on a disk representing the times at which edits had been made. Fostex provides software for its D-20 Edit Control System which is able to read EDLs in the CMX format (CMX is a well-known American manufacturer of video editors and its EDL format is something of a *de facto* standard). In this way, the DAT editing system is enabled to read the timecode locations at which video edits had been made, and can then automatically copy edit the original DAT audio which accompanied the picture to match the video edits. The user selects the reel of videotape whose edit commands are to be used from the CMX EDL. The edited DAT master can then be laid back to the edited video master using a synchroniser to lock the two machines.

Such an approach, with the appropriate software, could be used for other digital recording formats as well. It would also be possible to achieve similar results with tapeless systems, and examples exist of such systems which automatically copy first-generation audio from master videotapes during video editing, along with original timecode, making it possible subsequently to use these tracks as the basis for audio editing and post-production (sweetening). The sync audio plus any added effects and music can then be laid back to the edited videotape.

Chapter 15

Synchronous operation of disk-based systems

Much of the foregoing discussion of synchronisation applies as much to disk-based digital audio as it does to tape recording. Certainly all the points about signal synchronisation are still valid, since it is no less important that a disk-based digital recorder has a separate sync input, and can be made to lock to composite video, AES/EBU or WCLK. A major difference lies in the fact that disk recorders do not have a timecode track, because sound is simply stored in files which are made up of storage blocks on the disk (see section 3.7). This does not mean that such systems cannot be synchronised to timecode, because indeed they can.

15.1 Overview

Tapeless systems made for audio editing or video post-production have timecode inputs to allow timecode to be read at the same time as original audio is recorded on disk. Rather than being recorded, as it would be with a tape recorder, the timecode at which the file starts and ends is noted in the directory entry which accompanies each file (see Figure 15.1). This can then be displayed in the catalogue of files which reside on the disk, if required. Synchronous recording (see section 14.8) ensures that timecode and sample clock are locked, and in some systems a table is stored which allows timecode values to be referenced to the disk locations of a file, so that the correct relationship can be maintained between timecode and audio on replay. One

File name	TC start	TC finish
Car engine 1	03:53:12:19	03:53:19:02
Car engine 2	03:55:42:03	03:55:46:14
Door slam 1	01:29:00:01	01:29:02:17
Tyre squeal	19:01:25:23	19:01:29:05
etc...		

Figure 15.1 A typical cue list for a tapeless sound file directory, showing original timecode start and end points for each file

FACT FILE 30 An example of disk system synchronisation

External SMPTE/EBU timecode is converted, using a suitable 'gearbox ratio', to an internal system timecode, which will be called the 'sample address'. This sample address is a count of samples elapsed since midnight. Associated with any file held in the store will be the original sample address, that is the one which prevailed at the time of recording, either transferred with the samples over an AES/EBU interface, or derived from incoming SMPTE/EBU timecode. During replay of sound files, there will be a system sample address which increments steadily as replay time elapses, and there will necessarily be a third sample address which accounts for any offsets between the system address and the original sample addresses of files to be replayed; we will call this the offset sample address. Lastly, and not to be forgotten, is the *physical* address of each sound file in the store.

As shown in (a), files may be written to the store, along with a record of their starting and ending sample addresses (the original address). An index or look-up table is generated for each file which relates original sample addresses to physical block addresses in the store, and this is also stored. During synchronised replay (as shown in (b)) a system sample address will be derived which relates the appropriate frame rate to the appropriate sampling rate. From this are derived the various offset sample addresses which may be required to access different original sound files at various times, dictated by the replay schedule, to be routed to different outputs. In order for this to work correctly it will be important that a replay schedule has been determined, otherwise the system will not know which files are to be played at which times, and what offset sample addresses must be used.

Files with different sampling rates could be accommodated, provided that the gearbox ratio between timecode and sample address were modified accordingly. As far as the user is concerned, the direct handling of sample addresses will usually be unnecessary, and the system may convert these to SMPTE/EBU timecode format for display and keypad entry. There is one further twist in that more than one file may have the same original sample address (if two files were recorded on different days for example), and thus the *name* of the file will be important in determining which of them is to be replayed at a particular time.

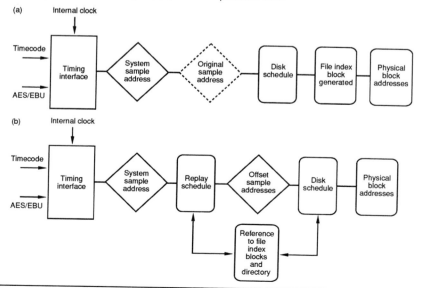

example of a method used for synchronisation of a disk-based system is shown in Fact File 30.

Most tapeless systems are self-synchronising: that is, they accept a timecode input on replay and will lock to it, plus or minus an offset compared with the system's internal timecode. This is often used for locking a tapeless system to a VTR for video post-production. There is a significant difference, though, between those systems which simply trigger the replay of selected sound files at certain timecode locations, and those which remain synchronised throughout the replay of the file. The former may be useful for the insertion of sound effects stored as disk files at pre-programmed instants, but it may not be adequate for the long-term synchronisation of a half-hour programme being dubbed against a picture. In the case of long-term lock to picture it is important that files have been recorded synchronously, and that replay is also synchronous, with reference being made regularly to timecode values from the VTR in order to detect any jumps or discontinuities. Furthermore, if the only link between the VTR and the tapeless recorder is the timecode from the VTR's timecode track, it is important that the tapeless recorder correctly 'chases' the VTR, starting when it starts and stopping when it stops. Some tapeless dubbing systems have a control interface to a VTR for the purpose of controlling the two systems with one set of transport commands.

(a)

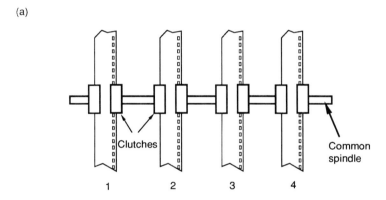

(b)

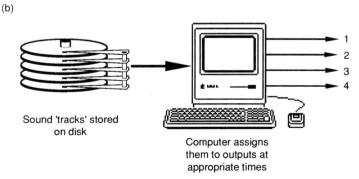

Figure 15.2 In film sound editing, as shown in (a), separate sound tracks are locked to a common spindle using clutches, and may be 'slipped' in time with relation to each other. In (b) the disk-based editor follows a similar approach, allowing sound tracks stored on disk to be assigned to any output at any time

15.2 Timecode-locked dubbing with tapeless systems

The tapeless system is an ideal basis for dubbing sound to picture because of its random access nature. No matter what timecode accompanied a file when it was recorded, it can be replayed at any other time, along with other files from different recording times. As discussed above, the tape recorder has a timecode track which runs alongside the audio tracks, and thus there is a physical relationship between the timecode track and a location along the tape. If a certain offset is established between a VTR and an ATR, then all the sounds recorded on the ATR will be bound to occur at fixed points with relation to the picture. If any sound is to be moved, it must be re-recorded elsewhere, so as to establish the correct offset.

Tapeless systems avoid this problem by allowing each file (each being an individual sound recording) its own offset, such that any sound may be placed virtually anywhere with relation to master timecode, under control of a computer. As shown in Figure 15.2, this is much more akin to the film-dubbing process where tracks may be slipped with relation to each other, but is even more flexible than this because sounds are not even restricted to a particular track in tapeless dubbing, provided that enough channel outputs are available (see section 3.11).

15.3 Synchronous recording of sound files

In order to enable the synchronous recording of sound files it is common for a system to present the user with a 'recording page' on the display, which will allow the selection of such things as the appropriate inputs to be used and the sampling rate, as well as allowing the naming of the file(s) to be recorded. Timecode should be connected to the tapeless recorder from the source device, together with a digital input from the source, and the tapeless system should be set to an external sync mode. Occasionally, if timecode is inserted into the incoming AES/EBU channel status data, it may be possible to carry both timecode and audio information over one AES/EBU link. If AES/EBU is not used for transfer then it may be necessary to use a separate synchronising signal to lock the tapeless recorder to the sampling rate of the source, unless the whole system is operating with reference to house sync anyway (see section 13.2).

During the recording of sound files it may be possible to label points within the file, such that important junctures may be located easily during subsequent editing, using their labels. By pressing a 'mark' or 'label' button at the relevant point, the user might be prompted to enter the name of the label, or the system might automatically number the labels sequentially so that a number of labels could be entered in quick succession without the need to type in titles. By recording and naming files of varying lengths, the user will build up a library or database of sound files which can subsequently be used in the editing process. These files might be the takes from a recording session, or extracts from a collection of sound effects to be used in picture dubbing, for example. Along with these will usually be stored a record of the original timecode values which prevailed during recording (see above). After initial recording it may be possible to 'top and tail' files so that unwanted sections are removed before final storage, and this can help in optimising the usage of storage space.

If the database of sound files is to be well organised, such that files of a similar type may be grouped together to aid subsequent location, it is desirable to be able

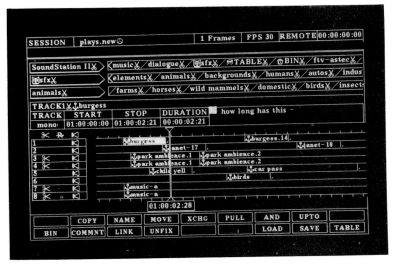

Figure 15.3 This touch-screen panel from the Digital Audio Research *SoundStation 2* shows clearly the 'virtual tape' with eight tracks just above the bottom of the display. Sound file segments are labelled for clarity. (Courtesy of DAR)

to build 'folders' or 'directories', within which may lie further nested sub-folders. In the collection of sound effects, for example, one could have folders for 'weather noises', 'animal noises' and 'people noises', and within the 'animal noises' folder could be kept 'dog', 'cat' and 'toad' noises, with further sub-grouping if necessary.

15.4 Synchronous replay and dubbing

In order to build up the montage of sounds which will accompany a picture, the user will place sound files in particular time locations, perhaps editing them at the same time in order to make them fit the scene in question. Some sound files will contain 'sync dialogue' and 'sync effects', and these will be sound material which was recorded at the same time as original picture material. In addition to this there will be 'wild' effects (non-synchronous with the original picture), ambience and music, all inserted at artistically appropriate times. Most of the time, sync dialogue and effects will need to remain fixed with relation to the picture, no matter what other material is edited into the same 'track' or channel in the dub, and most systems designed for this purpose allow the user to select whether or not sound files should be 'anchored' to a particular timecode location or whether they should slide up or down in time as material is inserted. The latter approach is more appropriate in music editing, as described in section 11.10.

The technique of displaying the programmed replay schedule (see section 5.14) graphically, as a piece of moving tape with a number of tracks, has been adopted widely. With this technique a virtual 'head' passes across a virtual 'tape' (or vice versa), the head representing 'now' (the current timecode location), with each track on the tape representing a different physical output or channel. The example shown in Figure 15.3 shows the display from the Digital Audio Research SoundStation II which illustrates a number of these points.

At the top of the display is a line showing the current session name ('plays.new') and various details of the timecode in use. Below this are three lines displaying 'directories', as described above, in which the file library is represented. In the upper directory are shown the main directories of 'music', 'dialogue' and 'sfx' (sound effects), and we can see that the 'sfx' directory is open in the directory below, listing 'elements', 'animals', 'backgrounds', 'humans', 'autos', etc., as further sub-directories of effects. Below this, we can see that the 'animals' sub-directory is open, showing further subdivisions of 'farms', 'horses', and so on.

Buttons at the bottom of the display may be pressed to set different modes, most of which are self-explanatory: for example, PULL will 'pull' a file from one of the directories at the top and allow it to be placed onto the virtual tape shown in the middle of the display, whereas BIN will dispose of a selection. The virtual tape has eight channels or 'tracks', and the loudspeaker symbols show that the channel is armed for playback (unmuted). On each of the eight tracks can be seen sections of sound files, named as required, all of which have anchors to show that they are anchored to their timecode locations and will not move, as described above. These are therefore 'sync' sounds. The arrowed line across the tape shows the 'replay head', and the current system timecode is shown in the box at the bottom of this line. The details of the highlighted file, 'burgess', are given in the area above the tape. Files, locations and buttons are selected or highlighted by touching the appropriate areas of the screen.

The process of editing and dubbing tends to be similar to the cut- or copy-and-paste techniques described in section 11.5, whereby the user can cut or copy items from one location and 'paste' them into another. This process can be extended as far as necessary, such that, for example, sections of audio may be cut from one track and pasted to another (so that they are routed to a different output), or moved from one timecode location to another, with the system internally keeping track of these movements and adjusting the replay schedule accordingly. It should be noted that

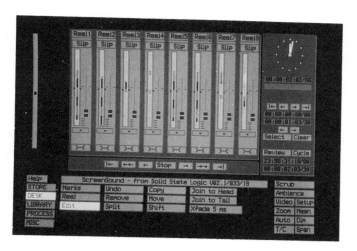

Figure 15.4 This display from SSL's *ScreenSound* shows how sound tracks may be represented 'film-style', in the form of vertical bars which correspond to reels of sound film. Each reel may be slipped and edited separately. (Courtesy of SSL)

it is perfectly feasible for edited sound files to be treated as entities in their own right, and that it is not necessary to copy the whole of a sound file from one location to another if that is not needed. A sound file from the library may be broken up into sections by the editing and compilation process, and these short sections may, in some systems, be placed back into the library as database entries in their own right. It may only be necessary for one copy of the sound file to reside in the store, even if parts of that file exist as other database entries, as long as the system can keep track of these subdivision and renaming processes, since the replay of the same file at a number of different times is a simple matter.

One commercial example of interest (SSL ScreenSound) is a product which displays each audio channel as a separate tape, or reel, which might appeal more to the film sound editor (see Figure 15.4). Each of these reels rolls past its replay head vertically, and the reels may be locked together or 'slipped' against each other so as to offset them in time. This is perhaps a more appropriate way of showing the concept of independent channels than to display the equivalent of a multitrack tape, as the multitrack tape implies some fixed relationship between the tracks.

Appendix 1

From analogue to digital and back

In the following appendix, an overview of the principles of A/D and D/A conversion will be given, showing how an analogue signal is converted into a digital signal and vice versa. It is not intended here to cover the subject of conversion in depth, but rather to provide an introduction to the topic which is appropriate to the level of this book.

A1.1 A/D conversion

A1.1.1 Sampling

An analogue audio signal is a time-continuous electrical waveform, and the analogue-to-digital convertor's task is to turn this into a time-discrete sequence of binary numbers. The process involved is shown in Figure A1.1. It will be seen that the continuous audio waveform is used to modulate a regular chain of pulses which are then quantised. The frequency of these pulses is known as the sampling frequency. Before modulation all these pulses have the same amplitude (height), but after modulation the height of the pulses is modified according to the instantaneous amplitude of the audio signal at that point in time. The process is known as pulse amplitude modulation (PAM). The frequency spectrum of the modulated signal is as shown in Figure A1.2. It will be seen that in addition to the 'baseband' audio signal (the original spectrum before sampling) there are now a number of additional spectra, each centred on multiples of the sampling frequency. Sidebands have been produced either side of the sampling frequency and its multiples, and these extend above and below the sampling frequency and its multiples to the extent of the base bandwidth. In other words these sidebands are pairs of mirror images of the audio band, reflected about the sampling frequency.

A1.1.2 Filtering and aliasing

It is necessary to filter the baseband audio signal before the PAM process, so as to remove any components having a frequency higher than half the sampling frequency (known as the Nyquist frequency), otherwise these components will be folded back into the baseband or 'aliased'. Looking at Figure A1.2 it may be appreciated that an extension of the baseband above the Nyquist frequency would result in the lower sideband of the first spectral repetition overlapping the upper end

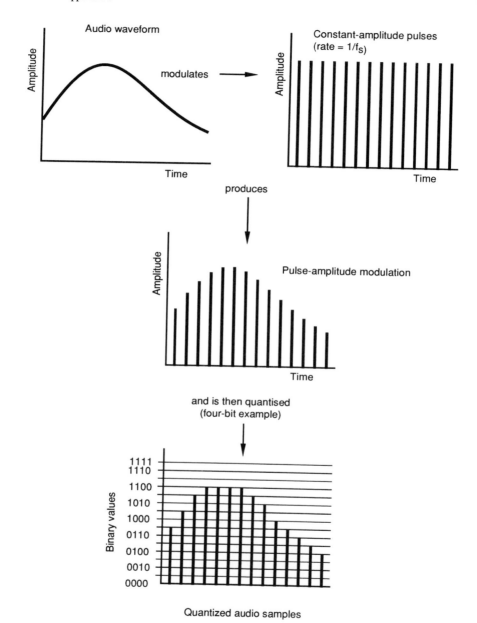

Figure A1.1 In analogue-to-digital conversion an analogue waveform is used to modulate a pulse train, resulting in pulse amplitude modulation. The modulated pulses are then assigned binary values according to their size (pulse code modulation). Positive sample values only are shown

of the baseband, since the first lower sideband is a mirror image of the baseband. Such a situation is shown in Figure A1.3. The audible effect of aliasing is that unwanted signal components are heard within the wanted signal. For example, if the

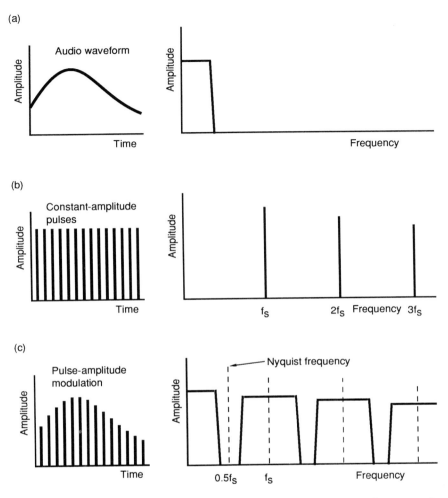

Figure A1.2 Spectra of signals at different stages in A/D conversion. (a) Baseband spectrum of analogue audio signal. (b) Spectrum of sampling pulses before modulation shows a fundamental at the sampling frequency plus harmonics at multiples of the sampling frequency. (c) Spectrum after modulation shows sidebands around multiples of the sampling frequency (audio baseband also shown)

sampling frequency were 40 kHz, making the Nyquist frequency 20 kHz, and a tone were introduced at 22 kHz into the baseband without being filtered out, an alias component would appear at 18 kHz in the reconstructed baseband.

In real systems, and because filters are not perfect, the sampling frequency chosen is slightly higher than twice the upper audio frequency to be represented, allowing for the filter to roll off more gently. The filters incorporated into convertors have a pronounced effect on sound quality, since they determine the linearity of the frequency response within the audio band, the slope with which it rolls off at high frequency, and the phase linearity of the system. In a non-oversampling convertor, the filter must reject all signals above half the sampling frequency with an

(a)

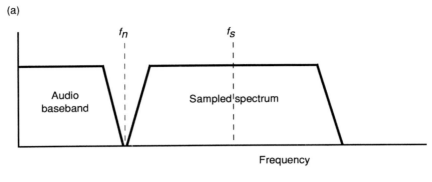

(b)

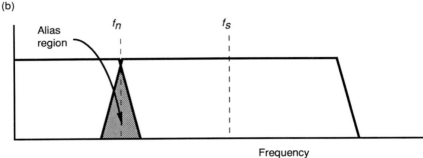

(c)

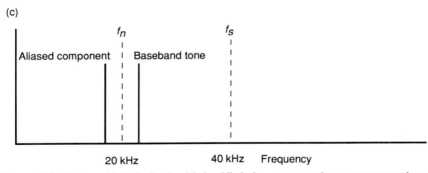

Figure A1.3 Aliasing. (a) Audio baseband is band-limited so as to contain no components above the Nyquist frequency, f_n. No aliasing results. (b) Audio baseband is allowed to contain components above f_n and thus the lower sideband of the first spectral repetition overlaps the upper end of the audio baseband. Aliasing results. (c) Example of aliasing. A baseband tone introduced above f_n results in an aliased component within the baseband

attenuation of at least 80 dB. Steep filters tend to have erratic phase response at high frequencies, and may exhibit 'ringing' due to the high 'Q' of the filter. Steep filters also have the added disadvantage that they are complicated to produce. Although filter effects are unavoidable to some extent, manufacturers such as Apogee have made considerable improvements to analogue anti-aliasing and reconstruction filters, and these may be retro-fitted to many existing systems with poor filters. A positive effect is normally noticed on sound quality.

The process of oversampling (see below) has helped to ease the problems of analogue filtering, since it shifts the first repetition of the baseband up to a much higher frequency, allowing the use of a shallower filter.

A1.1.3 The time domain

It is less easy to visualise the concepts of sampling, filtering and aliasing in the time domain. It requires acceptance of a certain amount of theory which is beyond the level of this book, but it is possible to explain the principles. At low frequencies it is relatively easy to see intuitively how a waveform may be represented by a string of pulses of varying amplitude (see Figure A1.4), but at high frequencies, where there may only be a few samples per cycle, it is not so straightforward. The information theorem, as put forward by either Shannon or Kotelnikov (depending on whether you are American or Russian), shows that it is necessary to have at least two samples per cycle of the waveform which you wish to reconstruct. If you have this, then any sine wave component up to half the sampling frequency may be reconstructed perfectly by integrating (low-pass filtering) the sequence of pulses of varying amplitude after D/A conversion, using a low-pass reconstruction filter which cuts off at the Nyquist frequency.

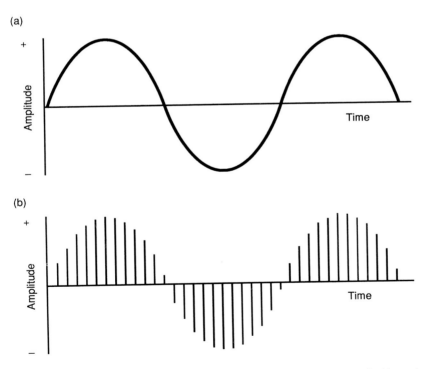

Figure A1.4 Intuitively it is easy to see how the shape of a waveform, as shown in (a), can be represented by samples, as shown in (b), whose rate is many times greater than the frequency of the analogue signal

(a)

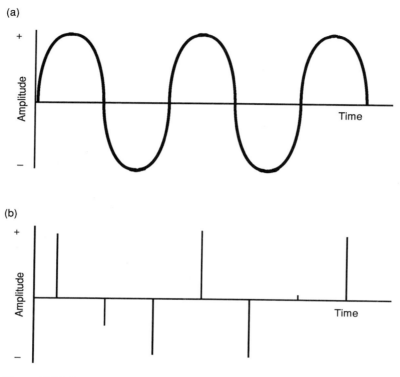

(b)

Figure A1.5 It is difficult to accept the validity of the sampling process when an analogue waveform, as shown in (a), is sampled just below the Nyquist frequency, as shown in (b), but there is still only one waveform which can result from these pulses which will pass through the reconstruction filter, and that is the sine wave shown

Figure A1.5 shows the situation with a sampled sine wave just below the Nyquist frequency, and it may be appreciated that there is only one baseband sine wave which can be drawn through the points shown which could have (a) passed through the original anti-aliasing filter, but more importantly (b) which can pass through the low-pass reconstruction filter after D/A conversion. It would be possible to draw a more unusual and jagged waveform through the points shown, but this waveform would have contained frequency components above the cut-off frequency of the reconstruction filter, and thus would not be reproduced. The result would still be a sine wave at the original frequency. The limiting situation, with a sine wave at the Nyquist frequency, is a 'red herring', always confuses people, and should not be dwelled upon, since worries may develop about what happens if there are only two samples per cycle, and when these samples occur at the zero-crossing points of the sine wave. The fact is that even in this condition there is only one acceptable sine wave that could be drawn through the points concerned, and that is a sine wave at the Nyquist frequency, although at this point the filter cut-off would have to be infinite. Many theorems, when investigated intuitively in the limiting condition, appear not to hold up, and one must resort to mathematics to be satisfied. The reader is referred to Shannon, C.E. (1948) A mathematical theory of communication. *Bell System Technical Journal* **27**, p 379, if he or she is interested in pursuing this further.

(a)

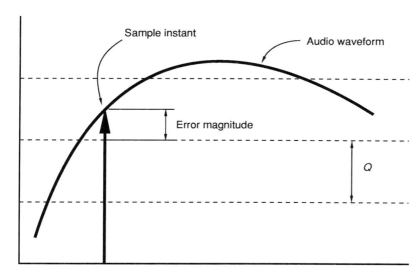

(b)

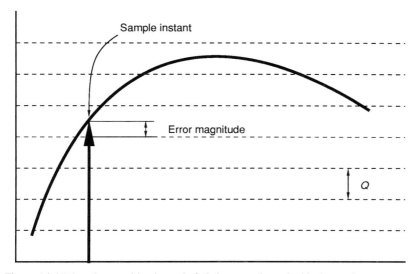

Figure A1.6 When the quantising interval, Q, is large, as shown in (a), the maximum error magnitude is greater than it would be if a greater number of quantising intervals were used to cover the same range, as shown in (b)

A1.1.4 Quantisation

After PAM, the modulated pulse chain is subjected to quantisation. Quantisation is the process of assigning binary values to the pulse amplitudes (samples). In a linear

16 bit system, 16 bit words are used to describe the amplitude of each sample, allowing for a possible 65 536 (2^{16}) discrete levels to be represented. Each step represents an equal increment of signal voltage. Clearly there may be an error involved in quantisation, since there are only a limited number of discrete levels available to represent the amplitude of the signal at any time. The error size will only ever be a maximum of plus or minus half the amplitude of the least significant bit (LSB), and a greater number of bits per sample will result in a smaller error (see Figure A1.6). This error, provided that the audio signal covers a number of quantising levels (is well above the threshold) and is a broadband 'random' signal, will manifest itself as white noise spread evenly across the bandwidth of the system (up to the Nyquist frequency). An intentional low-level noise source known as 'dither' is often used to 'force' the quantising noise to be random, no matter what the nature of the audio signal, since otherwise the effect of the error may be 'grainy', step-like and unpleasant on low-level signals.

A1.1.5 Use of dither

The use of dither in digital audio is now widely accepted as correct, since it has the effect of linearising a normal convertor (in other words it effectively makes each quantising interval the same size), and makes quantising distortion into a random, noise-like signal at all times. Dithering an audio signal in the analogue domain involves the addition of a low-level signal (having the amplitude of approximately one-third of a quantising interval), which may be white noise, or a waveform at half the sampling frequency, or a combination of the two, depending on the type of dither employed. A signal which has not been correctly dithered during the A/D conversion process cannot thereafter be dithered with the same effect, since the signal may have been irrevocably distorted by a non-linear conversion process.

Dither endows a digital signal with a quiescent noise floor close to the minimum theoretical limit of the system and may facilitate the reconstitution of audio signals below the theoretical limit (it has been shown to be possible to reconstitute audio signals which were up to 20 dB below the theoretical noise floor in systems using dither). Undithered audio signals begin to sound 'grainy' and distorted at low signal levels. In systems which allow dither to be switched off it may be that the apparent quiescent hiss will disappear, but this will have the side effect of increased distortion with low signal levels.

Dither is also used in digital processing devices such as mixers, but this time it is introduced in the digital domain as a random number sequence. In this context it is used to remove low-level distortion in signals whose gains have been altered, and to optimise the conversion from high resolution to lower resolution during post-production (see sections 10.4 and 10.5).

A1.2 Sampling parameters and signal limits

The sampling rate and the number of bits per sample both affect sound quality. They also affect the bandwidth required to store or transmit the signal (see section 3.1). Sampling rate is linked directly with frequency range, whilst number of bits per sample is linked with dynamic range or signal-to-noise ratio. The upper limit of frequency response of a system cannot be greater than half the nominal sampling rate, and the theoretical dynamic range of a linear PCM system is approximately

6 dB per bit. Thus a 16 bit system is theoretically capable of around 96 dB dynamic range. Unfortunately the situation in practice is nothing like so straightforward, since many systems are capable of reproducing signals below the theoretical limit due partly to modulation of the dither signal, and oversampling convertors with noise shaping exhibit noise characteristics which do not obey the laws of straightforward linear PCM. Additionally, many so-called 16 bit convertors do not have full 16 bit linearity, and thus the resulting noise floor may be higher than predicted in theory. Further, modulation of the signal caused by timing jitter (see section 13.3) will also worsen the dynamic range.

A1.3 Oversampling

Oversampling spreads the quantising-noise power spectrum over a wider range of frequencies, since in oversampled convertors the Nyquist frequency is above the upper limit of the audio band. This has the effect of reducing the in-band noise by around 3 dB per octave of oversampling (that is a system oversampling at twice the nominal rate of 48 kHz (96 kHz) would see the noise power within the audio band reduced by 3 dB). This is not the same as simply increasing the sampling frequency, which would not in itself reduce noise, since the process of decimation is used in oversampling to limit the bandwidth of the oversampled signal to the Nyquist frequency of the nominal sampling rate, and this is the process which results in the noise improvement. Noise shaping (see Fact File 31) offers a further improvement in audible quantising noise.

Oversampling convertors are really the key to improved sound quality on both the A/D and D/A sides of a system, since oversampling removes the need for steep analogue filters and offers better linearity in conversion, both of which have a beneficial effect on sound quality. Oversampling convertors are also more robust than non-oversampling types in the face of short-term timing errors (jitter), having a less tight requirement for clock stability. Most manufacturers of digital equipment have realised this, and modern products nearly all use oversampling convertors of one type or another. There is also a burgeoning market in third-party oversampling convertors which can be connected to digital equipment using the AES/EBU interface (which can carry 20–24 bits of audio data).

Although oversampling A/D convertors often quote very high sampling rates of up to 128 times the nominal rate of 48 kHz (corresponding to some 6 MHz), the actual rate at the digital output of the convertor is no more than the normal 48 kHz, since samples acquired at the high rate are often only converted to a few bits' resolution and then subjected to 'decimation'. Decimation involves reducing the sampling rate by dropping samples from the oversampled stream, followed by low-pass filtering of the signal in the digital domain to avoid the aliasing which would otherwise occur. Noise shaping is used prior to decimation, and this allows samples at the output of the decimator to be increased in length to perhaps 20 bits with a noise floor to match, since much of the original quantising noise has been shifted out of band before decimation.

The result of this process is a digital audio signal of perhaps 18 or 20 bit resolution with a nominal sampling rate of 48 or 44.1 kHz (or any other rate defined by the input word clock). The acquisition of samples at the initially high rate avoids the need for steep anti-aliasing filters; indeed many such convertors do not use analogue filters at all, preferring to eliminate alias products by digital filtering as part of the

FACT FILE 31 Noise shaping

Noise shaping is a means by which noise within the audio frequency range is reduced at the expense of increased noise above this range, using a process which 'shapes' the spectral energy of the quantisation noise, thus making it less audible. It is possible because of the high sampling rates used in

Noise power

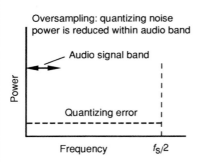

Non-oversampling: quantizing noise lies almost totally within audio band

Oversampling: quantizing noise power is reduced within audio band

oversampling convertors, since a high sampling rate extends the frequency range over which quantising noise is spread.

Quantising noise energy extends up to the Nyquist frequency, and if the audio signal only occupies a small part of this band then, for the same quantising error, the noise within the audio band will be lower than if the audio signal had extended up to the Nyquist frequency.

In A/D conversion, noise shaping involves the use of an integrator (low-pass filter) before the convertor, and a negative feedback loop, as shown below. The result is that the quantising noise (introduced after the integrator) is given a rising frequency response at the input to the decimator, whilst the input signal is passed with a flat response. There are clear parallels between such a circuit and analogue negative-feedback circuits.

Without noise shaping, the energy

Noise shaping

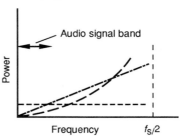

Quantizing noise power
- - - - - no noise shaping
—·—·— with 1st order filter
— — — with 2nd order filter

spectrum of quantising noise is flat up to the Nyquist frequency, but with first-order shaping this energy spectrum is made non-flat. With second-order shaping the in-band gains are such that the in-band noise is well below that achieved without noise shaping.

Noise-shaping ADC

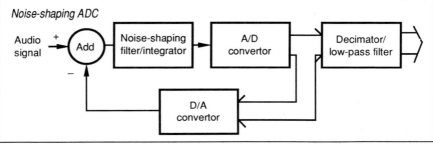

decimation process. The process is shown diagrammatically in Figure A1.7.

Oversampling A/D convertors which offer 20 bit output resolution are often switchable to 18 or 16 bit resolution also, the truncation being performed intelligently within the convertor in order to preserve the maximum accuracy at the chosen resolution. Because of this, a noticeable improvement in sound quality is often achieved by using such a convertor in place of the fitted convertors in a 16 bit system, since the 16 bit accuracy of a 20 bit convertor tends to be better than the 16 bit accuracy of a 16 bit convertor.

In the case of D/A oversampling convertors, similarly high sampling rates are used, but in this case the additional samples required for conversion at the higher rate are produced by digital sample rate conversion of the data coming from the tape, CD or other digital source (see Fact File 24). Samples are acquired from the digital source at the nominal rate (say 48 or 44.1 kHz) and converted to a mathematically accurate stream of samples at the oversampled rate. These samples are then converted back to analogue at the higher rate, again avoiding the need for steep filters, often with further noise shaping to move quantising noise to areas of the spectrum where it is not subjectively annoying. This process is shown diagrammatically in Figure A1.8.

Oversampling D/A convertors used in hi-fi systems often claim 18 bit performance, but this claim should be regarded warily when such convertors are used with a 16 bit medium such as the CD. As stated earlier, it is not possible to extract from a signal information (or sound quality) which was never there in the first place,

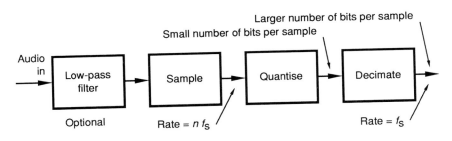

Figure A1.7 In an oversampling A/D convertor samples are first taken at many times the nominal sampling rate of the system, often only to a low quantising resolution. The decimation process reduces the sampling rate to the nominal rate at the same time as introducing digital low-pass filtering to increase sample resolution

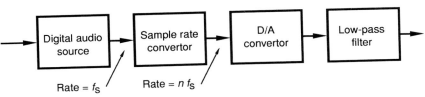

Figure A1.8 In an oversampling D/A convertor samples taken from the digital source at the nominal rate are sample rate converted to a high sampling rate. Samples are then converted to the analogue domain at this high rate, sometimes using a lower resolution and noise shaping to distribute the quantising noise so that it lies outside the audio band. The high sampling rate allows the use of a shallow low-pass filter with fewer audible artefacts

although it is possible to reduce the subjective effects of quantising noise by noise shaping. One problem with so-called 'minimally audible noise shaping' is that it may make noise audibly less annoying at the expense of a poorer *measured* noise performance, and work is in progress to achieve both good subjective *and* measured results. It may be that a new noise-weighting curve is required for digital audio purposes.

A1.4 D/A conversion

The D/A conversion process is shown in Figure A1.9. Audio sample words are converted back into a staircase-like chain of electrical levels corresponding to the sample values. This is achieved in simple convertors by using the states of bits to turn current sources on or off, making up the required pulse amplitude by the combination of outputs of each of these sources. This staircase is then 're-sampled' to reduce the width of the pulses before they are passed through a low-pass reconstruction filter, whose cut-off frequency is half the sampling frequency. Without this re-sampling the averaging effect of the filter would result in a reduction in the amplitude of high-frequency audio signals (due to the so-called 'aperture effect'), and this effect may be reduced by limiting the width of the pulses to perhaps one-eighth of the sample period. Equalisation is required to correct for aperture effect.

A1.5 Binary data

Numbers are represented in a digital audio system using binary form. Each digit of a binary number represents a power of two, just as each digit of a decimal number represents a power of ten (see Figure A1.10). The advantage of binary representation is that each digit of a number may be represented by a simple true or false state, such as the presence or lack of a voltage on a wire. Data is handled in groups of binary digits, called bytes. A byte is eight binary digits, and it is still a very common division of a data string, although many systems will work with data words of 16 and 32 bits. A form of shorthand called 'hexadecimal' is often used when discussing binary numbers, and this uses the numbers 0–9 and the letters A–F to represent binary numbers in the base 16. It follows that for each combination of 4 bits ($2^4 =$ 16) there is a hexadecimal character, as shown in Table A1.1.

A1.6 Two's complement

The output of a quantiser is a parallel binary word with certain bits set high and low, depending on the amplitude of the sample. A number system known as 'two's complement' is often used to represent audio signals, since it allows for the representation of negative numbers. An AC audio signal consists of both positive- and negative-going phases (see Figure A1.11), and this is represented digitally by using the most significant bit (MSB) of the sample to represent the sign. A one in this position represents a negative number and a zero represents a positive number. Thus, in the 16 bit example shown in Figure A1.11, the positive range goes from 0000000000000000 to 0111111111111111 (hexadecimal 0000 to 7FFF), and the

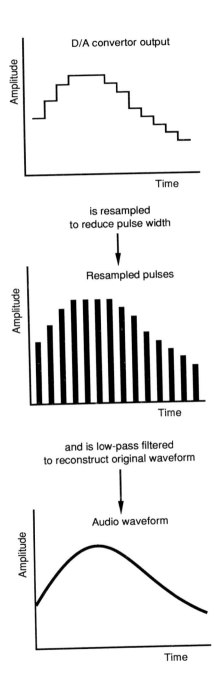

Figure A1.9 After D/A conversion, the staircase waveform is resampled to produce a train of finite-width pulses. These are then low-pass filtered to reconstruct the original audio waveform

Table A1.1 Binary-to-hexadecimal conversion

Binary	Hexadecimal	Decimal
0000	0	0
0001	1	1
0010	2	2
0011	3	3
0100	4	4
0101	5	5
0110	6	6
0111	7	7
1000	8	8
1001	9	9
1010	A	10
1011	B	11
1100	C	12
1101	D	13
1110	E	14
1111	F	15

Binary	1	0	1	0	0	0	1	0
Power of 2	2^7	2^6	2^5	2^4	2^3	2^2	2^1	2^0
Decimal	128	64	32	16	8	4	2	1

N.B: The binary word above represents a decimal value of:
128 + 0 + 32 + 0 + 0 + 0 + 2 + 0 = 162

Figure A1.10 Binary digits (bits) represent powers of two. The least significant bit (LSB) represents 2^0, or decimal 1, whilst the most significant bit (MSB) in this example represents 2^7, or decimal 128

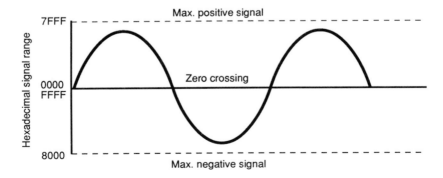

Figure A1.11 Two's complement binary numbering allows for negative values to be represented. In the 16 bit example shown, positive values range from hexadecimal (&) 0000 to &7FFF, whilst negative values range from &FFFF to &8000. Binary values change from all zeros to all ones at the zero-crossing point

negative range goes from 1111111111111111 to 1000000000000000 (hexadecimal FFFF to 8000). It will be seen that the bits all change from zeros to ones as the signal crosses the centre-line (zero volts in analogue terms). The advantage of two's complement numbering is that mathematical operations may be performed on the samples, adding positive and negative numbers together for example, and the result will still be correct.

Troubleshooting guide

The following guide may help in locating the source of difficulties encountered when operating digital recording systems, and is grouped under headings relating to the type of problem. This is a guide to initial trouble-shooting, and is no substitute for proper and regular maintenance. Many of the problems referred to below could be classed as 'finger-trouble'. Many aspects are referred to further in relevant sections of the main chapters of the book.

1. No signal from recorder's analogue or digital output when monitoring E–E (straight through) or recording

- Check that machine is turned on. Many will not link input to output without power.
- If device is a PCM adaptor check that a video link exists between Video In and Video Out.
- Check that record muting is turned off.
- Check that input gain is turned up.
- Some machines need to be in a record–pause mode before giving an output in E–E mode.
- Check that correct input is selected (analogue or digital). Check that machine is not in a dub or copy mode, unless copying from another digital machine.
- Check for implementation of SCMS in DAT machines if copying from a digital input.

2. No signal from output whilst replaying

- Check error lights to see if excessive error rate exists. If so refer to (3) below.
- Check meters to see if signal is showing here. If it is, check output gain and subsequent signal chain.
- Recording may be badly out of alignment. Try replaying it on the machine it was made on and copying it.
- Check that tracking is adjusted correctly on video recorders used with PCM adaptors.
- Check that monitoring is switched to replay on machines with confidence replay.

3. High error rates (see also Chapter 9)

- Clean heads or use cleaning tape.
- Check tracking on VTRs with PCM adaptors.
- Could be the result of poor tape quality, or a poorly aligned recording.
- Check for excessive humidity or static.
- Could be the result of worn heads.
- Check transport and/or electronics alignment.

4. Digital interfaces not communicating (see also Fact File 15)

- Sampling rates different on transmitter and receiver.
- Receiver not locked to transmitter sampling rate.
- Copy protection flag set.
- SCMS flag set in DAT system.
- Machines locked to different sync references.
- Cabling faulty, mismatched or too long.
- Poor signal quality. Check eye height and jitter.
- Incompatibility in channel status, user or validity data (IEC interfaces).
- Consumer data not accepted by professional device.

5. Noises and distortion

- Dither not turned on or set to wrong resolution (low-level distortion if not turned on, too much noise if set for lower resolution than system).
- Tracking error on VTR resulting in break-up of sound and high error rate.
- High error rate resulting from other factors (see above).
- Recording made at low level, resulting in noise/distortion. Cannot be corrected.
- Recording peaking over peak level resulting in clipping. Cannot be corrected.
- Possibly you are monitoring the analogue cue tracks as opposed to the digital tracks.
- Sync slippage (regular clicks at low level). Check all machines locked to same sync reference.
- Errors on digital input (clicks, spits, break-up). Check quality of interface signal.
- Fault in convertor.
- DC offset in convertor (check alignment).
- Recording copied from high-resolution system to lower-resolution system without optimal level correction or re-dithering.

6. Sync problems (see also Chapters 13–15)

- 'Sync' or 'locked' indicator flashing or out normally means that no sync reference exists or that it is different from that of the signal at the digital input. Check that sync reference and input are at correct rate and locked to the same source. Decide on whether to use internal or external sync reference, depending on application.
- If problems with 'good lock' or drifting offset arise when locking to other machines or when editing, check that timecode is synchronous with video and sampling rate. If not, tape must be re-striped with timecode locked to the same reference as the recorder.

7. Poor frequency response

- Machine is resorting to interpolation, which signifies a high error rate (see above).
- Check that you are monitoring the digital tracks and not the analogue cue tracks.

Glossary

A/D convertor Analogue-to-digital convertor – a device which converts an **analogue** audio waveform into a digital pulse-code-modulated (**PCM**) signal.

A/V Audio-to-video

Access time The time taken to access a requested block of data held on a mass storage device. In a disk drive it is the combination of **seek time** and **rotational latency**. Access time is usually quoted as an average, or with stated criteria, as it may vary.

Address A binary number describing the location of a piece of **data** held in a storage device.

AES Audio Engineering Society.

AES/EBU interface A digital audio interface carrying two channels of audio plus auxiliary information over a single balanced line.

Aliasing The effect which results in digital audio systems when spectral products from the sampled domain appear within the audio **baseband**. This will occur if baseband components are allowed to exceed the **Nyquist frequency**. An anti-aliasing filter is normally incorporated before the input to an A-to-D convertor to prevent components higher than the Nyquist frequency entering the system.

Analogue Used to denote a signal represented by a continuously-varying waveform, either acoustic, electrical, optical or magnetic.

ANSI American National Standards Institute.

Baseband The spectrum of a signal prior to **modulation**.

Binary A means of representing information in two-state form, e.g.: by means of on/off, true/false, or high/low states.

Bit One **binary** digit.

Block The smallest addressable unit of data in a mass storage device, often 512 or 1024 bytes. Alternatively, may be used to denote a group of samples within which an **interleave** pattern is complete.

Buffer A block of memory which provides for the smoothing of timing discontinuities in an erratic data stream.

Byte A digital word made up of eight **bits**.

CAV Constant angular velocity — referring to a disk drive which rotates at a constant speed. (**Winchester**, most **WORM** and **M-O** drives use CAV recording.)

CD Compact Disc.

CD-E Erasable CD.

CD-I   Interactive CD.

CD-R   Recordable CD.

Channel code   A **modulation** method used in digital communications to provide data with suitable characteristics for recording or transmitting (e.g. MFM, Miller)

CLV   Constant linear velocity — referring to a disk drive whose rotational speed varies in order to maintain a constant linear velocity of the head in relation to the disk track, depending on the position of the head. (Compact Disc uses CLV recording.)

Codec   A coder and decoder pair.

Coefficient   A **binary** value used in the mathematical manipulation of **data**, acting as a multiplier.

Compansion   Compression followed by expansion.

Composite digital   A digital audio signal **modulated** so as to appear like a video signal, in order that it may be recorded on a **VTR**.

Contiguous   A term meaning either 'adjacent' or 'adjoining'.

CPU   Central processing unit — a microprocessor device which executes pre-programmed commands and performs mathematical operations on data, in order to control the functionality of a larger computer system.

CRC   Cyclic redundancy check — used to detect errors in digital audio replay.

Crossfade   A crossfade is initiated between two pieces of audio material when they are joined together, to give a smooth transition, and is performed by fading one signal down whilst fading the other up, mixing the two resulting signals together.

Cylinder   Used to describe all the tracks which reside vertically above each other in a **Winchester** drive.

D/A convertor   Digital-to-analogue convertor - a device which converts a digital **PCM** signal into an **analogue** audio waveform.

DATR   Digital audio tape recorder.

DASH   Digital audio stationary head — a tape recording format.

Data   A sequence of **binary** information, usually divided into **bytes**.

Digital   Information represented in **binary** numerical form, e.g. an audio waveform.

DMA   Direct memory access — a means of transferring **data** quickly to and from **RAM** without involving the **CPU**.

DQPSK   Differential quadrature phase-shift keying — modulation method used in **NICAM** 728.

DSIS   Dual-channel sound-in-syncs.

DSP   Digital signal processing - a process involving high-speed mathematical operations on data in order to simulate, in audio terms, functions such as equalisation (EQ), compression, and cross-fading.

EBU   European Broadcasting Union.

EDL   Edit decision list — a stored list of commands which indicate which recordings/takes/sound files are to be played at what timecode point, and where they are to be edited together.

EIAJ   Electronic Industries Association of Japan.

Fragmentation   The intentional or forced subdivision of data into remote blocks on a storage medium such as a disk.

Frame   A definable block or group of blocks of data which is repeated at a regular rate.

HF   High frequency.

IEC   International Electrotechnical Commission.

IF   Interface

IMD   Intermodulation distortion.

Interleaving   The process by which the original order of samples or blocks is re-arranged according to a rule, either for error-correction purposes or for efficiency in a disk drive.

Jitter   Small, fast timing variations in an analogue or digital signal. Jitter may cause the blurring of clock or data bit edges, such that it becomes difficult to tell at what precise time the edge occurred.

kbyte   Kilobyte — equals 1024 **bytes**. A unit measurement of **data**.

LF   Low frequency.

M-O   Magneto-optical.

MADI   The multi-channel audio digital interface — a serial interface carrying up to 56 channels of audio over a single coaxial cable or optic fibre.

Mbyte   Megabyte — equals 1024 **kilobytes**. A unit measurement of **data**.

MIDI   The musical instrument digital interface — a serial interface carrying control data between musical devices (and some audio equipment).

Modulation   A process by which **baseband** signals are used to modify one or more characteristics of another signal (called the carrier), in order that they may be transmitted or recorded, for example. Sampling is a modulation process, because here an audio signal is used to vary the amplitude of a carrier which consists of a train of pulses (see **PAM**).

NICAM   Near-instantaneously-companded audio multiplex.

NTSC   National Television Standards Committee; used in reference to the 525-line, 59.97 Hz colour TV transmission standard in the US, Japan and elsewhere.

Nyquist frequency   A term used to mean 'half the sampling frequency' in a digital system. The Nyquist frequency is that frequency above which no **baseband** components must be allowed, otherwise **aliasing** will occur.

Oversampling   A means of raising the **sampling rate** in a digital system, so as to improve audio quality.

PAL   Phase alternate lines; used in reference to the 625-line, 50 Hz TV standard in Europe and elsewhere.

PAM   Pulse amplitude modulation — a **modulation** process in which a series of pulses of finite width are amplitude-modulated by an **analogue** signal (sometimes called sampling).

PCM   Pulse code modulation — a means of coding an **analogue** waveform by sampling it and representing the amplitude of the sample pulse by a **binary** word of fixed length (eg: sixteen bits).

PD   ProDigi — a tape recording format.

Post-production   The process of editing, mixing and further treatment of original material in order to produce a finished entity.

PQ   Two of the subcode channels in the **CD** format

Quantisation   The process of assigning **binary** values to **PAM** samples in **PCM** systems. The quantisation accuracy depends on the number of **bits** in the binary word. A greater number of bits allows for more accuracy and less **quantising error**.

Quantising error   The error which results when a **PAM** pulse of a certain height is represented by a particular **binary** value in **PCM**. As there are only a limited number of binary values, it is likely that there will be an error between the original level of a sample and its quantised level.

R-DAT   Rotary-head digital audio tape.

RAM   Random access memory — a form of solid state memory which has fast access time and can be used for the temporary storage of **data**.

RAR   Read after read — a system of double replay error protection.

Reconstruction filter   **Analogue** low-pass filter which serves to reconstruct an analogue waveform from **PAM** pulses at the output of a digital-to-analogue convertor. Its cut-off should be complete at the **Nyquist frequency**.

Rotational latency   The amount of time taken for a disk to rotate until a requested **block** arrives under the head.

Sample   A single **PCM** word or **PAM** pulse which represents the amplitude of an audio waveform at a particular point in time.

Sampling rate   The rate at which **PAM** pulses are generated in a convertor: i.e. the number of audio samples taken per second. Typical sampling rates in professional audio are 32, 44.1 and 48 kHz.

Sampling   See **PAM**.

SCMS   The serial copy management system; used to prevent multiple digital copying in DAT machines.

SCSI   Small computer systems interface — a standard interface for the connection of mass storage devices and other equipment to computers.

SDIF   The Sony digital interface — a serial interface carrying one channel of digital audio **data** plus auxiliary information.

Sector   Used to describe all the blocks which reside physically above each other in a **Winchester** drive.

Seek time   The time taken for a head to traverse the surface of a disk in order to arrive at the correct track for the **block** of **data** it requires.

Sideband   A spectral component resulting from the **modulation** process.

SIS   Sound in syncs

SMPTE/EBU timecode   A **digital** code representing time in hours, minutes, seconds, frames format, which may be recorded on tape and used to measure the passage of recorded time. Used widely as a synchronisation reference in audio and video operations.

SPDIF   The Sony/Philips digital interface — a serial interface carrying two channels of digital audio plus auxiliary information.

SPG   Sync pulse generator.

Take   A section of audio from a recording session which is to form part of a finished master, e.g. 'Take 32' — 2nd movement, bars 33–125.

TC   Timecode

TDM   Time division multiplex

Track   Used to describe the concentric rings of blocks containing data in a **Winchester drive**. Also used to describe one channel of audio on a multitrack tape.

Transfer rate   The rate at which **data** may be transferred from a storage device once the data has been accessed. This will be measured in kilo or mega bits or bytes per second. There is a difference between the instantaneous transfer rate, which is the maximum intermittent 'burst' rate, and the sustained rate, which is that which can be sustained over a longer period.

Varispeed   The action of slowing down or speeding up a tape machine so that the pitch and speed of audio changes.

VTR   Video tape recorder.

Winchester drive   A sealed magnetic disk drive containing fixed rigid disks rotating together on a common spindle, each disk surface having its own read/write head.

WORM   Write Once Read Many — the term used in reference to mass storage media which may be written-to once, but not erased thereafter.

Bibliography

Abbott, C. (1984) Efficient editing of digital sound on disk. *Journal of the Audio Engineering Society*, **32.6**, June, pp 394–402.

AES (1985) AES recommended practice for digital audio engineering - serial transmission format for linearly-represented digital audio data. *Journal of the Audio Engineering Society*, **33**, pp 975–984.

AES (1990) AES10-19XX, AES recommended practice for a serial multichannel audio digital interface (MADI) (draft).

AES (1990) AES17-19XX, AES standard method for measurement of digital audio equipment (draft).

AES (1990) AES11-19XX, AES recommended practice for synchronisation of digital audio equipment in studio operations (draft).

Borish, J., *et al* (1985) SoundDroid: a new approach to digital editing and mixing of sound. *BKSTS Journal*, November, pp 616–621.

Bush, D. (1989) Recording timecode in the DAT subcode. Presented at the *Digital Information Exchange* (London, 1989).

Cabot, R. (1989) Measuring AES/EBU interfaces. In *Proceedings of the AES/EBU Interface Conference* (London, 1989), Audio Engineering Society.

Caine, R. (1989) Routing digital audio. *Broadcast Systems Engineering*, October.

Cellier, C. (1990) The Nagra-D digital audio recorder. *International Broadcast Engineer*, May.

Croft, S. (1990) Nagra's digital dream. *Broadcast Systems Engineering*, September.

Davidson, G. *et al* (1990) Low-complexity transform coder for satellite link applications. Presented at the *89th AES Convention* (Los Angeles, 1990), preprint no. 2966 (F-I-6), Audio Engineering Society.

Davies, G. (1989) Television and SIS. In *Proceedings of the AES/EBU Interface Conference* (London, 1989), Audio Engineering Society.

Doi, T. (1981) Channel codings for digital audio recordings. Presented at the *70th AES Convention* (New York, 1981), Audio Engineering Society.

Doi, T. (1982) A design of professional digital audio recorder. Presented at the *71st AES Convention* (Montreux, 1982), preprint no. 1885 (G-2), Audio Engineering Society.

Duggan, R. (1989) Digital audio metering. *Studio Sound*, December.

Evans, P. (1989) AES signals within a broadcast centre. In *Proceedings of the AES/EBU Interface Conference* (London, 1989), Audio Engineering Society.

Evans, P. (1990) Digital audio in the broadcast centre. *EBU Review – Technical*, No 241/242, June–Aug.

Faulkner, T. (1983) Inside the PCM-F1. *Studio Sound*, March.

Fourré, R. *et al* (1990) 20-bit evolution. *Studio Sound*, May.

Fox, B. (1990) Business column (re: Philips DCC). Studio Sound, *December*.

Gaskell, P. S. (1985) A hybrid approach to the variable-speed replay of digital audio. Presented at the *77th AES Convention* (Hamburg, 1985), preprint no. 2202 (B-1), Audio Engineering Society.

Gerzon, M. (1990) The gentle art of digital squashing. *Studio Sound*, May.

Hampshire, N. (1989) Mass media. *Personal Computer World*, April, pp 160–164.

Harding, W.B. (1984) Audio coding methods to extend the DBS sound coverage. In *Proceedings of the International Broadcast Convention* (Brighton, 1984), pp 185–187, Institute of Electrical Engineers, London.

Hauser, M.W. (1990) Overview of oversampling A/D conversion. Presented at the *89th AES Convention* (Los Angeles, 1990), preprint no. 2973 (G-1), Audio Engineering Society.

Hawksford, M.O.J. and Wingerter, W. (1990) Oversampling filter design in noise-shaping digital-to-analog conversion. *Journal of the Audio Engineering Society* **38.11**, pp 845–856, November.

Ingebretsen, R. B. and Stockham, T. G. (1984) Random access editing of digital audio. *Journal of the Audio Engineering Society*, **32.3**, September, pp 114–121.

Ishida, Y. *et al* (1985) On the signal format for the improved professional use 2-channel digital audio recorder. Presented at the *79th AES Convention* (New York, 1985), preprint no. 2270 (A-4), Audio Engineering Society.

Kogure, T. *et al* (1983) The DASH format: an overview. Presented at the *74th AES Convention* (New York, 1983), preprint no. 2038 (A-9), Audio Engineering Society.

Lagadec, R. (1990) New frontiers in digital audio. Presented at the *89th AES Convention* (Los Angeles, 1990), preprint no. 3002 (K-2), Audio Engineering Society.

McLeod, J. (1988) Optical storage may fulfill its promise – after years of trying. *Electronics*, May 12, pp 75–77.

McLeod, J. (1988) Wringing Winchester speed from erasable optical disks. *Electronics*, May 12, pp 85–87.

McNally, G. W. (1984) Variable-speed replay of digital audio with constant output sampling rate. Presented at the *76th AES Convention* (New York 1984), preprint no. 2137 (A-9). Audio Engineering Society.

McNally, G. W. (1985) Fast edit-point location and cueing in disc-based digital audio systems. Presented at the *78th AES Convention* (Anaheim 1985), preprint no. 2232 (D-10), Audio Engineering Society.

McNally, G. W. (1986) Variable-speed operations for digital audio. In *Proceedings of the International Broadcast Convention*, (Brighton, 1986), pp 131–135, Institute of Electrical Engineers, London.

McNally, G. W. and Gaskell, P. S. (1984) Editing digital audio. BBC Research Department report.

McNally, G.W., Gaskell, P.S. and Stirling, A. J. (1985) Digital audio editing. Presented at the *77th AES Convention* (Hamburg, 1985), preprint, Audio Engineering Society.

Mee, C. D. and Daniel, E. D. (1988) *Magnetic Recording, Volume 2: Computer Data Storage*. McGraw-Hill.

Moorer, J.A. (1990) Hard disk recording and editing of digital audio. Presented at the *89th AES Convention* (Los Angeles, 1990), preprint no. 3006 (K-6), Audio Engineering Society.

Mornington-West, A. (1989) Signal analysis. In *Proceedings of the AES/EBU Interface Conference* (London, 1989), Audio Engineering Society.

Pohlmann, K. (1985) CD pre-mastering. *MIX*, **10.7**.

Pohlmann, K. (1985) *Principles of Digital Audio*. Howard W. Sams and Co.

Pohlmann, K. (1989) The Compact Disc. Oxford University Press.

Rumsey, F. J. (1988) Direct access recording – a survey of the state of the art. In *Proceedings of the Institute of Acoustics*, **10.7**, Institute of Acoustics.

Rumsey, F.J. (1989) *Stereo Sound for Television*. Focal Press.

Rumsey, F.J. (1989) The apt-X 100 digital audio compression system. *International Broadcast Engineer*, November.

Rumsey, F.J. (1990) *MIDI Systems and Control*. Focal Press.

Rumsey, F.J. (1990) *Tapeless Sound Recording*. Focal Press.

Sakamoto, N. *et al* (1984) On high-density recording of the compact-cassette digital recorder. *Journal of the Audio Engineering Society*, **32.9**, September.

Shelton, T. (1989) Synchronisation of digital audio. In *Proceedings of the AES/EBU Interface Conference* (London, 1989), Audio Engineering Society.

Smyth, S.M. (1989) Digital audio compression – a practical solution. Presented at the *National Association of Broadcasters Convention* (Las Vegas, 1989).

Sony/Philips (1983) Specification of the 3/4-inch cassette-type CD master tape, DAG 320-83 12 23.

Stevens, R. and Croney, B. (1990) The 'Temple' project at Thames TV, part two, digital audio. *Broadcast Hardware International*, September.

Sypha Consultants (1989) *The Tapeless Directory*. Sypha, 216a Gipsy Rd, London SE27 9RB.

Tanaka, K. (1986) The PD format. *Studio Sound*, November.

Vanderkooy, J. and Lipshitz, S. (1984) Resolution below the least-significant bit in digital systems with dither. *Journal of the Audio Engineering Society* **32.3**, pp 106–112, March.

Watkinson, J. (1984) DASH format and the PCM-3324. *BKSTS Journal*, April.

Watkinson, J. (1988) *The Art of Digital Audio*. Focal Press.

Watkinson, J. (1990) *Coding for Digital Recording*. Focal Press.

Watkinson, J. (1990) R-DAT: the irrepressible format. *Broadcast Systems Engineering*, July.

Weisser, A. and Komly, A. (1986) Description of an audio editing system using computer magnetic hard disk. Presented at the *80th AES Convention* (Montreux, 1986), preprint no. 2317 (A-5). Audio Engineering Society.

Wiffen, P. (1990) The fibre-optic studio. *Audio Media*, June.

Wilton, P. (1987) Interface and control for digital recorders. *Broadcast Systems Engineering*, January, pp 39-42.

Wilton, P. (1989) MADI (Multichannel Audio Digital Interface). In *Proceedings of the AES/EBU Interface Conference*, pp 117–130, Audio Engineering Society.

Index